Roland Berger Strategy Consultants – Academic Network

Editorial Council

Prof. Dr. Thomas Bieger, Universität St. Gallen
Prof. Dr. Rolf Caspers, European Business School, Oestrich-Winkel
Prof. Dr. Guido Eilenberger, Universität Rostock
Prof. Dr. Dr. Werner Gocht, RWTH Aachen
Prof. Dr. Karl-Werner Hansmann, Universität Hamburg
Prof. Dr. Alfred Kötzle, Europa Universität Viadrina, Frankfurt/Oder
Prof. Dr. Kurt Reding, Universität Gesamthochschule Kassel
Prof. Dr. Dr. Karl-Ulrich Rudolph, Universität Witten-Herdecke
Prof. Dr. Johannes Rüegg-Stürm, Universität St. Gallen
Prof. Dr. Leo Schuster, Katholische Universität Eichstätt
Prof. Dr. Klaus Spremann, Universität St. Gallen
Prof. Dr. Dodo zu Knyphausen-Aufseß,
         Otto-Friedrich-Universität Bamberg

Dr. Burkhard Schwenker, Roland Berger Strategy Consultants

Titles published in English by the Academic Network

G. Corbae · J. B. Jensen · D. Schneider
Marketing 2.0
VI, 151 pages. 2003. ISBN 3-540-00285-5

Soumitra Dutta · Arnoud De Meyer
Amit Jain · Gérard Richter
Editors

T‎ ‎ ‎ ety
i‎ ‎ ‎ ⇒

Wi
an

 Springer

Roland Berger
Strategy Consultants

Professor Soumitra Dutta
Professor Arnoud De Meyer
INSEAD
Bd de Constance
77300 Fontainebleau
France
E-mail: soumitra.dutta@insead.edu
E-mail: arnoud.de.meyer@insead.edu

Amit Jain
Research Program Manager
INSEAD
Bd de Constance
77300 Fontainebleau
France
E-mail: amit.jain@insead.edu

Gérard Richter
Partner
Roland Berger Strategy Consultants
Arabellastraße 33
81925 München
Germany
E-mail: gerard_richter@de.rolandberger.com

Cataloging-in-Publication Data
Library of Congress Control Number: 2006920774

ISBN-10 3-540-26221-0   Springer Berlin Heidelberg New York
ISBN-13 978-3-540-26221-3   Springer Berlin Heidelberg New York

Springer is a part of Springer Science+Business Media
springeronline.com

© Springer-Verlag Berlin Heidelberg 2006
Printed in Germany

Cover design: Erich Kirchner
Production: Helmut Petri
Printing: Strauss Offsetdruck

SPIN 11497738   Printed on acid-free paper – 42/3153 – 5 4 3 2 1 0

Acknowledgement

Soumitra Dutta, Amit Jain and Arnoud De Meyer, the editors at INSEAD, gratefully acknowledge the assistance of SAP in supporting prior research into the information society in Europe. This research inspired the more recent and comprehensive analysis presented in this book.

Foreword

In descriptions of modern society, the term "information society" is frequently used, and rightly so. Information is no longer one element among many: today, it is the crucial element which characterizes society as a whole.

The dissemination of information has become indispensable. An increasing number of people are involved in creating information, and just as many spend their free time consuming it. The reason for this is obvious: information helps justify decisions. It clarifies, or at least provides, both the reasons behind decisions and their consequences. We request information to overcome ignorance, and we hope that it helps us make better decisions.

It is no wonder, then, that information is set to become a key factor in politics, business and in the lives of individuals in a rational, enlightened and democratic Europe. To gain acceptance, politicians are increasingly obliged to inform the public of their decisions. Information and communication technologies make political decisions more transparent, and therefore help legitimize them.

Business also increasingly depends on information. Technological progress has led to an ever-growing range of opportunities. This, in turn, has led to a greater need for making and justifying decisions. Companies are constantly facing new challenges such as realigning business strategies, adapting to changing environmental conditions, and deciding whether to outsource production to another country. All of these challenges require that companies make major decisions; to do this, they need an abundance of information – from market research to consulting services – which is transferred and saved securely through IT support.

As consumers of information, individuals also have to make decisions on a daily basis. Which products should I buy? Where and how should I spend my free time? Even the most mundane decisions can be difficult without the right information. More importantly, information and the knowledge that is derived from it is the best way to maximize career opportunities and improve one's personal wealth.

Access to information has therefore become critical. Today, access to the modern information and communication technologies that have made the information society possible has become a pre-requisite for equal opportunities and social justice as well as for success in business.

The following volume therefore focuses on the current status of the information society in a new, enlarged Europe. The authors present a detailed look at the information societies in 25 EU member countries and three accession states: They shed light on the process of transformation that both old and new member states have experienced on their way to becoming information societies. The authors examine how information and communication technologies have influenced social cohesion, and look at the role of European governments in a digitalized economy. They also discuss ways in which companies are dealing with information management. The only available comprehensive data on the European information society collected at the industry and country level is included. All of them make this book indispensable for anyone who wants to gain valuable insight into the European information society.

Prof. Dr. h.c. mult. Roland Berger
Chairman, Roland Berger Strategy Consultants

Table of Contents

Introduction

"The objective of this Action Plan is to provide a favorable environment for private investment and for the creation of new jobs, to boost productivity, to modernize public services, and to give everyone the opportunity to participate in the global information society."

eEurope 2005: An Information Society for All. (European Union, June 2002)

The series of eEurope Action Plans drawn up by the European Commission manifests the desire of European Union countries to not only develop and nurture an equitable information society, but also to benchmark the relative level of development of the member states. Various benefits from the presence of an information society have been identified: notably, economic benefits such as improved productivity and efficiency, in addition to the creation of new jobs and employment. Seen in this light, assessing the level of development of the information society in a given country takes on considerable importance. The eEurope 2005 Action Plan provides a suitable benchmarking framework for this purpose.

The year 2004 witnessed the accession of ten new members to the group of 15 incumbent European Union members. This enlargment of the European Union from 15 to 25 countries increases not only its scope, but also its diversity. The new member states have varying historic legacies. They include former Soviet-controlled states such as Lithuania, alongside former Czechoslovakian and former Yugoslavian states.

It is against the backdrop of EU enlargement that this book seeks to explore some of the key issues centering around the information society in Europe. It achieves this objective by examining differences in the development of the information society at all levels: at country level, industry level and individual level. In addition, it studies the extent to which the three most important stakeholders – individuals, businesses and the government – make use of information and communications technology (ICT).

This book is divided into three main sections: essays, country profiles and data tables. The essay section draws on the expertise of scholars, practitioners and business leaders. The country profiles section provides a detailed snapshot of the relative developmental status of the information society in each economy. Data tables that rank the economies based on the assortment of variables discussed in this book are presented in the final section of the book.

The first chapter, "An assessment of the relative level of development of an information society in the enlarged European Union" by Soumitra Dutta and Amit Jain, presents the results of research measuring the level of diffusion of an information society at the country level, based on the computation of the eEurope 2005 Index. The benchmarking indicators defined for the eEurope 2005 Action Plan lay the foundation on which this research seeks to identify two things: the competitiveness of member states in the field of ICT; and the degree to which the new member states align with the incumbent EU nations. Drawing on the results of index computation and the relative performance of the 25 countries studied, the authors classify these countries into five distinct categories: 1) Global leaders 2) Totally aligned 3) Somewhat aligned 4) Development required 5) Significant development required. The authors further investigate the impact of Gross Domestic Product per capita on each country's overall index score, as well as exploring the link between the index score and the number of Internet users per 100 inhabitants. Examples of best practices in the new member states are presented throughout the discussion.

In the second chapter, "Electronic business in the European Union: an assessment of the digital divide in business", George Karageorgos and Hannes Selhofer present research conducted at the eBusiness W@tch exploring the extent to which there is a digital divide in the use of ICT and in electronic business practices between companies in the new EU member states and the EU-15 countries. The level of analysis thus shifts to that of the sector or industry within the countries of the European Union. Karageorgos and Selhofer attempt to respond to two key hypotheses: first, whether a digital divide exists between the EU-15 countries and the new member states. This hypothesis is tested by comparing the use of ICT on a sector-by-sector basis. Second, whether the performance of different sectors is heterogeneous across the countries studied. While no consistent pattern is found across all countries and all sectors, Karageorgos and Selhofer do identify some gaps between the EU-15 and the new member states. In other words, they do discover evidence of a digital divide. This underscores the message of the first chapter by Dutta and Jain on the alignment of the new member states with the EU-15 countries.

In the third chapter "The impact of ICT on social cohesion: looking beyond the digital divide", Tobias Hüsing, Karsten Gareis and Werner B. Korte assess whether the potential of ICT can help policy-makers in the new member states to counter threats to social cohesion. This chapter looks at the impact of ICT at both the macro and micro (individual) levels within a country. At the macro level, they explore whether the information society is merely a question of economic development, i.e. whether GDP per capita is the only factor that determines the level of ICT development. If this were the case, there would presumably be little scope for policy strategies to cultivate the information society. At the level of the individual, the authors ask whether or not using computers, the Internet and other technologies largely reflect those dimensions of social structure that shape other individual opportunities and social inclusion or exclusion. Hüsing et al. find that the new member states, with the exception of Estonia, lag behind the EU-15, and that there is indeed evidence of a digital divide, though its extent varies. Nevertheless, individual skills in the use of ICT are found to have a significant impact in reducing the probability of unemployment.

In the next chapter, "The role of European governments in the digital economy", Arnoud de Meyer postulates that governments can play an important role in at least four ways to foster the development of e-government and an information society: 1) By stimulating the development of infrastructure. 2) By investing in improved services. 3) By stimulating an e-friendly environment. 4) By creating an all-inclusive information society. De Meyer identifies the four pillars of an effective e-government strategy: 1) A clear e-government *vision*. 2) *Publication* of government information on an Internet portal. 3) *Interaction:* the development of secure transactional capabilities and progress towards bidirectional information flows. 4) Building *knowledge workers* in the public sector. According to de Meyer, one key to successful implementation of e-government is to facilitate technological innovation on a broad scale. He therefore argues that policy-makers should concentrate on developing the enabling structures and links that can apply to all agents in the innovation process.

In the fifth chapter, "Value-based information management in European ICT strategies", Kai Bender and Julia Hoerauf of Roland Berger Strategy Consultants outline how IT can be leveraged to address business challenges and create real business value. The authors stress the importance of performance indicators for IT project success. In their view, the crucial factor is not whether IT projects are completed on time and on budget: What is more important is how much value they add by reducing process times, slashing process costs and raising quality. These messages could be of tremendous significance to policy-makers as they seek to evaluate the benefits and impacts of proposed IT policies and projects. The authors illustrate their thinking with real-world examples, providing an intriguing case study of how they applied their methodology in one particular situation: Germany's "Toll Collect" project, where the project was completely turned around and successfully delivered by Roland Berger.

In the next chapter, "Finland – a prototypical knowledge economy", Petri Rouvinen and Pekka Ylä-Anttila present a country case study that gives a fascinating insight into the key factors and the process leading to the transformation of Finland into one of Europe's ICT powerhouses. The authors describe how Finland has evolved from a situation where it had close ties to the former Soviet Union (a situation similar to that of many of the new member states) and heavy dependency on natural resources (forestry) to become a world leader in mobile telecommunications and high technology. The authors trace the emergence of Nokia, Finland's leading mobile communications company, discuss the factors leading to its success as a global ICT player and explore the impact of this growth on Finland's technology landscape.

In the final chapter, "Data analysis and index computation: methodology", Amit Jain describes the methodology used to compute the eEurope 2005 Index (presented in the first chapter). An insight is provided into the data collection process, the selection of key indicators and the statistical treatment of these indicators.

The second section of the book contains country profiles for each of the 25 countries studied while evaluating the eEurope 2005 Index. This is followed by the third and final section, a presentation of the data tables listing the variables used to compute the eEurope 2005 index. These last two sections of the book give the reader a deeper understanding of the key indicators identified as measures/factors contributing to the information society in the European Union. This can help policy-makers compute their current information society competitiveness trajectory and take measures to ensure that progress continues in the direction they desire.

Ultimately, the development of a competitive information society remains an important goal for policy-makers in most countries, and especially so in the ten new member states of the European Union. The information society promises key advantages, not only for individuals, but also for businesses and governments. As such, it can contribute to Europe's overall economic and social development and cohesion.

Soumitra Dutta
Arnoud De Meyer
Amit Jain
Gérard Richter

Part 1: Chapters

1 An Assessment of the Relative Level of Development of an Information Society in the Enlarged European Union

Soumitra Dutta and Amit Jain, INSEAD

Preface

INSEAD has long been studying the role of information and communications technology (ICT) as a catalyst for organizational transformation and change. As a consequence, gaining a better understanding of the economic and business impact of ICT has been identified as a key research priority, giving rise to a multitude of research streams. In this spirit, the eEurope 2005 Index discussed in this report aims to shed light on the ICT situation in Europe, given the context of the accession of ten new countries to the European Union.

ICT forms the "backbone" of several industries, such as banking, airlines and publishing, and is an important value-adding component of consumer products such as television sets, cameras, cars and mobile handsets. ICT is today a dominant force in enabling companies to exploit new distribution channels, create new products and deliver unique value-added services to customers. It is also an important catalyst for social transformation and national progress. For reasons such as these, it is important to align the new member states with the levels of ICT development in the countries of the European Union, and to identify both areas of strength and areas in need of development.

The European Union outlines its aims and objectives for the ICT development of member countries in its eEurope Action Plans. The eEurope 2005 Action Plan succeeds the eEurope 2002 Action Plan. It aims to help member nations tap the vast potential of an information society, to improve productivity and quality of life. According to the Commission of the European Communities[1]:

---

[1] eEurope 2005: An information society for all, May 28, 2002, Commission of European Communities.

"The objective of this Action Plan is to provide a favorable environment for private investment and for the creation of new jobs, to boost productivity, to modernize public services, and to give everyone the opportunity to participate in the global information society. eEurope 2005 therefore aims to stimulate services, applications and content based on a widely available broadband infrastructure."

This chapter presents results of the research done at INSEAD with the aim of benchmarking the new member states of the European Union against the incumbent EU-15 countries[2]. The eEurope 2005 Index, which is based on the eEurope 2005 framework[3] elaborated by the European Commission, was computed on the basis of this research. The discussion in this chapter is divided into five main sections. First, there is a brief outline of the eEurope Action Plans and their aims and objectives. Second, previous ICT benchmarking research is discussed, in particular with respect to the European Union. Third, the results of the research and analysis are presented – the relative ranking of nations based on their degree of alignment with the EU-15 countries. Next, we take a closer look at the five component indexes that make up the eEurope 2005 index and how various countries have fared on each of these dimensions. The final section investigates the relationship between the eEurope 2005 index and two key variables: GDP per capita and Internet usage. It also spells out some of the key challenges faced while conducting the study.

The eEurope 2005 Action Plan

eEurope 2005

eEurope 2005 focuses on building on the achievements of eEurope 2002: stimulating services, applications and content that create new markets, reduce costs and eventually increase productivity throughout the economy. The plan recognizes the important role of market mechanisms in developing content, services and applications, and in the roll-out of the underlying infrastructure. In this light, the Action Plan concentrates on those areas

---

[2] Three countries – Cyprus, Malta and Turkey – could not be included in the analysis due to data availability limitations.

[3] The eEurope 2005 Action Plan was recommended for implementation in the Council Resolution of February 18, 2003, as published in the Official Journal of the European Union, pp. C48/2 to C46/8.

where public policy can provide added value and contribute to creating a positive environment for private investment.

While eEurope 2002 focused on creating a knowledge economy by extending Internet connectivity in Europe, eEurope 2005 aims to translate increasing levels of connectivity into economic activity and thus generate growth. Services such as e-government, e-health, and e-education are prioritized in addition to efforts to promote e-commerce. Strong emphasis is given to broadband, as this increases the speed of connectivity and hence the effective use of networks. Since diffusing the benefits of the Internet increasingly depends on the availability of high-speed Internet access amongst citizens and businesses, increasing the usage of broadband is a significant goal of the eEurope 2005 plan, in line with the aim of the previous plan to "create an information society for all".

eEurope 2002

The eEurope 2005 Action Plan succeeds the eEurope 2002 Action Plan that was endorsed by the Feira European Council in June 2000. It is a part of the Lisbon strategy to make the European Union "the most competitive and knowledge-based economy" in order to create a knowledge economy with improved employment and social cohesion by 2010.

eEurope 2002 focused on developing the level of Internet penetration. Growth was seen to be created by translating connectivity into economic activity. Significant progress was achieved during the eEurope 2002 Action Plan, as outlined in box 1.

Box 1

Progress During eEurope 2002

- Internet penetration in homes has doubled
- Telecom framework is in place
- Internet access prices have fallen
- Almost all companies and schools are connected
- Europe now has the world's fastest research backbone network
- Legal framework for e-commerce is largely in place
- More government services are available online
- A smart card infrastructure is emerging
- Web accessibility guidelines have been adopted and recommended in Member States

Source: European Commission

Effective usage of e-commerce and e-transactions depends upon the security of networks. The more ubiquitous the usage of networks, the more security becomes important and a necessity. As a consequence, the eEurope 2005 plan lays strong emphasis on online security. Box 2 summarizes the key goals of the eEurope 2005 Action Plan.

A benchmarking framework has been developed by the Commission and presented in the Official Journal of the European Union (28/2/2003). The benchmarking indicators developed encapsulate the aims and objectives of the e-Europe 2005 Action Plan. A schematic representation of these indicators is shown in figure 1.

Box 2

eEurope 2005 Action Plan Goals

By 2005 European member states should have:

* Modern online public services
  - E-government
  - E-learning services
  - E-health services

* A dynamic e-business environment

* And, as an enabler for these
  - Widespread availability of broadband at competitive prices
  - A secure information infrastructure

Five broad categories of indicators have been identified: Internet indicators, modern online public services, a dynamic e-business environment, a secure information infrastructure, and broadband. In all, 14 policy indicators and 22 supplementary indicators have been provided which cumulatively indicate the degree of alignment of a country or community with the objectives of eEurope.

1. *Internet indicators:* The Internet indicators capture the degree to which individuals have access to the Internet. It comprises 3 main categories (see figure 1), namely: citizens' access to and use of the Internet; enterprise access to and use of the Internet; and Internet access costs,
2. *Modern online public services:* This category aims to benchmark the different European countries based on the degree of availability of online public services and the level of their usage by Europeans. Three broad categories of public services have been identified: e-government, e-learning and e-health,
3. *A dynamic e-business environment:* This category aims to capture the level of e-commerce in different European nations. It consists of two main categories: buying and selling online and e-business readiness,

4. *A secure information infrastructure:* This category aims to evaluate the level of security of Internet access and of online commerce across different European countries,
5. *Broadband:* Broadband aims to measure the level of availability and usage of broadband services across European nations.

Based on this benchmarking framework, an eEurope 2005 Index has been computed for this research project to facilitate an understanding of the degree to which the new member states (NMS) and candidate countries are aligned with the 15 current member countries of the European Union.

Previous Work in This Field

Taking a step back, one could ask why new efforts to gauge the ICT competitiveness of nations are at all necessary. Several research projects have already focused on evaluating a countries' e-readiness (see table 1). For instance, the Cap Gemini study of the "Online Availability of Public Services" sought to benchmark the progress of online public services in 18 European countries. The Economist's 2003 E-Readiness Ranking provides a benchmark to compare and assess countries' e-business environments. Similarly, the Networked Readiness Index, a joint study by INSEAD and the World Economic Forum (WEF), benchmarks the level of ICT development of nations worldwide.

The country coverage of these research streams varies. The Cap Gemini study focuses on 18 European nations, while the Economist study targets 60 countries worldwide. The Networked Readiness study conducted by INSEAD and the WEF evaluates 104 nations. What can be seen from these and other research projects in the same area is that no single study addresses the subset of EU-15 countries, the new member states and the candidate countries. In addition, no research stream addresses the problem of alignment of NMS on the basis of the eEurope Action Plans or in accordance with EU guidelines.

Table 1: Previous ICT research projects

	E-Europe 2005 Index (current study) (2005)
Aims and objectives	**New member state benchmarking** To evaluate the degree of development of the 25 EU countries with respect to ICT. To study the degree to which the ten new member states are aligned with the 15 incumbent members of the European Union 15, with due account for the eEurope 2005 Action Plan and the benchmarking framework.
Country coverage	**25 countries:** Austria, Belgium, Bulgaria, Czech Republic, Denmark, Estonia, Finland, France, Germany, Greece, Hungary, Ireland, Italy, Latvia, Lithuania, Luxembourg, Netherlands, Poland, Portugal, Romania, Slovak Republic, Slovenia, Spain, Sweden and the United Kingdom
Model/output	The e-Europe 2005 framework is used to benchmark countries. This framework has 5 key components: 1. **Internet indicators** 2. **Modern online public services** 3. **Dynamic e-business environment** 4. **Secure information infrastructure** 5. **Broadband** Based on a cumulative e-Europe Index calculated using the above framework, countries are classified into different categories depending on their level of ICT development and alignment with the incumbent EU nations: 1. **Global leaders** 2. **Totally aligned** 3. **Somewhat aligned** 4. **Development required** 5. **Significant development required**
Data used	Data was obtained from leading international sources such as the World Bank, Pyramid Research, ITU and the World Economic Forum.
Strengths	• Focus on the assessment of new member states with respect to incumbent nations • Adherence to the eEurope 2005 benchmarking framework

Table 1 (continued)

Cap Gemini: Online availability of public services (January 2004)	INSEAD and World Economic Forum (February 2005 – see Appendix 1)
E-government benchmarking To benchmark the progress of online public services in Europe; to measure the online sophistication of basic public services available on the Internet; and to measure the percentage of public services fully available online. This work pertains in particular to the benchmarking of the e-government part of the e-Europe Action Plans.	**Global ICT benchmarking** To provide an established benchmark to compare and assess different countries' ICT environments, e-readiness and ICT usage. A unique feature of the study is that it has been repeated for four consecutive years.
18 countries: Austria, Belgium, Denmark, Finland, France, Germany, Greece, Iceland, Ireland, Italy, Luxembourg, Netherlands, Norway, Portugal, Spain, Switzerland, Sweden and the United Kingdom.	**104 countries** from every continent are covered by the study.
This study classifies the countries into 4 categories that reflect their "availability of public services online": 1. **Information:** The information necessary to start the procedure of obtaining this public service is available online. 2. **One-way interaction:** The public-domain website allows users to start the procedure of obtaining a given service via non-electronic channels (by downloading forms). 3. **Two-way interaction:** The public-domain website offers the possibility of electronic interaction, with an official electronic form of authentication for the (physical or legal) person requesting the services in order to reach stage 3. **Full electronic case handling:** The public-domain website allows users to complete entire public services, including decisions and delivery, on the website.	The framework is based on three major indicator areas: 1. **Environment for ICT** 2. **Readiness for ICT** 3. **Usage of ICT** Each indicator category consists of several variables and is used to evaluate three major ICT stakeholders: • **Individuals** • **Businesses** • **Governments** The overall result is indicated by the Networked Readiness Index (NRI). The NRI results for 2004-05 are detailed in Appendix 1.
Survey conducted by Cap Gemini Ernst and Young in the 18 countries in question.	The majority of the data was sourced with the World Economic Forum and international agencies such as the ITU and the World Bank.
• Clear analysis of online availability of public services • Conducts time series analysis of countries, taking into consideration previous studies by the company in the same field	• Comprehensive model covering different aspects of ICT readiness and usage • Possibility of time series analysis due to availability of benchmarking results over four years

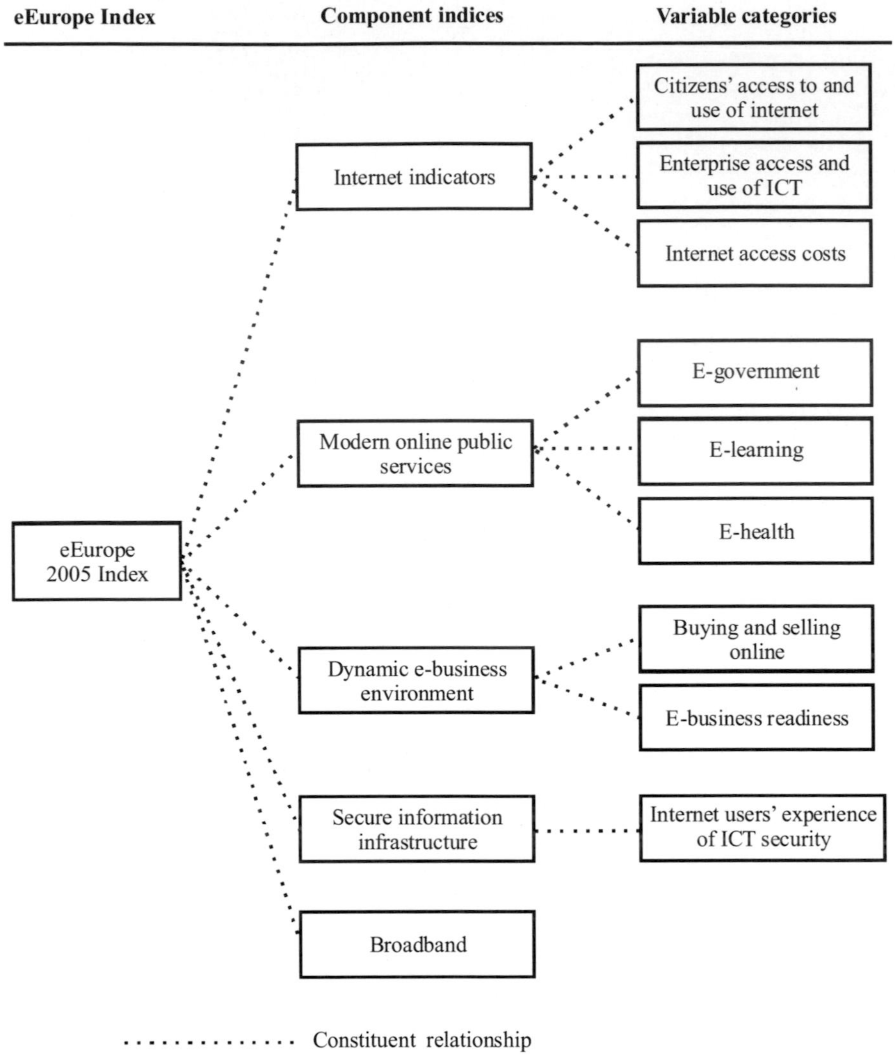

eEurope Index	Component indices	Variable categories

.... Constituent relationship

Source: Based on the European Union's eEurope 2005 framework

Fig. 1: The eEurope 2005 framework

This lack of relevant research in the context of the enlarged European Union was one of the primary reasons that motivated the current research effort by INSEAD. The current research uses the eEurope 2005 benchmarking framework infrastructure to determine the degree of similarity between the incumbent European Union nations, the new member states and the candidate nations.

eEurope 2005 Index Results

The overall results for the eEurope 2005 Index[4] are presented in table 2. Denmark comes out with the top rank, followed by the United Kingdom and Sweden. Finland, Germany and the Netherlands occupy fourth, fifth and sixth place respectively. Austria, Belgium, Ireland and Estonia follow and are currently represented in the top ten.

While chapter 7 ("Data analysis and index computation: methodology") provides technical details on how the eEurope 2005 Index is calculated, a few words of explanation are in order for the country scores reported in this chapter. For the specific technical reasons outlined in chapter 7, reported index scores are standardized with a mean of 0. This results in the scores of the countries being distributed above and below the mean score of zero. A positive score merely reflects the fact that the country concerned is doing better than the mean performance across the countries studied. Likewise, a negative score implies that its ranking is below the mean performance of the countries included in this study.

New Member States and Candidate Countries

The top ranked new member states are Estonia and Slovenia, which respectively rank 10th and 17th with scores of 0.37 and -0.44 on the eEurope index. Estonia in particular is placed in the middle of the EU-15 group of countries, exhibiting a higher level of ICT development than a number of them based on the indicators used in this study.

Lithuania and Latvia occupy third and fourth place respectively among the NMS and rank 18th and 19th among the EU-25. The Czech Republic follows in 20th slot. Poland, the Slovak Republic and Romania come next. The last two NMS/candidate countries are Hungary and Bulgaria.

Alignment of the New Member States

The degree to which the NMS are aligned with the current member states of the European Union is shown in figure 2. The countries are classified

---

[4] The eEurope 2005 Index presented in this chapter/book are the result of analyses and research conducted at INSEAD in collaboration with various research partners. They are not official EU eEurope 2005 scores and have not been produced/endorsed by the European Union.

into five distinct groups according to their performance on the computed index: global leaders, totally aligned, somewhat aligned, development required and significant development required.

Group I: Global Leaders

Group I consists of countries that are global leaders – outstanding performers at international level in the ICT realm. This group of countries has an eEurope Index score greater than 0.75 on a standardized[5] scale and comprises seven countries: Denmark, the United Kingdom, Sweden, Finland, Germany, the Netherlands and Austria. These countries also rank very highly in the Networked Readiness Index (2004-2005) (see Appendix 1), with three of them among the top ten (out of a group of 104 countries). Due to their high level of ICT development, this group of countries proveides a rich set

Box 3

eEurope 2005	Rank	Score
Denmark	1	1.30
United Kingdom	2	1.06
Sweden	3	0.95
Finland	4	0.93
Germany	5	0.84
Netherlands	6	0.83
Austria	7	0.82

of best practices and case studies that can be used by other nations who wish to improve their own ICT development.

---

[5] The eEurope 2005 index is standardized. The mean scores of all countries considered is 0. Positive index scores represent above-average countries. Any countries with negative index scores have an eEurope 2005 index score below the average.

Table 2: eEurope 2005 Index

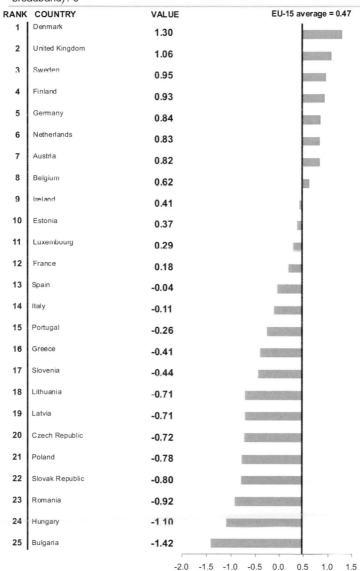

eEurope 2005 Index = (Internet indicators + modern online public services + dynamic e-business environment + secure information infrastructure + broadband) / 5

RANK	COUNTRY	VALUE
1	Denmark	1.30
2	United Kingdom	1.06
3	Sweden	0.95
4	Finland	0.93
5	Germany	0.84
6	Netherlands	0.83
7	Austria	0.82
8	Belgium	0.62
9	Ireland	0.41
10	Estonia	0.37
11	Luxembourg	0.29
12	France	0.18
13	Spain	-0.04
14	Italy	-0.11
15	Portugal	-0.26
16	Greece	-0.41
17	Slovenia	-0.44
18	Lithuania	-0.71
19	Latvia	-0.71
20	Czech Republic	-0.72
21	Poland	-0.78
22	Slovak Republic	-0.80
23	Romania	-0.92
24	Hungary	-1.10
25	Bulgaria	-1.42

EU-15 average = 0.47

-2.0 -1.5 -1.0 -0.5 0.0 0.5 1.0 1.5

Source: INSEAD 2005

18   S. Dutta and A. Jain

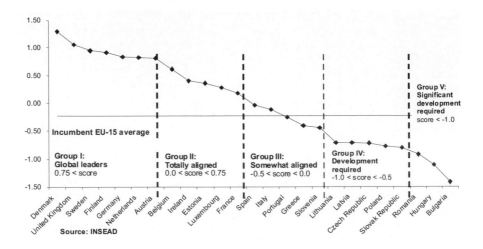

Source: INSEAD

Fig. 2: New member state and candidate country alignment analysis

Group II: Totally Aligned (EU-15 Average)

Group II countries are countries that reflect the average European Union level of development with respect to information and communications technologies. These countries have an eEurope 2005 index score between 0 and 0.75. They have very good ICT infrastructures and a high degree of usage of ICT by the three stakeholders: individuals, businesses and the government. This group com-

Box 4		
eEurope 2005	Rank	Score
Belgium	8	0.62
Ireland	9	0.41
Estonia	10	0.37
Luxembourg	11	0.29
France	12	0.18

prises five countries: Belgium, Ireland, Estonia, Luxembourg and France. These countries rank relatively highly in the Networked Readiness Index (2004-2005) (Appendix 1), all of them figuring among the top thirty (out of a group of 104 countries). While this group reflects the EU-15 average, its level of development is relatively high in terms of global comparison.

Of note in this group is Estonia, which ranks 10th out of 25 countries in the eEurope 2005 Index and 25th out of 104 countries on the NRI. Estonia is the top-ranked NMS and is fully aligned with the EU-15 countries in respect of the eEurope 2005 benchmarking indicators and the level of ICT development.

Group III: Somewhat Aligned

Group III countries have a level of ICT development below the European Union average level. They have eEurope 2005 scores between 0.0 and -0.5, compared to the EU-15 average of 0.47. Group III thus represents a group of countries whose eEurope benchmarking indicators are aligned to some degree with the average score of the EU-15 countries. This group comprises five countries: Spain, Italy, Greece and Slovenia. These five countries: Spain, Italy, Por-

Box 5		
eEurope 2005	**Rank**	**Score**
Spain	13	-0.04
Italy	14	-0.11
Portugal	15	-0.26
Greece	16	-0.41
Slovenia	17	-0.44

tugal, Greece and Slovenia. These five countries all rank within the top fifty countries in the Networked Readiness Index (2004-2005) (see Appendix 1). Two facts are of note in this group:

1. Four countries – Spain, Italy, Portugal and Greece – share the lowest level of ICT development among the EU-15 countries,

2. One new member state, Slovenia, is present in this group.

Group IV: Development Required

Group IV countries are countries that require some development before they come into line with the EU-15 countries with respect to the eEurope benchmarking indicators. This group of countries has an eEurope Index score under -0.5 and over -1.0, compared to the EU-15 average of 0.47. Group IV comprises five NMS: Lithuania, Latvia the Czech Republic, Poland, the Slovak Republic and one candidate country, Romania.

Box 6		
eEurope 2005	**Rank**	**Score**
Lithuania	18	-0.71
Latvia	19	-0.71
Czech Republic	20	-0.72
Poland	21	-0.78
Slovak Republic	22	-0.80
Romania	23	-0.92

Confirmation of this analysis of the level of ICT development comes from the observation that these six countries also rank relatively far down in the Networked Readiness Index (2004-2005) (Appendix 1).

Group V: Significant Development Required

Group V countries are countries that require significant development before they come into line with the EU-15 countries with respect to the eEurope benchmarking indicators. This group of countries has an eEuropa Index score below -1.0

Box 7		
eEurope 2005	Rank	Score
Hungary	24	-1.10
Bulgaria	25	-1.42

compared to the EU-15 average of 0.47. Group V comprises one NMS (Hungary) and one candidate country (Bulgaria).

Interpreting the Results

The eEurope 2005 Index permits business leaders and public policy-makers to investigate the reasons leading to a nation's ranking and its de-gree of alignment with the EU-15 countries with respect to ICT develop-ment. It captures key factors relating to the Internet, online public services, e-business/e-commerce, online security concerns and broadband penetra-tion. It can also be used to understand the performance of a nation or even a region with regard to ICT development. The component index and sub-index rankings serve to identify key areas where a nation is under or over-performing. One would, for instance be able to identify relative imbalances in development across the five component indexes or even go one level deeper[6].

We would like to emphasize that, while rankings are useful as relative in-dicators of a nation's ICT excellence, there are several limitations to the analytic process. For one, caution should be exercised when comparing countries that are closely ranked. For instance, countries ranked close to-gether can evidence very small variations in their index scores. Lithuania (index = -0.71, rank = 18) and Latvia (index = -0.71, rank = 19) actually have the same overall score. In this case, Lithuania had an overall index score marginally higher than that of Latvia, albeit the discrepancy occurred only at the third decimal place. Additionally, small differences in the index

---

[6] For example, Estonia, whose overall ranking is 10, has scores ranging from 6 for the broadband component index to 22 for the secure information infrastructure component index. One could explore the reasons for this imbalance by examin-ing the sub-indices and variables that make up the secure online infrastructure dimension and studying Estonia's performance in each area.

may be beyond the limits of statistical significance due to the fact that a number of missing observations were estimated using analytic techniques such as regression and clustering. Chronic shortage of data was a particular problem for Cyprus, Malta and Turkey, which were therefore excluded from the analysis. Nevertheless, our opinion is that the eEurope 2005 Index provides a good indication of the relative level of ICT development across the 25 countries in question.

Finally, the complexity of ICT issues in a nation can become obscured behind the numerical score in the eEurope 2005 Index. Countries have vastly different problems and performance issues, ranging from low levels of economic development with low GDP per capita (Romania and Bulgaria), to legacy effects of the transition from Communism to market economies (Lithuania and Romania), to effects of national fragmentation (ex-Czechoslovakia and the ex-Yugoslavian countries), to high performance (Estonia). Any composite index provides an average picture of the level of ICT development. By its very nature, however, it cannot take into consideration effects that are specific to national contexts, such as those just mentioned.

Exploring the eEurope 2005 Index

The eEurope 2005 Index provides a quick and relative benchmark of the level of development of the information society in 25 European countries. It also gives an indication of the extent to which the NMS align with the incumbent European Union member states. While this is useful, it may still be necessary to gain further insights into areas of a nation's over and underperformance, and to understand the key drivers determining the results. This can be done by looking at the five component indexes: Internet indicators, modern online public services, dynamic e-business environment, secure information infrastructure and broadband. Table 2 through table 6 show the results of each component index. A deeper understanding may be gained by examining the 37 variables that make up each component index. Appendix 2 (at the end of this chapter) explains how the indices were computed. Figure 3 is a schematic diagram of the relationships between the various indexes. It shows how they add up to form the eEurope 2005 Index.

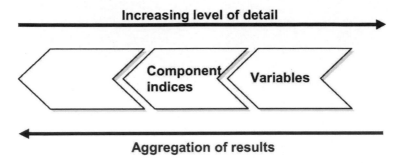

Fig. 3: Disaggregating the eEurope 2005 Index

1.1   Internet Indicators

The Internet indicators capture the degree of access to the Internet by individuals. It consists of three main categories (see figure 1), namely: citizens' access to and use of the Internet; enterprise access to and use of the Internet; and Internet access costs. The results of how the 25 countries performed in this dimension are shown in table 3. The Netherlands, Finland and Sweden occupy the top three places.

New Member States

Estonia is the top-ranking NMS. coming eleventh with a score of 0.33 (compared to the EU-15 average of 0.41). Slovenia (13), Lithuania (18), and the Czech Republic (19) are the next best-performing NMS. Estonia and Slovenia are relatively well aligned with the EU-15 countries in the Internet indicators dimension. Lithuania and the Czech Republic, Hungary, Poland and the Slovak Republic have scores close to those of southern European countries such as Spain, Portugal and Greece, and are somewhat aligned in the Internet indicators dimension. The remaining NMS need some development before they match the level of development of the current European Union members.

Box 8 outlines efforts made by the Slovak Republic to promote ICT-related skills among their citizens and hence develop ICT usage by individuals and businesses. Box 9 summarizes the efforts of Estonia to set up public Internet access points to promote the use of the Internet by their citizens.

Box 8

Infovek – Slovak Republic[7]

The Infovek (InfoAge) program aims to prepare young citizens of the Slovak Republic for the challenges of the information society, especially in light of the country's accession to the European Union.

The program has ambitious objectives to provide Internet access to about 2,500 primary schools and 800 secondary schools by the year 2005. It is forecast that, as a result of this effort, Internet penetration in schools will increase from 20 percent at the end of 2001 to 35 percent by the end of 2002.

Box 9

Public Internet Access Points – Estonia[8]

According to the Estonian Information Act, each Estonian citizen should have access to free public information. In order to comply with this target, public Internet access points (PIAPs) are being set up in all public libraries. So far, about 550 PIAPs have been installed under this program and at least 100,000 people have been trained to use the Internet.

1.2   Modern Online Public Services

Modern online public services aim to benchmark the different European countries on the degree of availability of online public services and the level of their usage by Europeans. Three broad categories of public services have been identified: e-government, e-learning, and e-health. Table 4 displays the results of the 25 countries studied in the online public services dimension. Overall, Denmark, the Netherlands and the United Kingdom occupy the top three places.

New Member States

Estonia (8) and Slovenia (15) lead the group of NMS and candidate countries. The next-ranked NMS is the Czech Republic, with a score of -0.42

---

[7] Source: Prisma.

[8] Source: eEurope+ 2003 Progress Report, February 2004.

and rank of 17, compared to the EU-15 average of 0.38. Lithuania comes next, in 18th place with a score of -0.58, followed by the Slovak Republic in 19th place with a score of -0.75. Estonia, Slovenia and the Czech Republic can be considered closely aligned in terms of their online public services.

It is worth noting that, if alignment is considered to lie within the lower limit of the range of the EU-15 scores, then the lowest EU-15 country is Greece, which ranks 22nd with a score of -0.95. Seen from this angle, two other NMS – Latvia (20) and Hungary (21) – would have scores within this range and would also be deemed aligned in addition to the countries cited above.

Box 10 presents some of the efforts Malta has undertaken to promote e-government. Box 11 highlights the ID card used in Estonia.

Box 10

E-government Passport Service – Malta[9]

Passport emission in Malta has been enabled online as part of a program to promote e-government in this country. Applicants submit their information online. This information is processed by the relevant authorities. Once passports are ready, individuals are notified and can pick up their passports from the passport service.

Box 11

ID card – Estonia[10]

Electronic identification can now be based on digital signatures in Estonia. A national ID card has been introduced. In parallel, a universal system named DigiDoc has been developed to handle the necessary authentication. By early January 2004, over 360,000 ID cards had been issued.

---

[9] Source: eEurope+ 2003 Progress Report, February 2004.

[10] Source: eEurope+ 2003 Progress Report, February 2004.

1.3   A Dynamic e-Business Environment

The dynamic e-business environment indicator aims to capture the level of e-commerce in different European nations. It consists of two main categories: buying and selling online and e-business readiness. Table 5 displays the results of the dynamic e-business environment component index. The top three countries in this component index are the United Kingdom, Denmark and Sweden. The EU-15 average score is 0.53.

New Member States

Estonia and Slovenia are the top-ranked NMS, occupying 7th and 13th places respectively with scores of 0.71 and -0.25 (compared to the EU-15 average of 0.53). The Czech Republic (16), Lithuania (18) and the Slovak Republic (19) follow as the next best-performing NMS. Estonia is well aligned with the EU-15 countries in the dynamic e-business environment dimension. Slovenia, the Czech Republic, Lithuania, the Slovak Republic, Romania and Hungary have scores close to that of southern European countries such as Italy, Spain and Greece and are somewhat aligned in the Internet indicators dimension.

Box 12 shows one example of a best e-business practice among the NMS: the use of e-banking in Estonia.

Box 12

Internet Banking – Estonia[11]

95 percent of all Estonian banking transactions are handled through electronic channels. Only the remaining 5 percent take place in branch offices. The top four banks together have over 740,000 Internet banking clients (in a country of 1.37 million people).

1.4   A Secure Information Infrastructure

This indicator aims to evaluate the relative security of Internet access and online commerce across different European countries. Table 6 displays the results for the 25 countries studied in the secure information infrastructure dimension. Overall, the United Kingdom, Ireland and Italy occupy the top

---

[11] Source: eEurope+ 2003 Progress Report, February 2004.

three places. The EU-15 average score is 0.81. Interestingly, some of the EU-15 countries that score highly overall rank relatively poorly in the dimension of "secure information infrastructure". Examples include Sweden, in 15th place, and the Netherlands, in 17th place.

New Member States

The top-ranked NMS is Poland, with a score of 0.48 and rank of 10, compared to the EU-15 average of 0.81. Latvia and the Slovak Republic are the next best-ranked NMS and are relatively well aligned with the EU-15 countries in this dimension. The remaining NMS need to work towards the goal of developing a secure information infrastructure and educating citizens about both the opportunities presented by the Internet and the associated issues of security and privacy.

1.5   Broadband

The broadband indicator captures the degree diffusion of high-speed access to the Internet in a given country. The results of the performance of the 25 countries in the Internet indicators dimension are shown in table 7. Belgium, Austria and the Netherlands occupy the top three places. The EU-15 average score in the broadband component index is 0.20.

New Member States

Estonia is the top-ranked NMS, in 6th place with a score of 1.03 (compared to the EU-15 average of 0.20). Estonia's score is thus well above the EU-15 average. The next three NMS are Hungary (12), Latvia (13) and Lithuania (14). These countries are well aligned with respect to the average level of broadband penetration in the EU-15 countries.

Table 3: Internet indicators

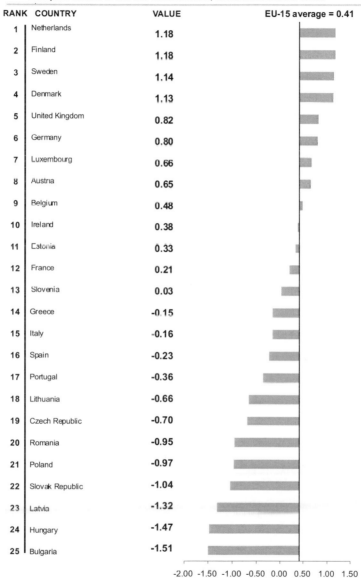

This indicator captures the degree of access to the internet by individuals. It consists of three main categories: citizens' acces to and use of the Internet; enterprise access to and use of the Internet; and Internet access costs.

RANK	COUNTRY	VALUE	EU-15 average = 0.41
1	Netherlands	1.18	
2	Finland	1.18	
3	Sweden	1.14	
4	Denmark	1.13	
5	United Kingdom	0.82	
6	Germany	0.80	
7	Luxembourg	0.66	
8	Austria	0.65	
9	Belgium	0.48	
10	Ireland	0.38	
11	Estonia	0.33	
12	France	0.21	
13	Slovenia	0.03	
14	Greece	-0.15	
15	Italy	-0.16	
16	Spain	-0.23	
17	Portugal	-0.36	
18	Lithuania	-0.66	
19	Czech Republic	-0.70	
20	Romania	-0.95	
21	Poland	-0.97	
22	Slovak Republic	-1.04	
23	Latvia	-1.32	
24	Hungary	-1.47	
25	Bulgaria	-1.51	

-2.00 -1.50 -1.00 -0.50 0.00 0.50 1.00 1.50

Source: INSEAD 2005

Table 4: Modern online public services

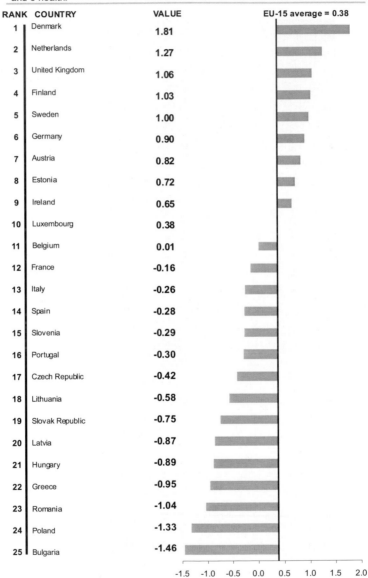

This indicator measures the degree of availability of online public services. It consists of three broad categories of public services: e-government, e-learning, and e-health.

RANK	COUNTRY	VALUE
1	Denmark	1.81
2	Netherlands	1.27
3	United Kingdom	1.06
4	Finland	1.03
5	Sweden	1.00
6	Germany	0.90
7	Austria	0.82
8	Estonia	0.72
9	Ireland	0.65
10	Luxembourg	0.38
11	Belgium	0.01
12	France	-0.16
13	Italy	-0.26
14	Spain	-0.28
15	Slovenia	-0.29
16	Portugal	-0.30
17	Czech Republic	-0.42
18	Lithuania	-0.58
19	Slovak Republic	-0.75
20	Latvia	-0.87
21	Hungary	-0.89
22	Greece	-0.95
23	Romania	-1.04
24	Poland	-1.33
25	Bulgaria	-1.46

EU-15 average = 0.38

Source: INSEAD 2005

Table 5: A dynamic e-business environment

This indicator captures the level of e-commerce in different European nations. It consists of two main categories: buying and selling online, and e-business readiness.

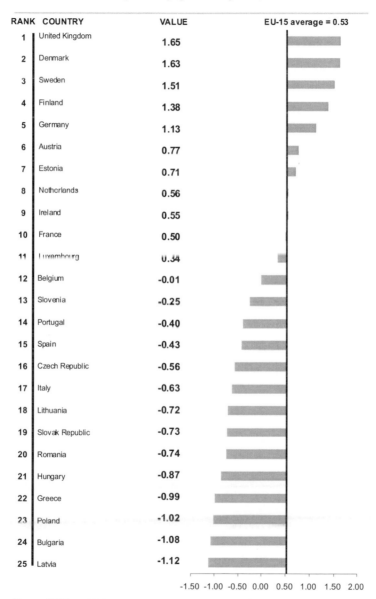

RANK	COUNTRY	VALUE
1	United Kingdom	1.65
2	Denmark	1.63
3	Sweden	1.51
4	Finland	1.38
5	Germany	1.13
6	Austria	0.77
7	Estonia	0.71
8	Netherlands	0.56
9	Ireland	0.55
10	France	0.50
11	Luxembourg	0.34
12	Belgium	-0.01
13	Slovenia	-0.25
14	Portugal	-0.40
15	Spain	-0.43
16	Czech Republic	-0.56
17	Italy	-0.63
18	Lithuania	-0.72
19	Slovak Republic	-0.73
20	Romania	-0.74
21	Hungary	-0.87
22	Greece	-0.99
23	Poland	-1.02
24	Bulgaria	-1.08
25	Latvia	-1.12

EU-15 average = 0.53

-1.50 -1.00 -0.50 0.00 0.50 1.00 1.50 2.00

Source: INSEAD 2005

Table 6: A secure information infrastructure

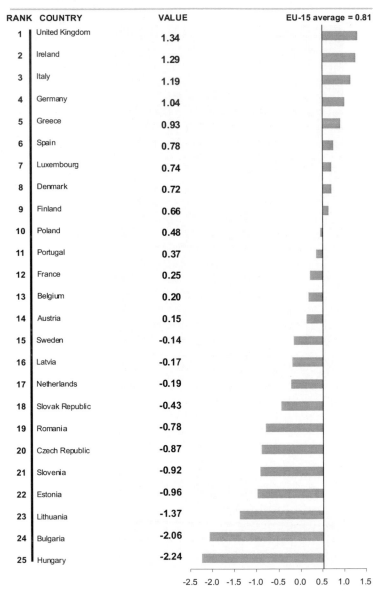

This indicator evaluates the level of security of Internet access and of online commerce across different European countries.

RANK	COUNTRY	VALUE	EU-15 average = 0.81
1	United Kingdom	1.34	
2	Ireland	1.29	
3	Italy	1.19	
4	Germany	1.04	
5	Greece	0.93	
6	Spain	0.78	
7	Luxembourg	0.74	
8	Denmark	0.72	
9	Finland	0.66	
10	Poland	0.48	
11	Portugal	0.37	
12	France	0.25	
13	Belgium	0.20	
14	Austria	0.15	
15	Sweden	-0.14	
16	Latvia	-0.17	
17	Netherlands	-0.19	
18	Slovak Republic	-0.43	
19	Romania	-0.78	
20	Czech Republic	-0.87	
21	Slovenia	-0.92	
22	Estonia	-0.96	
23	Lithuania	-1.37	
24	Bulgaria	-2.06	
25	Hungary	-2.24	

-2.5 -2.0 -1.5 -1.0 -0.5 0.0 0.5 1.0 1.5

Source: INSEAD 2005

Table 7: Broadband

Broadband measures the level of availability and usage of broadband services across European nations.

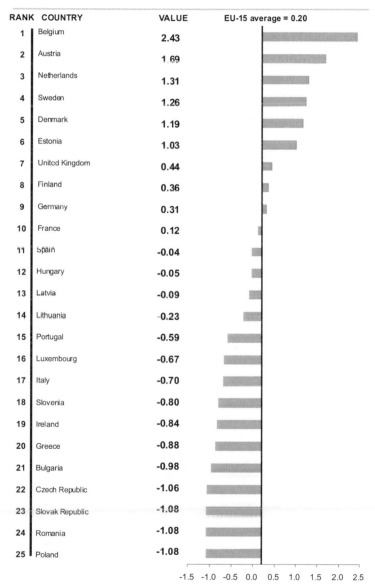

RANK	COUNTRY	VALUE	EU-15 average = 0.20
1	Belgium	2.43	
2	Austria	1.69	
3	Netherlands	1.31	
4	Sweden	1.26	
5	Denmark	1.19	
6	Estonia	1.03	
7	United Kingdom	0.44	
8	Finland	0.36	
9	Germany	0.31	
10	France	0.12	
11	Spain	-0.04	
12	Hungary	-0.05	
13	Latvia	-0.09	
14	Lithuania	-0.23	
15	Portugal	-0.59	
16	Luxembourg	-0.67	
17	Italy	-0.70	
18	Slovenia	-0.80	
19	Ireland	-0.84	
20	Greece	-0.88	
21	Bulgaria	-0.98	
22	Czech Republic	-1.06	
23	Slovak Republic	-1.08	
24	Romania	-1.08	
25	Poland	-1.08	

-1.5 -1.0 -0.5 0.0 0.5 1.0 1.5 2.0 2.5

Source: INSEAD 2005

Understanding eEurope 2005 Alignment

The degree of alignment with respect to the eEurope 2005 framework is the result of a multitude of effects. Our research started with a set of over 130 different variables or indicators to evaluate networked readiness. Statistical analysis then reduced these to a set of 37. These 37 variables were grouped into the five component indices that make up the eEurope 2005 benchmarking framework. This provides us with an opportunity to study some of the correlations that exist across the variables and the components/sub-indices in the eEurope 2005 framework.

GDP and the eEurope 2005 Index

Any attempt to use a single measure to approximate the eEurope Index must necessarily be a simplification. One of the most intuitive and appealing measures that one may be tempted to use as a proxy is a country's Gross Domestic Product (GDP) per capita. A closer look at the eEurope results shows that Estonia, with GDP per capita of € 5,143, has an eEurope score of 0.37 and ranks 10th overall. Poland, with very similar GDP per capita of € 5,176, nevertheless scores -0.78 and has an overall ranking of 21st. One thus sees a wide spread in the eEurope score for a given level of GDP per capita.

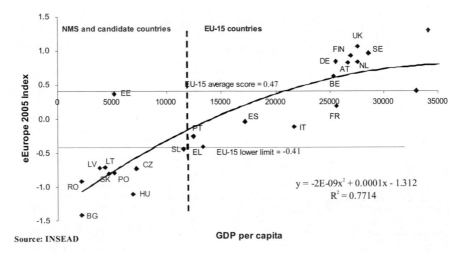

Fig. 4: eEurope 2005 Index and GDP per capita

It is, however, still possible to look at the relation between eEurope and GDP to obtain a better understanding of trends, and also to identify over- and underperformers with respect to each trend. A country's per-capita income or its relative wealth influences the investment decisions made by policy-makers, the budget they have for ICT and the relative importance of ICT in their budget allocation. It is to be expected that nations with high levels of GDP per capita will invest more in ICT to enhance their economic competitiveness. Figure 4 plots a curve linking GDP per capita to the eEurope 2005 Index. It is apparent that there is a strong relationship between GDP per capita and the eEurope 2005 Index with a regression R^2 value of 0.7714. Other notable features of the chart are as follows:

- The 25 countries divide neatly into NMS and EU-15 countries based on GDP per capita. The country with the highest GDP per capita amongst the NMS and candidate countries (Slovenia) has a GDP per capita inferior to that of the EU-15 country with the lowest GDP per capita (Portugal),
- For a given GDP per capita, there is a clear spread in the eEurope scores around the regression curve.

Countries widely distanced from the regression curve could be examples of underperforming or overperforming countries. For instance, Denmark evidently leads the eEurope ranking and is a clear overperformer, whereas France underperforms on the overall eEurope 2005 score. Similarly, Estonia strongly overperforms on its eEurope score with respect to its GDP per capita.

Internet Users per 100 Inhabitants and the eEurope 2005 Index

It is tempting to use a country's number of Internet users as a proxy estimate of its eEurope Index. Figure 5 plots a curve linking the number of Internet users per 100 inhabitants to the eEurope 2005 Index. The existence of a significant relationship between these variables becomes apparent on observing that the linear regression curve has a high regression R^2 value of 0.7738. The eEurope Index is much richer than the Internet users measure, since it takes into account diverse factors such as online public services, e-commerce, online security and broadband. For instance, two countries with the same level of Internet users per 100 inhabitants may have a different index score if they differ in relative terms across other parameters of the index.

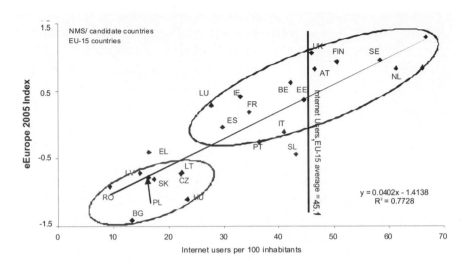

Fig. 5: eEurope 2005 Index and Internet users per 100 habitants

Figure 5 shows the distribution of NMS and EU-15 member countries along the axes of the eEurope 2005 Index and Internet users per 100 inhabitants. The formation of two distinct sets of countries is clearly visible, as is the presence of Estonia and Slovenia among the EU-15 member countries. Likewise, Greece is seen to be more similar to the NMS than to the EU-15 in these two dimensions.

Research Challenges

Finding the facts: The best-designed frameworks can face seemingly insurmountable obstacles to implementation due to the lack of accurate and reliable data. The overriding aim in our research and analysis has been to provide a scientific and credible interpretation of reality. The first step in our research was therefore to collect the most complete and highest-quality set of data that relates to ICT and is pertinent to both the eEurope 2005 Action Plan benchmarking indicators and the EU benchmarking guidelines[12].

---

[12] The eEurope+ Progress Report dated February 2004 states the guidelines for data collection as follows:
- *Data should be recent* in order to be relevant (the agreed data measurement point was set at June 2003),

We used two types of data in our research: soft data, which is subjective data gathered from questionnaires (such as the Global Competitiveness Survey, Sibis), and hard data, which is driven by statistics collected by reputed independent agencies (such as the World Bank and ITU). Both these sets of data play a crucial role in the overall analysis. The soft data is critical in determining the opinion of the decision-makers and opinion leaders who have an intimate knowledge of a nation's economy. On the other hand, the hard data captures fundamental elements related to the development of infrastructure, human capital and ICT.

Absence of key usage metrics: Key ICT metrics required for the eEurope 2005 framework, such as data pertaining to e-commerce and businesses, is difficult to obtain. Future research projects must seek to improve in this area. In addition, accurate usage metrics are difficult, if not impossible, to obtain and/or are seldom up to date. In the absence of such usage metrics, the challenge is to devise ways to best estimate the development of a country's ICT. For example, metrics based on realized cost savings, high-speed Internet access costs and usage, key measures of policy and regulation, and the use of ICT by governments all remain elusive.

Data estimation: Despite our best efforts to collect data from all major international sources, it was at times necessary to cope with incomplete sets of data for the countries surveyed. To compensate for this, statistical procedures (mainly regression and clustering techniques) were used to estimate missing data. Control procedures and checks were devised to ensure that estimations were reasonable and not overly favorable or disadvantageous in their representation of a given country.

- *Data should be consistent* and critically assessed for comparability, as far as possible,
- *Data should be cross-referenced* with existing public and private sources as far as possible,
- *Data should be compared with relevant EU figures,* usually an EU average, to allow a benchmark of the situation. Data trends over the past three years should be shown where possible.

Summary

This chapter presents the eEurope 2005 Index, which is based on the eEurope 2005 Action Plan defined by the European Union. The level of ICT development in 25 countries – the 15 incumbent European Union member states, eight new member states (NMS) and two candidate countries – was studied based on the eEurope 2005 benchmarking framework. Two new member states (Cyprus and Malta) and one candidate country (Turkey) were excluded from the analysis due to limitations in the availability of data.

The eEurope 2005 Index attempts to interpret the underlying complexity of the development and use of ICT and the Internet in an intuitive, readily understandable model. The overall index is an aggregate measure of a nation's ability to participate in and benefit from the networked economy. In addition, the eEurope 2005 Index provides guidance to business leaders and public policy-makers to enhance the impact of ICT. It does this by providing summary as well as detailed analysis of each country's strengths and weaknesses.

Based on the calculated index, the level of alignment of the NMS was determined. Countries were divided into five distinct groups: global leaders; EU-15 average or aligned countries; somewhat aligned countries; countries requiring some development; and countries requiring a significant level of development. It was found that Estonia belongs to the group II countries that are fully aligned with the EU-15 countries. Somewhat aligned NMS (group III) include Slovenia. Group IV NMS/candidate countries must work to develop their ICT infrastructure. This group includes Lithuania, Latvia, the Czech Republic, Poland and the Slovak Republic. Group V countries require significant development in ICT in order to line up with the incumbent EU-15 countries. This group consists of Bulgaria, Hungary and Romania, all of which are countries with lower GDP per capita.

The essence of the eEurope 2005 Index extends beyond any single metric. Overall, some countries are evidently overperforming while others underperform. Some have put ICT high on the national agenda and worked hard to make it an area of excellence. Others have not done so. The former countries have succeeded in transcending individual measures of national income or national ICT spending in an effort to provide an optimal environment for ICT development. In so doing, they have promoted high levels of e-readiness and usage among all three key stakeholders. Of the NMS, Estonia is one such example. Among the EU-15 countries, Denmark, Sweden and the United Kingdom rank as leaders and could serve as role models for other nations in their quest for ICT excellence. The eEurope 2005 Index allows a nation to benchmark its ICT performance and determine the effectiveness of policy. It also permits a country to learn from the policy and performance of other countries with similar profiles, and to identify best practices.

ICT holds the keys to develop our practices in many areas: education, work, personal relationships, work effectiveness and national productivity. One interesting characteristic of ICT components such as the Internet is that there is no linear correlation between overall value added and the number of connected individuals and organizations. Increasing the levels to which developing countries participate in ICT creates benefits not only for these countries, but also gives all relevant stakeholders greater potential to realize value.

References

Council Resolution of February 18, 2003, on the implementation of the eEurope 2005 Action Plan. *Official Journal of the European Union.* February 28, 2003.

Flash Eurobarometer 135, "Internet and the Public at Large". *Eurobarometer.* November 2002. http://www.gesis.org/en/data_service/eurobarometer/.

Dutta, S., B. Lanvin, and F. Paua (editors), 2003. *The Global Information Technology Report 2002-2003: Readiness for the Networked World.* New York: Oxford University Press. January 2003.

Dutta, S., B. Lanvin, and F. Paua (editors), 2004. *The Global Information Technology Report 2003-2004: Towards an Equitable Information Society.* New York: Oxford University Press. February 2004.

Dutta, S. and A. Lopez-Claros (editors), 2005. *The Global Information Technology Report 2004-2005: Efficiency in an Increasingly Connected World.* New York: Palgrave MacMillan. March 2005.

eEurope+ 2003 Progress Report. February 2004. http://www.emcis2004.hu/dokk /binary/30/17/3/eEurope__Final_Progress_Report.pdf.

Information Society Statistics, 2003 edition. *Eurostat.* http://europa.eu.int/comm/ eurostat/.

International Telecommunication Union. 2002. *World Telecommunications Indicators.* Online. http://www.itu.int/home/index.html.

Online Availability of Public Services: How is Europe Progressing? 2004. *Cap Gemini Ernst & Young.*

Organization for Economic Co-operation and Development. *Science, Technology and Industry Outlook: Drivers of Growth: Information Technology, Innovation, and Entrepreneurship.* 2001.

Sabol, Thomas. 2003. eGovernment in Selected EU Accession States. *Prisma Strategic Guideline*, April 8, 2003.

Sibis Pocket Book 2002/2003. *Sibis.* http://www.empirica.biz/sibis/.

The 2003 e-Readiness rankings. 2003. *Economist Intelligence Unit.*

World Bank Group. 2002. *World Development Indicators 2001.* Online. http:// www.worldbank.org/data/wdi/index.htm.

WP4-D4.3.3 eEurope 2005 Key Figures for Benchmarking EU 15. *Database Consulting*. http://www.empirica.biz/sibis/.

Appendix 1: Networked Readiness Index 2004-5

Source: Dutta and Lopez-Claros, 2005

Country	Score	Rank	Country	Score	Rank
Singapore	1.73	1	Tunisia	0.39	31
Iceland	1.66	2	Slovenia	0.37	32
Finland	1.62	3	Bahrain	0.37	33
Denmark	1.60	4	South Africa	0.33	34
United States	1.58	5	Chile	0.29	35
Sweden	1.53	6	Thailand	0.27	36
Hong Kong	1.39	7	Cyprus	0.25	37
Japan	1.35	8	Hungary	0.24	38
Switzerland	1.30	9	India	0.23	39
Canada	1.27	10	Czech Republic	0.21	40
Australia	1.23	11	China	0.17	41
United Kingdom	1.21	12	Greece	0.17	42
Norway	1.19	13	Lithuania	0.13	43
Germany	1.16	14	Jordan	0.10	44
Taiwan	1.12	15	Italy	0.10	45
Netherlands	1.08	16	Brazil	0.08	46
Luxembourg	1.04	17	Mauritius	0.08	47
Israel	1.02	18	Slovak Republic	0.03	48
Austria	1.01	19	Jamaica	-0.03	49
France	0.96	20	Botswana	-0.10	50
New Zealand	0.95	21	Indonesia	-0.13	51
Ireland	0.89	22	Turkey	-0.14	52
United Arab Emirates	0.84	23	Romania	-0.15	53
Korea	0.81	24	Morocco	-0.17	54
Estonia	0.80	25	Namibia	-0.21	55
Belgium	0.74	26	Latvia	-0.23	56
Malaysia	0.69	27	Egypt	-0.24	57
Malta	0.50	28	Croatia	-0.25	58
Spain	0.43	29	Trinidad and Tobago	-0.28	59
Portugal	0.39	30	Mexico	-0.28	60

Country	Score	Rank	Country	Score	Rank
Costa Rica	-0.29	61	Tanzania	-0.71	83
Russian Federation	-0.36	62	Venezuela	-0.72	84
Pakistan	-0.38	63	Macedonia	-0.73	85
Uruguay	-0.39	64	Nigeria	-0.73	86
Ghana	-0.41	65	Madagascar	-0.77	87
Colombia	-0.42	66	Guatemala	-0.78	88
Philippines	-0.43	67	Bosnia and Herzegovina	-0.86	89
Vietnam	-0.46	68	Peru	-0.91	90
Panama	-0.47	69	Georgia	-0.94	91
El Salvador	-0.49	70	Mali	-0.96	92
Sri Lanka	-0.49	71	Malawi	-0.98	93
Poland	-0.50	72	Zimbabwe	-1.02	94
Bulgaria	-0.51	73	Ecuador	-1.08	95
Gambia	-0.52	74	Mozambique	-1.11	96
Kenya	-0.62	75	Honduras	-1.19	97
Argentina	-0.62	76	Paraguay	-1.20	98
Uganda	-0.63	77	Bolivia	-1.25	99
Dominican Republic	-0.65	78	Bangladesh	-1.30	100
Serbia and Montenegro	-0.65	79	Angola	-1.36	101
Algeria	-0.66	80	Ethiopia	-1.52	102
Zambia	-0.68	81	Nicaragua	-1.61	103
Ukraine	-0.68	82	Chad	-1.69	104

Appendix 2: Constructing the eEurope 2005 Index

The eEurope 2005 Index is made up of five component indexes: Internet indicators, modern online public services, a dynamic e-business environment, a secure information infrastructure and broadband. Starting from a set of over 130 ICT-related variables, we divided these variables among the five indexes. We then eliminated variables based on the number of countries for which data was available and on the use of analytical procedures such as factor analysis and reliability tests (e.g. Cronbach's Alpha). Our final index computation was therefore based on a set of 37 variables[13].

Definitions of the eEurope 2005 Index and Component Indexes

The eEurope 2005 Index is defined as follows:

eEurope 2005 Index = 1/5 Internet indicators + 1/5 modern online public services + 1/5 dynamic e-business environment + 1/5 secure information infrastructure + 1/5 broadband

   A.   **Internet indicators:** a component index consisting of three broad categories of data: citizens' access to and use of the Internet; enterprise access to and use of ICT; and Internet access costs

       1.   Data variables relating to "citizens' access to and use of the Internet":

1.01	Home Internet access
1.02	Internet usage
1.03	Internet usage intensity
1.04	E-mail
1.05	Internet users
1.06	DSL Internet subscribers
1.07	ISDN subscribers
1.08	Home Internet usage
1.09	Internet usage at work
1.10	Internet access in schools

---

[13] Our research used the most recent data available from the relevant sources (such as the World Economic Forum's Global Competitiveness Survey 2003-2004 questionnaire and data from the World Bank, SIBIS and ITU).

1.11   Households online
1.12   Personal computers

2. Data variables relating to "enterprise access to and use of ICT":

2.01   Employees with Internet access
2.02   Business PCs
2.03   Teleworking usage
2.04   Teleworking intensity

3. Data variables relating to "Internet access costs":

3.01   Residential telephone connection charge
3.02   Business telephone monthly subscription
3.03   Business telephone connection charge

B. **Modern online public services:** a component index consisting of data that can be grouped into three distinct categories: e-government, e-learning, and e health

1. The "e-government" group consists of the following data variables:

4.01   Government online presence
4.02   Government online services
4.03   Online book search
4.04   Government prioritization of ICT
4.05   Online tax returns
4.06   Government ICT promotion

2. "E-learning" is defined by the following variables:

5.01   Internet access in schools
5.02   Online learning
5.03   Offline electronic learning

3. "E-health" is defined by the following variables:

6.01   Online health searches
6.02   Internet usage by the disabled

C. **A dynamic e-business environment:** a component index consisting of data that can be divided into the following two categories: buying and selling online and e-business readiness.

1. "Buying and selling online" is defined by the following variables:

    7.01   Online purchases
    7.02   B-to-C e-commerce

2. "E-business readiness" is defined by the following variables:

    8.01   Laws relating to IT

D. **A secure information infrastructure:** a component index consisting of Internet users' experience of ICT security. It comprises the following variables:

    9.01   Online privacy
    9.02   Secure online commerce

E. **Broadband:** a component index consisting of the following variables:

    10.01   DSL broadband access
    10.02   Broadband subscribers

2 Electronic Business in the European Union: An Assessment of the Digital Divide in Business

Hannes Selhofer, empirica GmbH
George Karageorgos, European Commission

2.1 Introduction

This article is based on research that was carried out by the European Commission's *e-Business W@tch* in 2003 and 2004. It explores whether and to what extent there is a digital divide in the use of ICT and in electronic business practices between companies from the new EU member states and the former EU-15 countries.

The *e-Business W@tch*[1] is an initiative of the European Commission's Enterprise & Industry Directorate General. It was launched in late 2001, since when it has served as an observatory to monitor and analyze the adoption, development and impact of electronic business[2] practices in different sectors of the European economy. Special emphasis is placed on the implications of ICT and e-business for SMEs. The observatory was initiated in the wider context of the eEurope 2005 Action Plan, endorsed by the Seville European Council in June 2002, which confirmed the goal of promoting *"take-up of e-business with the aim of increasing the competitiveness of European enterprises and raising productivity and growth through investment in information and communication technologies (ICT), human resources (notably e-skills) and new business models"*.

---

[1] Since its launch, the *e-Business W@tch* has published impact studies on 17 different sectors of the European economy, three comprehensive synthesis reports, two statistical pocketbooks and data on the diffusion of e-business. All this material is available under 'publications' at www.ebusiness-watch.org.

[2] In accordance with a definition proposed by the OECD, electronic business is defined here as „automated business processes (both intracompany and intercompany) over computer-mediated networks".

After the Hype: The New Importance of ICT for Business

It is widely acknowledged that the use of ICT in business has far-reaching implications for the productivity of firms, the organization of the market (the way companies interact with their suppliers and customers) and competition within and between industries. Although the business implications of ICT were over-hyped during the boom phase of the Internet economy, there is no question that modern business cannot do without ICT. In fact, some major impacts on markets and competition have only become visible in the past two to three years.

The growing maturity and diffusion of ICT-based applications is nevertheless confronting firms with a new challenge. Doing business electronically, once an option to demonstrate innovation and strategic positioning, is about to become a "must" if companies are to stay in business. ICT is, to some extent, losing its innovative status and is instead becoming a basic technology. Against this background, it is even more important that all companies possess at least basic ICT infrastructure and skills to do some of their business electronically.

If this general assessment holds true, it is understandable that the demand for adequate ICT diffusion and adoption measures and the quest for better, innovative metrics to understand impacts still ranks highly on policy-makers' agenda. In the context of EU enlargement, the question arises to what extent the "e-maturity" of companies from the 10 new member states compares with the status of their counterparts in the former EU-15. On the basis of available data on household conditions, it was impossible to preclude the possibility of a considerable digital divide in the sophistication of e-business at companies in the new and existing member states. On the other hand, if ICT infrastructure and usage in companies from the new member states was found to be comparable to the average situation in the "old" ones, important preconditions for productivity and competitiveness would be met. This chapter provides some evidence on this issue.

The Importance of a Sectoral Perspective in e-Business

For the purposes of this article, four industries were selected as examples to explore the digital maturity level of firms in different countries. They include two manufacturing and two service industries:

- **The chemicals, rubber and plastics industries**, which account for about 15% of EU manufacturing output (in value terms),

- **The electrical machinery and electronics industry**, which is very suitable for e-business because of the high degree of product standardization, globalization of production and specialization of firms along the value chain,
- **The retail sector**, which represents a cornerstone of economic activity within Europe (around three million retail enterprises currently employ nearly 14 million people in the EU),[3]
- **The tourism sector** (including hotels, restaurants, travel agencies, tour operators, and air transport) which, in some respects, has always been a forerunner in using ICT, and where e-commerce is having a huge impact and challenging intermediaries.

The sectoral perspective is important because ICT assumes different functions for enterprises depending on the nature of their business activity. It depends, for example, on whether firms deal with large numbers of consumers or mainly with smaller numbers of other businesses, on the kinds of goods or services they produce, and on the specifics of the industry value chain.

For firms from manufacturing sectors, for example, increasing the efficiency of supply chain processes was a key objective for many e-business projects in 2003/04. Moreover, large manufacturers have set up or use sophisticated e-procurement platforms to cut down on procurement costs. Service sectors, on the other hand, are less homogeneous in themselves. Retail companies, for instance, focus on procurement and logistics-related opportunities. By contrast, tourism is experiencing the power of the Internet as a new channel for marketing and sales, with significant impacts on the value chain.

Evidence presented in this article tests whether the average relative "e-maturity" of firms from a given country (compared to their counterparts in other countries) can vary from one sector to another, depending, for example, on the relative importance of that sector in the country's economy.

---

[3] Based on Eurostat New Cronos. Cf. Sector Study on Retail (2004), www.ebusiness-watch.org.

2.2 Methodology

2.2.1 Data Sources

The data used in this analysis is based on primary research, namely on a representative survey of decision-makers at European enterprises about their firms' use of ICT and e-business (E-Business Survey 2003). The survey comprised more than 10,800 telephone interviews conducted in the period March-November 2003, including enterprises from 11 sectors, all EU member states and Norway.[4]

The sample drawn was a random sample of companies from the respective sector population in each country (where the respective sector was to be surveyed), the objective being to achieve a representative share (strata in respect of company size classes) of at least 10 percent of large companies (250+ employees) per country-sector cell, 30 percent of medium-sized enterprises (50-249 employees) and 25 percent of small enterprises (10-49 employees). The average number of interviews per sector in a given country was between 75 and 100.

Two weighting methods were applied: weighting by employment and by the number of enterprises. Data used for the research presented in this article is weighted by employment. This means that percentages describing a certain share of firms should be read as "enterprises comprising x% of employees (in the given sector or country)". The reason for using employment weighting is that there are many more micro-enterprises than non-micro-enterprises. The unweighted figure would effectively represent mainly the smallest sizes of firm. Weighting was based on the latest available universe figures about the industry by Eurostat. Missing or undisclosed universe data had to be imputed.

2.2.2 Hypotheses

Based on the general assumptions and perspective on e-business outlined in the introduction, and on findings of the *e-Business W@tch* sector studies in 2004, the special analysis carried out for this article took the following two hypotheses as its point of departure:

---

[4] Not all sectors could be surveyed in all countries. The matrix of country/sector cells covered by the survey and further information about the methodology is available in the methodology annex of the European E-Business Report 2004.

H1:   There is no general digital divide between enterprises in the two groups of countries, i.e. between the EU-15 on the one hand and the new EU member states on the other. Rather, different levels of e-maturity exist between firms in individual countries.

H2:   The e-maturity of firms in specific countries can vary by sector. There is no "equidistance" between the e-maturity of firms in a given country and the EU average across all sectors.

2.2.3 Indicators and Construction of the Index

The instrument used to test whether the two hypotheses hold true for the selected sectors was the E-Business Scoreboard, which was developed by *e-Business W@tch* in 2004.[5] This scoreboard uses 16 key indicators to compare the importance of ICT and e-business applications (for example across sectors or countries).

The 16 component indicators for ICT and e-business are grouped into four categories according to the business functions to which they refer. The four categories translate into first level sub-indices. They can then be further aggregated to an overall compound index known as the E-Maturity Index. The four sub-index categories of the scoreboard are:

A.   **Basic ICT infrastructure** ("connectivity") of the enterprise: This category relates to the standard and functionality of the company's ICT network,

B.   **Internal business processes**: The second category indicates to what extent firms use ICT to automate internal business processes,

C.   **Supplier-facing processes**: The third category looks at electronic procurement activities and the level of supply chain integration in firms,

D.   **Customer-facing processes**: The fourth category computes indicators about the intensity of firms' electronic marketing and sales activities.

---

[5] The main application of the scoreboard in 2004 was to compare e-business activity in different sectors. Here, the scoreboard is used to compare companies from different countries (within a given sector).

The component indicators for each of the four dimensions are shown in figure 1. Some of the component indicators (such as indicator A.1, the percentage of companies using a local area network) can be derived directly from one specific question in the survey. Others are composites of more than one variable. One example is indicator A.2 (quality of Internet access), which considers not only whether or not a company has Internet access but also the maximum available bandwidth. A more detailed definition of the component indicators is available in the publications of the *e-Business W@tch.*[6]

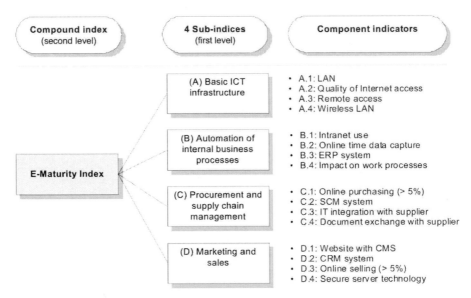

Fig. 1: The E-Business Scoreboard: component indicators and indices

Computation

Component indicators were extracted from the survey results (weighted by employment). Those indicators that consist of more than one variable were then computed, creating a set of 16 indicators for the four sectors.

No weighting procedure was applied to aggregate component indicators into first-level indices. Nor was this done to aggregate the overall E-

---

[6] Cf. Pocketbook of e-Business Indicators 2004. Luxembourg: Office for Official Publications of the European Communities.

Maturity Index (the second level). In other words, each indicator had the same weighting of 1.0.

The values on the E-Business Scoreboard, however, were computed and can be presented in two ways, both of which apply to both component indicators and indices:

- First, "simple" indexed values based on the percentages from the respective survey questions,
- Second, values expressed as relative distances between a unit and the mean value, measured as multiples of standard deviations to the mean value. These take into account the percentages (diffusion rates) for all units compared and show how a specific unit differs from the all-units average.

The constituting values for the second method are z-values, i.e. $z = (x - mean(x))/stddev(x)$. This procedure results in a distribution with $mean(z)=0$ and $stddev(z)=1$. Accordingly, the index values express the multiple of the standard deviation (1 or (-1)) for a specific unit and the selected indicator. 0 equals the mean value for all units, a value of $+1$ that the percentage is higher than the mean percentage of all units by the extent of the standard deviation. Negative values show that the percentage is lower than the mean percentage of all units.

In this article, the tables and bar charts are based on the first method, while the spider charts are based on the second method of computation.

Selected Countries

In light of data availability on the one hand and the research questions on the other, the following countries were selected for comparison:

- All countries from the new EU member states for which data was available for the respective sector from the E-Business Survey 2003,
- The aggregate of the five largest EU economies ("EU-5"), consisting of Germany, Spain, France, Italy and the UK. Data for the EU-5 total is available for all sectors. As these five countries represent about 70-75% of the EU economy (e.g. in terms of production value and GDP), their aggregate can be considered a good proxy for the EU-15 (if not for the EU-25) total,

- One Nordic country was included (subject to data availability), as these countries normally rank as leaders in the adoption of ICT. The objective of including a Nordic country was to get some indication about the digital divide within the former EU-15 (by comparing data with the EU-5 total), as compared to a possible gap relative to the new member states.

Following "conventional wisdom", a ranking could be expected which showed the Nordic countries to be the most e-mature economies, followed by the EU-5 aggregate and then by the new member states. Results show that this holds true in part, but that the distance between the leading economies and the followers can vary considerably across sectors.

2.3   Results

2.3.1   The Chemicals Industries

Profile and Background

The combined chemicals industries, as defined for the analysis by the *e-Business W@tch*, consist of two sectors in the sense of the NACE Rev. 1 classification of business activities: the manufacture of chemicals, chemical products and man-made fibers (NACE Rev. 1 Division 24); and the manufacture of rubber and plastic products (NACE 25).

Of the new EU member states, Poland, the Czech Republic and Hungary are the largest producers of chemical, rubber and plastic products. Together, these three countries account for about 80% of production and value added in the new member states. The *e-Business W@tch* estimates that these industries provide jobs for about 400,000 people in the new member states.[7]

The chemicals industries have been a rather conservative sector when it came to using ICT to link business processes and interact with their suppliers and customers. Part of the explanation may be found in the extremely stringent security requirements that apply in this sector. This is due to the sensitive nature of the goods produced (toxic potential) and the high level of research and development, at least in sub-sectors such as the

---

[7] Cf. Sector Study No. 02-I (2004), p. 15. www.ebusiness-watch.org (publications).

pharmaceuticals industries, requiring strict measures to protect company knowledge (data and patents).

However, conservative does not mean that companies refuse adoption and innovation. Quite the contrary: The sector as a whole exhibits some characteristics that are perfect for e-business. For example, many of its products are very suitable for standardization and, consequently, for online trading. However, the managers of chemical companies often press much harder for return-on-investment figures before approving the implementation of new IT architectures or software applications than may be the case in other sectors.

The sector is further characterized by a dichotomy between large companies on the one hand, which tend to be very advanced in exploiting ICT-related opportunities for e-business, and small firms on the other, many of which adhere to more traditional forms of trading.

E-Business Scoreboard 2003/04

Data from the E-Business Survey 2003 show that companies from Sweden are the most intensive users of ICT in the chemicals industry. There is a large gap between Swedish companies and the EU-5 average, particularly in the area of B2B trading. Nearly all data indicates that, in this sector, the adoption of systems for e-business is much more advanced in companies from Sweden than on average.

Among the new member states, companies from Estonia and the Czech Republic exhibit comparable levels of e-business activity as their counterparts in the EU-5. The pattern for Estonia is quite exceptional (cf. figure 3), as B2B trading activities and connectivity between enterprises is more widely deployed (relative to other countries) than the scale of its ICT infrastructure would suggest. The pattern for firms from the Czech Republic is very similar to the one for EU-5 companies.

For Latvia and Poland, however, the data shows that companies from the chemicals industry in these countries have not yet reached the same e-maturity level as in countries of the former EU-15. The gap is visualized in the spider charts in figure 3. The structure of the sector in these new member states, which have a higher share of small companies and less powerful ICT infrastructures, may help to explain this gap. In any case, the need for innovation in these countries seems to be greater if their companies are to stay competitive.

Country	Index A	Index B	Index C	Index D	Compound index
Sweden	100	100	100	100	100
EU-5	81	75	64	33	63
Estonia	70	50	86	46	63
Czech R.	78	82	49	37	61
Latvia	53	68	48	28	49
Poland	54	51	39	26	43

A = ICT infrastructure
B = Internal business process automation
C = Procurement and supply chain integration
D = Marketing and sales

Computed from simple percentages; ignores standard deviations from mean value. Indexed values (100 = Max.).

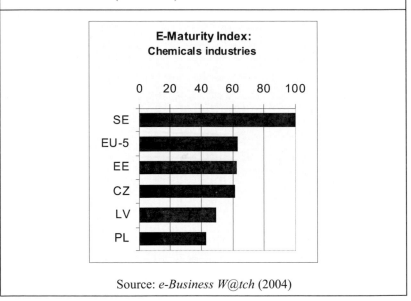

Source: *e-Business W@tch* (2004)

Fig. 2: The E-Business Scoreboard for the chemicals industries

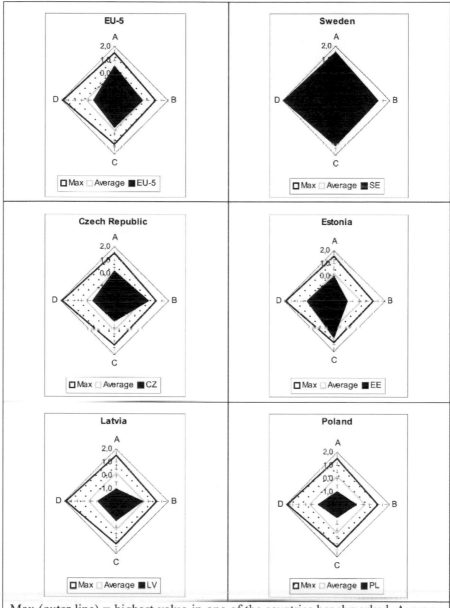

Max (outer line) = highest value in one of the countries benchmarked. Average (thick line) = mean value of all countries. Dark diamond = values for the respective country. Scale: distance from the mean value (= 0), measured by multiples of standard deviations.

Fig. 3: Benchmarking the e-maturity of chemicals companies from 6 countries

Conclusions: Alignment of the New Member States

In light of the very deliberate and careful application of ICT, it is unlikely that e-business will radically change the fundamentals of how chemical products are traded. This is not to say that there will be no impact at all. However, the major forces driving change in the chemicals, rubber and plastics industries can be seen in the internationalization of markets and in changes to the regulatory frameworks, rather than in information technology and e-business *per se*. If this general assumption holds true, it would be safe to conclude that ICT should not hamper the alignment of companies from the new member states in this sector, particularly since some of these countries appear already to be fairly closely "aligned" with the average EU level in respect to their companies' e-business activity.

The results furnished by the *e-Business W@tch* do not therefore suggest an urgent need for e-business-specific policies in the chemicals sector. ICT is being adopted and used in this sector in an evolutionary manner and is unlikely to cause dramatic changes or upheavals in the industry's value chain.

However, it is clear that basic use of ICT and e-business applications will – as in other sectors – be indispensable requirements for the conduct of business in future. It would therefore be important to monitor whether the digital divide can be narrowed between those countries that currently have a low level of e-maturity and the average for the European Union in this industry. This is no easy task. As electronic business has become much more mature and sophisticated than it was a couple of years ago, reaping the potential benefits requires more than just setting up a website. For small and medium-sized companies in particular, the cost of implementing the necessary infrastructure and systems can be substantial and require skilful change management. The main potential of e-business for the chemicals industries is currently to be found in improving the efficiency of internal and B2B processes by linking and automating processes electronically. It is important that companies, (including SMEs) in all EU member states participate in this development.

2.3.2 *Electrical Machinery and Electronics Manufacturing*

Profile and Background

This industry, as defined for the analysis of e-business, comprises activities within the following NACE Rev. 1 classifications[8]: the manufacture of office machinery and computers (DL 30); the manufacture of electrical machinery and apparatus (DL 31); and the manufacture of radio, television and communication equipment and apparatus (NACE Rev.1 92.2).

The EU's electrical machinery and electronics industry is heavily concentrated. Large firms account for only 2% of all companies in the sector but contribute 66% to its employment figure. Concentration is particularly pronounced in the electronics industries, where rapid technological progress and the production of standardized, high-volume electronic products have enhanced economies of scale and hence the concentration process. The manufacture of electrical machinery and apparatus requires more manpower than other sub-sectors of this combined industry, employing about 5 percent of total manufacturing labor.

The electronics industry in particular is a truly global business. Product design, production and related marketing activities are frequently carried out in different parts of the world, exploiting comparative regional advantages. Components and products are highly standardized, easy to describe and are traded in considerable quantities. Product life cycles are short and value chains complex and deep. Outsourcing is very common and requires intensive cooperation between enterprises, often across cultural and geographical borders.

In such a highly competitive global environment, companies from most of the new member states still lag behind their counterparts in the EU-15 countries in terms of production value and value added (at constant prices), although some of them are already well positioned. In Hungary and Poland, the industry has experienced promising and rapid development and plays an important role both in a national and international context.

---

[8] The "General Industrial Classification of Economic Activities within the European Communities", known by the acronym NACE and originally published by Eurostat in 1970, is the Statistical Classification of Economic Activities in the European Community. The current version is Revision 1.1.

E-Business Scoreboard 2003/04

Survey results indicate that basic Internet infrastructures are widely implemented within the electronics and electrical machinery industries across Europe. This is also true for most of the new member states. The lack of ICT infrastructures therefore does not constitute a major barrier to e-business.

However, considerable differences exist with respect to the availability of broadband Internet connections, remote and wireless access technologies and, in particular, the level of e-business activity in trading with suppliers and customers. In general, companies in the Nordic countries (Sweden and Finland) lead in these areas of ICT application. Companies from the new member states are found to lag behind in most e-business application areas, although there are exceptions depending on the precise application.

As already noted for the chemicals industry, the E-Business Scoreboard reveals companies from the Nordic countries to be the most intensive users of ICT and e-business, some way ahead of the EU-5 average. Unlike in the chemicals industry, however, there is a further considerable gap between companies from the EU-5 and most of the new member states in this sector. Figure 5 shows that firms from Slovenia and Estonia are closer to the EU-5 than their counterparts in Hungary and Poland, although the industry is relatively more important in the latter countries. Firms from Slovenia tend to have better ICT infrastructures, but companies from Estonia appear to be more active in terms of electronic trading activities.

Country	Index A	Index B	Index C	Index D	Compound index
Finland	100	100	100	100	100
EU-5	85	71	70	79	76
Slovakia	75	68	80	78	75
Estonia	63	55	76	56	62
Slovenia	82	78	25	48	60
Poland	58	39	38	46	46
Hungary	59	44	11	16	32

A = ICT infrastructure
B = Internal business process automation
C = Procurement and supply chain integration
D = Marketing and sales

Computed from simple percentages; ignores standard deviations from mean value. Indexed values (100 − Max,),

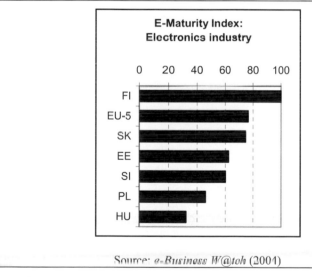

Source: e-Business W@tch (2001)

Fig. 4: The E-Business Scoreboard for the electrical machinery and electronics industry

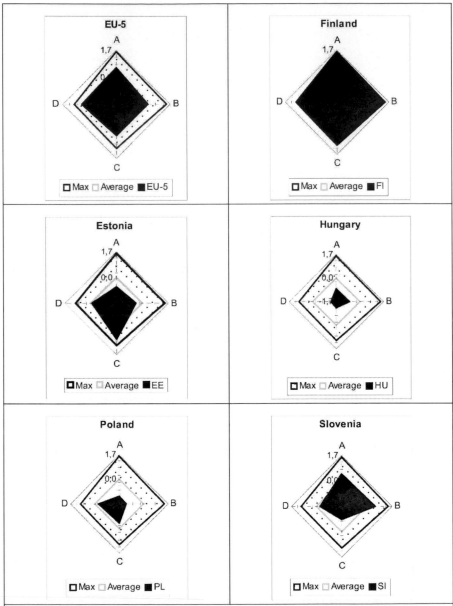

Max (outer line) = highest value in one of the countries benchmarked. Average (thick line) = mean value of all countries. Dark diamond = values for the respective country. Scale: distance from the mean value (= 0), measured by multiples of standard deviations.

Fig. 5: Benchmarking the e-maturity of companies in the electrical machinery and electronics industry from 6 countries

Conclusions: Alignment of the New Member States

Manufacturers of electronic equipment are naturally IT-savvy and open to experiment with IT-driven management solutions. The *e-Business W@tch* results have consistently shown that this sector in general, and the electronics industry in particular, is an early adopter of e-business. Above all, the very advanced status of large companies from this sector in the EU-15 and in the Nordic countries seems to be the most probable explanation for the significant digital divide that appears between them and firms from the new EU member states. On the basis of these results it is, therefore, fair to conclude that e-business alignment has not yet reached a satisfactory level in this sector.

Industries involved in the manufacture of electronics products are increasingly relying on partners for design and manufacturing activities. This trend, combined with a trend toward global sourcing, means that companies must manage end-to-end processes that extend beyond their company and across multiple tiers of their supply chain. In such a business environment, the efficient exchange of electronic information and the exploitation of B2B trading mechanisms will be important to stay competitive. Consequently, the e-maturity alignment between companies from the new member states and the EU-15 countries should accelerate with respect to both ICT infrastructure and basic applications.

In summary, hypothesis 1 ("... no general, clear-cut digital divide between companies from the 'old' and the new member states") must be partly rejected for the electrical machinery and electronics industry. Companies from most of the new member states are less advanced than their Western European counterparts. However, the situation in this sector is rather exceptional as large firms have already reached a very high level of e-maturity. This has also been observed in the new member states, where firms in this sector seem to be more advanced than their counterparts across sectors studied within the same country.

2.3.3 Retail

Profile and Background

The European and international retail trade (NACE Rev. 1 Division 52) has a complex structure comprising a large number of very small enterprises and some very large enterprises. The sector is increasingly being shaped by a few very large groups or chains that can exploit economies of scale, mixed in with many small shops that serve a local market.

Data available for the new EU member states indicates that more than 95 percent of the retail companies in these countries are micro-enterprises with less than 10 employees. Here, the retail industry structure is still a very traditional one made up of small specialized shops. Close to 900,000 people in the new member states are employed in retail, 47 percent of them in the Czech Republic and Slovakia.[9] Productivity rates were highest in Cyprus and Malta (ignoring variations in producer price indices), whose figures compare with those of some EU-15 countries (Spain and Portugal).

The structural characteristics of the retail sector should give ICT and e-business an important role. There is a need for more efficient upstream integration in the supply chain and, at the same time, for downstream communication with customers. In addition, particularly in the case of large companies, there is strong demand for auxiliary company-internal communication processes, for instance between field representatives and headquarters.

Consequently, the critical processes operated by companies in the retail industry involve procurement and the management of logistical flows. The main areas in which retailers are investing in applications are currently supply chain configurations, the management of store operations and interaction with customers.

E-Business Scoreboard 2003/04

Again, the Nordic country that was part of the sample (Norway in this case) exhibits the highest level of e-maturity. Estonia and the EU-5 aggregate show a similar propensity toward ICT, albeit with one exception: electronic procurement and supply chain logistics are less well developed among Estonian companies compared to the EU-5, in spite of their well-equipped ICT infrastructure. Retail companies from the other new member states fall behind in their e-business intensity, particularly those from Slovakia and Latvia. In these countries, electronic marketing and sales activities are practiced to a much lesser extent than in any other country surveyed in the retail sector.

---

[9] No data was available for Poland, the largest retail market, and Slovenia. These countries are missing from the quoted figure. Cf. Sector Study No. 06-I (2004), www.ebusiness-watch.org.

Country	Index A	Index B	Index C	Index D	Compound index
Norway	100	95	100	100	100
Estonia	87	100	48	85	81
EU-5	70	92	70	89	80
Lithuania	74	88	62	60	72
Cyprus	65	83	59	41	63
Poland	51	70	30	73	56
Slovakia	61	58	66	15	49
Latvia	57	33	35	15	37

A = ICT infrastructure
B = Internal business process automation
C – Procurement and supply chain integration
D = Marketing and sales

Computed from simple percentages; ignores standard deviations from mean value. Indexed values (100 = Max.).

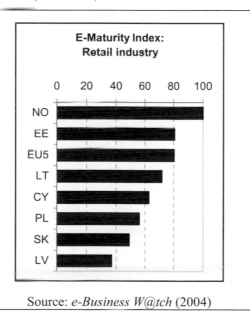

Source: *e-Business W@tch* (2004)

Fig. 6: The E-Business Scoreboard for the retail industry

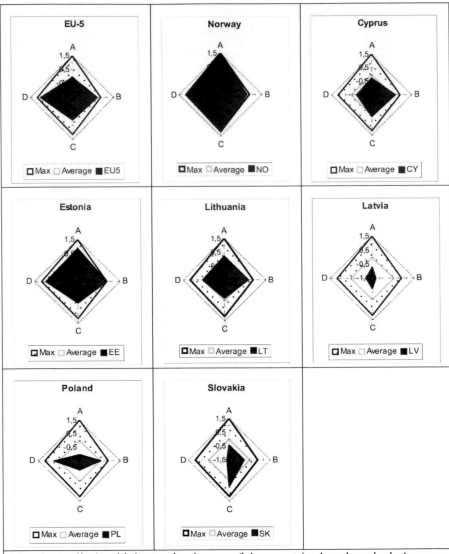

Max (outer line) = highest value in one of the countries benchmarked. Average (thick line) = mean value of all countries. Dark diamond = values for the respective country. Scale: distance from the mean value (= 0), measured by multiples of standard deviations.

Fig. 7: Benchmarking the e-maturity of retail companies from 8 countries

Conclusions: Alignment of the New Member States

Studies by the *e-Business W@tch* have shown that the diffusion of both e-commerce and e-business in the retail industry is far from a pervasive reality or even on a par with the standard diffusion of most other sectors. This is partly due to the industry structure, where SMEs still occupy the largest share in terms of both employment and the number of firms.

E-commerce is still very limited, increasing slightly with company size. The e-commerce advantages perceived by retailers are of an indirect nature. They are not seen in terms of sales volume or value, but in terms of marketing advantages such as customer retention/acquisition and the quality of the service delivered.

However, the *e-Business W@tch* studies also show that there is untapped e-business potential in this sector in particular, and that ICT can help small and medium-sized companies gain a competitive advantage, since many of their competitors are not yet advanced in this respect. As this sector is shaped by SMEs in the new member states even more so than in the EU-15, e-business related opportunities – but also risks, if the targeted innovation process is hampered by whatever circumstances – should be seriously considered. The promotion of modern technological e-business standards could help companies from the retail sector in the new member states at least to come into line with the average level for Western European retailers. Companies from the Nordic countries are more advanced in this respect. The gap between them and the European average can probably not be closed in the short term.

For the retail industry, hypothesis 1 (*"... no general, clear-cut digital divide between companies from the 'old' and the new member states"*) must be rejected: With a few exceptions, companies from the new member states are still lagging behind their West European counterparts in e-business development. The dominance of micro and small enterprises in these countries explains this situation to a large extent.

2.3.4 Tourism

Profile and Background

Tourism, as defined by the *e-Business W@tch* for its studies, involves the following business activities: hotels, restaurants, recreational and cultural activities (e.g. fairs, amusement parks and museums), travel agencies, tour operators and air transport. The tourism industry in Europe is represented by approximately two million enterprises who employ about 12 percent of the European workforce.[10]

Only a marginal percentage of these companies are large enterprises. The structure of the industry in the new member states resembles that of the EU-15 (in terms of size-class distribution).

The tourism sector is one of the fastest-growing industries in Europe and has a major impact on the European economy. Historically, the tourism sector has been among the first to use new technologies. Because it is an information-rich sector, it depends heavily on finding and developing new means to distribute travel and accommodation products and services, sell information to consumers and provide comfort and convenience to travelers.

Three main waves of innovation have impacted tourism's profile in recent decades: the development of the computer reservation system (CRS) in the 1970s; the development of the global distribution system (GDS) in the 1980s; and the Internet in the 1990s.

The Internet has deeply influenced and reshaped the sector profile. It has become the new medium for interaction that was previously carried out through different means (e.g. between hotel chains and their direct-to-counter customers). It has also allowed direct interaction between customers and suppliers (e.g. with tour operators), thus impacting the role of traditional intermediaries and favoring the entry of new e-intermediaries. Moreover, there has been a general trend toward the integration and concentration of the various players in the sector value chain.

E-Business Scoreboard 2003/04

Data collected by the *e-Business W@tch* shows that there are considerable differences in way "e-tourism" has developed in different European Union countries. However, the picture is not consistent across all ICT application areas. Firms from a specific country can be high level performers within a special area of e-business but still score average (or even low) grades in others. It is therefore impossible to establish an unambiguous country ranking – which, in any case, was not the objective of this research.

---

[10] Cf. Sector Study on Tourism, No. 07-I (2004), p. 10. www.ebusiness-watch.org (publications).

Generally speaking, it appears that companies from the Nordic countries (if Denmark, which was included in the survey, is regarded as representative) are certainly as advanced ICT users in this industry as in others. Otherwise, differences in e-maturity appear to be less pronounced than, for example, in the retail industry. On the basis of the E-Business Survey data, tourism firms from most of the new EU member states (Malta, Estonia, Slovenia and the Czech Republic) evidence similar levels of e-business usage as enterprises from the EU-5 (DE, ES, FR, IT, UK). Only firms from Poland appear to be lagging behind in this respect.

However, the scoreboard does point to some differences in specific application areas. For instance, the use of ICT for e-marketing and sales activities (e.g. online reservations) by firms in Malta appears to be remarkably low, especially in light of its advanced overall performance. The same applies to companies from the Czech Republic and Slovenia.

As for the other sectors, the underlying scoreboard data have been computed in a second step based on mean values and standard deviations. Results for the four sub-indices are visualized in the spider chart. These confirm the intensive use of ICT by tourism companies in Denmark and similar patterns for firms in most of the new member states and the EU-5. On the other hand, the same results indicate that tourism enterprises in Poland are trailing below the average in all four categories of ICT application.

Country	Index A	Index B	Index C	Index D	Compound index
Denmark	100	74	100	100	100
Malta	78	100	94	49	84
EU-5	63	68	71	65	71
Estonia	61	81	57	58	68
Slovenia	70	94	43	45	67
Czech R.	61	63	87	38	65
Poland	43	52	46	35	46

A = ICT infrastructure
B = Internal business process automation
C = Procurement and supply chain integration
D = Marketing and sales

Computed from simple percentages; ignores standard deviations from mean value. Indexed values (100 = Max.).

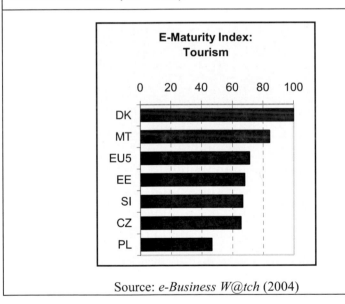

Source: *e-Business W@tch* (2004)

Fig. 8: The E-Business Scoreboard for the tourism industry

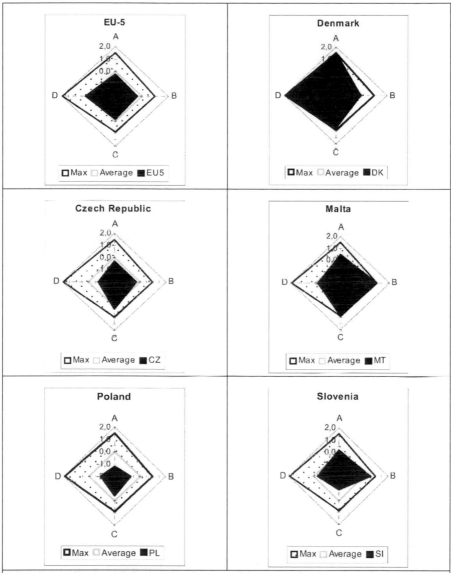

Max (outer line) = highest value in one of the countries benchmarked. Average (thick line) = mean value of all countries. Darkdiamond = values for the respective country. Scale: distance from the mean value (= 0), measured by multiples of standard deviations.

Fig. 9: Benchmarking the e-maturity of tourism companies from 6 countries

Conclusions: Alignment of the New Member States

The above analysis does not show a consistent picture across all ICT application areas and countries. With the exception of Poland, e-business diffusion among companies in the new member states appears to be on a similar level to the average among their counterparts in the EU-15, while enterprises from the Nordic countries come out as more advanced. It is difficult to explain these differences in detail. Nevertheless, the heterogeneity of the industries studied (in terms of the business activities covered) and the overall dichotomy between very small and large firms appear to have a significant influence on aggregate diffusion of ICT and e-business. These differences could also be explained on the basis of the relatively predominant sub-sectors in each specific sector in the respective country.

The enlargement of the EU in May 2004 was a very significant development for this sector in particular. For example, the electronic marketing of entire destinations will become even more important in the future. Analysis of the *e-Business W@tch* data shows that, notwithstanding some persistent gaps particularly in this e-business dimension, tourism companies in most of the new member states seem to be reasonably well aligned with their counterparts in the former EU-15.

For the tourism sector, hypothesis 1 (*"... no general, clear-cut digital divide between companies from the 'old' and the new member states"*) can thus be confirmed. In such a context, the challenge to the EU (and its member states) is to provide a framework that is conducive to the expansion and modernization of ICT infrastructure in the tourism sector across all member states, not just in the new ones. This would certainly help to raise the standards of ICT and e-business usage throughout the Union.

2.4 Summary

In November 2003, the *e-Business W@tch* interviewed decision-makers from more than 10,800 companies in the old and new EU member states about the use of ICT and e-business in their firms. The results suggest that the geographic digital divide in business may be smaller than expected, and that it is definitely smaller than the one in households. Firms from Slovenia and Estonia in particular, but also from the Czech Republic, were found to have reached the highest levels of e-maturity among the new members of the EU, apparently positioning themselves as the emerging "e-leaders" among the new EU members.

In reality, however, the picture is rather more complex. The situation is not consistent across sectors, and location is in no way a reliable predictor for a company's e-business activity. As a rule of thumb, gaps are more pronounced in the diffusion of more advanced e-business technologies and as regards the integration of applications within companies. Basic connectivity, such as Internet access, is in place at most companies in all member states. Even broadband access is widely deployed. Estonia is neck and neck with Germany, France and the UK when it comes to the share of firms that report being connected to the Internet with a bandwidth of 2 Mbps or more. Companies from other countries (for example from Poland, Hungary and Latvia) are trailing behind in this respect, but are not far short of the level of lower-tech regions in the current member states.

Coming back to the research hypotheses stated in the methodology section (see section 2.2), the findings are as follows (cf. figure 10):

- Hypothesis 1 (*"... no general, clear-cut digital divide between companies from the 'old' and the new member states"*) holds true for some sectors, definitely for tourism, but not for all sectors. It therefore needs to be modified,
- Hypothesis 2 (*"... relative e-maturity of firms from specific countries can vary by sector"*) can be confirmed. The geographic location of a company is in itself not a reliable predictor of its relative e-maturity. Depending on the industry structure in a given country, some sectors can be relatively more advanced than others.

Efforts to measure and assess e-business activity must therefore consider both the industry and the location as important contexts. One important factor is, for instance, whether a sector consists mainly of small firms, or whether medium-sized and large companies also play an important role.

Sector	Hypothesis 1: *"... no general, clear-cut digital divide between companies from the 'old' and the new member states"*	Hypothesis 2: *"... relative e-maturity of firms from specific countries can vary by sector"*
Chemicals	Generally confirmed: Level of e-business in firms from some new MS is similar to EU-5 level (but still a digital divide for some of the new MS)	
Electronics	Generally rejected: Digital divide between firms from most of the new MS and the EU-5 average (and especially the Nordic countries)	Mostly confirmed: Relative "performance" of firms in different countries varies by sector
Retail	Rejected: Can partly be explained by industry structures (SME dominance) in new member states	
Tourism	Confirmed: No consistent pattern to enterprises' e-business level by country	

Fig. 10: Confirmation/rejection of initial research hypotheses

Indication of Policy Implications

Even if there is no consistent pattern across all countries or sectors, some gaps are identifiable between the e-business performance of companies in the majority of the new member states and the corresponding average in the EU-15. There is, for instance, evidence of a persistent digital divide with respect to online procurement activities and supply chain integration. For example, only 19 percent of companies in Poland (in terms of their share of employment) say they order at least some of their input goods online, against 46 percent of companies from the current member states. The ratio is similar for related activities and IT-supported supply chain integration.

Electronic sourcing and procurement will also be important e-business applications to help many firms stay competitive in an increasingly networked economy. At the same time, some groundwork remains to be done especially in some of the new EU member states, where the telecommunications market structure is still rather old-fashioned. Broadband services, for example, are still quite expensive in some areas, a fact that constitutes a barrier to the efficient use of e-business.

Raising awareness and triggering innovation in this field may be a potential issue for e-business policies in the new member states. Recent initiatives by the European Commission, notably in the context of the E-Business Support Network[11], may support such policies, for instance by pooling good practices across the EU (including e-business policy practice) or by developing e-business software solutions adapted to the needs of SMEs.

---

[11] Cf. www.e-bsn.org.

References

e-Business W@tch (2004): The European E-Business Report 2004. A portrait of e-business in 10 sectors of the EU economy. 3rd Synthesis Report of the *e-Business W@tch* by the European Commission, DG Enterprise. Luxembourg: Office for Official Publications of the European Communities.

e-Business W@tch (2004): E-Business Sector Study: The chemical industries (2 reports). Study by empirica GmbH on behalf of the European Commission, DG Enterprise. www.ebusiness-watch.org.

e-Business W@tch (2004): E-Business Sector Study: Electrical machinery and electronics (2 reports). Study by IDATE / empirica GmbH on behalf of the European Commission, DG Enterprise. www.ebusiness-watch.org.

e-Business W@tch (2004): E-Business Sector Study: Retail (2 reports). Study by Databank Consulting / empirica GmbH on behalf of the European Commission, DG Enterprise. www.ebusiness-watch.org.

e-Business W@tch (2004): E-Business Sector Study: Tourism (2 reports). Study by RAMBOLL Management / empirica GmbH on behalf of the European Commission, DG Enterprise. www.ebusiness-watch.org.

3 The Impact of ICT on Social Cohesion: Looking Beyond the Digital Divide

Tobias Hüsing, Karsten Gareis and Werner B. Korte, empirica GmbH

The new member states of the EU face challenges in many different areas as economic restructuring continues in the aftermath of the fall of the Berlin Wall. The Information and Communications Technology Unit of the IPTS[1], which commissioned the research on which this chapter is based, has identified three challenges that are of utmost importance to the success of transformation in coming years. The first is to stabilize and foster economic growth rates in order to add new jobs and narrow the gap in standards of living relative to the old member states. The second, a consequence of the first, is to maintain and reinforce social cohesion and cushion the disparities that will almost inevitably accompany high growth rates. And the third is to ensure high-quality education to cope with demographic developments that threaten fiscal structures, social security systems and the existence of a highly qualified labor force, for example.

Of the three core challenges that the new member states will face in years to come, this research focuses on the second challenge identified above. It assesses the potential of information and communication technologies (ICT) to help policy-makers in the new member states avert threats to social cohesion.

Social disparities with regard to levels of income and access to jobs, education and basic infrastructures have been a permanent feature of economic development in the European Union ever since the Treaties of Rome. Disparities are present, for example, across different regions, social strata, ethnic groups and genders. Whereas recent years have brought some degree of convergence among EU countries at least at the national level, the latest round of enlargement has brought social divides back to the top of the European agenda. Not only do gaps still exist, however: They are in

[1] The Institute for Progressive Technological Studies (Seville), IPTS, DG JRC, European Commission, commissioned research under contract number 22200-2004-07 F1ED SEV DE that served as input to the present article. The authors wish to express their special gratitude to Marc Bogdanowicz and René van Bavel of the IPTS for their helpful comments on previous versions of this paper.

many cases actually widening as a result of selective economic restructuring, the increasing significance of the capacity of regions, companies, and communities to innovate, and differences in their ability to add value in the globally networked information economy.

Against this background, the discussion surrounding ICT tends to focus either on technology's potential to overcome and transcend existing social divides, or on the development of yet another – this time digital – social divide. Gainful employment, but also social participation and leisure activities, are increasingly becoming forms of information-based interaction that depend on one's ability to access, process, and transfer information. Thanks to the availability of broadband connections, work and other forms of interaction that hinge on information processing can increasingly be carried out "anytime, anywhere", be it synchronously or asynchronously. The threat posed by ICT, on the other hand, is seen as a logical result of the observation that both established social divides and newer digital divides seem to follow similar patterns of exclusion. This implies a strong likelihood that the two are reinforcing each other.

While there are strong arguments for both of these claims, there is a conspicuous lack of any serious attempts to establish evidence of correlations between the old and new divides. This is all the more surprising given that both EU and member-state policy continues to emphasize ICT's potential to contribute to social inclusion in areas such as adult education (e-learning), civic participation (e-government) and public welfare (e-health). E-services in these areas can generate direct and indirect benefits. Indirect benefits emerge as the quality of service improves due to government-to-government process optimization, back-office integration, and other activities that support coordination and delivery, for example. While such indirect benefits are generally indisputable, the direct benefits of ICT to the individual depend on the existence of match between supply and demand. Those on the downside of the social divide – those who are in one way or another disadvantaged – are arguably those who would benefit most from public services. However, they also appear to be the least likely to make use of ICT and public services delivered via electronic channels.

From a policy viewpoint, it is of special interest to explore whether and how ICT can realistically help bridge social divides and, if it can, what must be done to support such developments. Micro-data from the IST project SIBIS[2] provides country-specific information on both ICT uptake and various individual socioeconomic inclusion risks. This chapter analyzes this information to find evidence of the extent to which subgroups within the disadvantaged population make use of ICT and for what purposes.

Arguably, from a global perspective, ICT adoption is a matter of affluence. Trend-setting countries such as the USA, Canada and the Nordic countries also lead the world in terms of economic performance. The null hypothesis is therefore that it is all just a matter of economic development. This conclusion would leave little scope for policy strategies to foster the information society. To shed light on this debate, this chapter analyzes the relationship between GDP and ICT diffusion on a macro-level.

On an individual level, the basic assumption of the digital divide is that, regardless of the use of computers, the Internet and other technologies largely follow those dimensions of social structure that shape other individual opportunities and social inclusion or exclusion. In a simple initial model, ICT involvement can be expected to depend on an individual's supply of economic, social and cultural capital. Given the restrictions on available data, this assertion is examined especially in terms of education and income. Second, as ICT constitutes a set of relatively new and evolving technologies, cohort effects can be expected to take effect such that cohorts at whose educationally formative ages ICT did not exist or was not widespread will have fewer chances of involvement. Thirdly, ICT largely focuses on office tools. It is therefore mostly used by people in gainful employment in general and by white-collar employees in particular. The socioeconomic determinants of ICT diffusion are examined in light of a special emphasis on the correlation between skills, employability and education.

The report is structured as follows: The first section defines social cohesion, looks into the social and economic situation in the new member states, and then identifies the core challenges in this regard. The second section gives a brief overview of ICT adoption in general and then discusses the economic and social factors that determine individual and aggregate ICT uptake. It compares the social factors of ICT uptake with ex-

---

[2] SIBIS – Statistical Indicators Benchmarking the Information Society. See http://www.sibis-eu.org. SIBIS carried out representative sample surveys in all EU-15 countries, eight of the New Member States (Czech Republic, Estonia, Hungary, Latvia, Lithuania, Poland, Slovakia and Slovenia), Bulgaria, Romania and in Switzerland and the US. Sample sizes were about 1000 interviews in most countries. For methodological details cf. the website.

isting social divides. The third section explores how ICT can and does bridge social divides, focusing on an analysis of the relationship between employability and ICT skills. The fourth section includes country-specific case studies that illustrate matching or mismatching social and digital divides. A final section summarizes the findings and their policy implications.

3.1 Social Divides: The Challenge to Cohesion in the New Member States

Bits and Pieces of a Definition

Social cohesion is rarely defined explicitly. As a sociological term, cohesion refers to the degree of interconnectedness in social networks. In the public domain and in the political arena, social cohesion connotes and is sometimes used synonymously (or antonymously) with terms such as poverty, living standards, quality of life, social and political participation, social inclusion, integration, social divides and social inequality. Definitions often include aspects such as living standards and sufficient incomes, integration in the labor market, educational opportunities, social capital, shared values and the "fabric of society", health, housing conditions and the absence of discrimination. Conceptually, there is no broad consensus on a distinction between social cohesion and social inclusion.

Both terms, cohesion and inclusion, seem to involve the concept of participation and the capability (economic, social, physical, etc.) and opportunity to do so. They imply a sense of dichotomy – being included or excluded, being part of cohesive extended network or not – as does the term "divide", which has recently been used as a near-synonym for polarization. Vranken et al. (no date) propose a conceptual typology that does not contain social cohesion, but that emphasizes the dichotomous nature of the notions of inclusion and exclusion:

From this angle, the concept of social inclusion or exclusion posits divisions on the basis of social inequality. The continuum of social inequality is split into those social elements that are in a state of inclusion and those in a state of exclusion. Vranken et al. hence conceptualize social exclusion in terms of polarization, discrimination, poverty and inaccessibility.

Table 1: A typology in terms of hierarchy and fault lines

	Hierarchy	
Fault lines	No	Yes
No	Social differentiation	Social inequality
Yes	Social fragmentation	Social exclusion

Source: Vranken et al. (2001)

Social cohesion is a similar concept, sometimes even used as a synonym for social inclusion. Jenson (2002) identifies four traits of the literature on cohesion. First, social cohesion is seen as a process rather than a final state. Second, "social cohesion involves a definition of who is 'in' and who is not, to whom members of society owe solidarity and to whom they do not". While these two dimensions are identical with the dimensions of the exclusion concept, this is not necessarily true of the third and fourth characteristics. "Third, social cohesion is considered to require and be based on shared values" (ibid.). This observation adds the relevance of social capital to the notion of cohesion. Jenson also includes a fourth trait that is seldom found in the literature – institutions of political democracy and conflict resolution and their legitimacy – in his definition of social cohesion.

The EU's notion of social cohesion regularly emphasizes the geographical dimension, i.e. the disparities in economic development between regions and countries, as in the context of the Structural Funds. This implies an aggregate approach at the level of regions or countries, as opposed to an approach at the level of the individual.

On the other hand, the term social inclusion tends to be used to frame individual life chances and circumstances in the European policy context. In its 2001 report on social inclusion (CEC 2001), the European Commission identifies ten risk factors: monetary poverty; unemployment and quality of employment; education; the family situation; disability; health problems and difficult living conditions; housing conditions and neighborhood disadvantages; immigration; ethnicity; and racism and discrimination. The Laeken indicators (cf. Guio 2004, CEC 2003b) endorsed by the European Council to measure social inclusion comprise indicators of the four dimensions financial poverty, employment, health and education, but also add and emphasize the importance of housing conditions. Finally, Eurostat (2002) complements monetary indicators by using standard-of-living indicators such as the enforced lack of household durables, the absence of basic housing facilities, problems with accommodation and the environment, lack of ability to afford basic essentials, and an inability to meet payment schedules.

We will now look at both aspects: cohesion in its geographical dimension (by comparing country-level indicators of societal characteristics with regard to aggregate convergence or polarization) and cohesion among or inclusion of members of a society in terms of poverty and life chances.

Income Inequality and Poverty

The economic transition from the Communist regime triggered an economic shock in many of the new member states. Poverty emerged as a major issue in most countries during the late 1990s, although the Czech Republic and Slovenia stand out as examples of swift responsive intervention (CEC 2003a: 176). The overall income level is well below the average for the 15 old members of the EU (the "EU-15"). The gap is smallest in Cyprus and Slovenia. Poland and the Baltic States exhibit relatively low levels of both per-capita GDP and of the at-risk-of-poverty thresholds, which are related to the median income.

The at-risk-of-poverty rate ranges from 8 percent in the Czech Republic to 18 percent in Estonia. Social groups that need particular attention with regard to poverty risks are older people in Cyprus, the unemployed in Malta and the Baltic States, and the less well educated probably in many countries, although no specific at-risk-of-poverty data is available. The income distribution is most even in Slovenia and the Czech Republic. The Baltic States and Poland evidence the most severe income inequalities.

Table 2: Selected indicators of the income situation in the new member states

Income and poverty level		CY (1997)	CZ (2001)	EE (2002)	LV (2002)	LT (2001)	HU (2001)	MT (2000)	PL (2001)	SL (2000)	SK	EU10 (2001)	EU15 (2001)
At-risk-of-poverty threshold (single person)	PPS	6658	4045	2440	2301	2346	3369	5510	2859	6295	:	3210	8253
	EUR	5312	1897	1327	1215	1124	1641	5038	1742	4180	:	1818	8319
At-risk-of-poverty threshold (2 adults, 2 children)	PPS	13983	8494	5124	4833	4926	7075	11572	6004	13219	:	6741	17332
	EUR	11155	3984	2787	2552	2360	3446	10581	3658	8778	:	3818	17469
Per-capita GDP (PPS, EU-15 =100) (all data 2001)		86.2	58.8	38.5	30.0	33.3	51.1	56.3	39.4	69.4	47.9		100
Poverty risks													
At-risk-of-poverty rate (after social transfers)		16	8	18	16	17	10	15	15	11	:	13	15
0-15 years		12	12	18	19	20	14	21	21	9	:	18	19
65+ years		58	6	16	10	12	9	20	6	21	:	8	19
Women		18	8	19	16	17	10	15	15	12	:	13	16
Dependent employees		5	3	9	9	9	5	6	7	4	:	6	6
Self-employed		9	5	13	22	33	3	1	19	10	:	15	16
Unemployed		23	31	48	42	41	31	50	37	43	:	36	38
Income distribution													
Income quintile ratio (S80/S20)		4.4	3.4	6.1	5.5	4.9	3.4	4.5	4.5	3.2	:	4.2	4.4
Relative median poverty risk gap		24	16	24	20	22	16	18	22	18	:	20	22
Gini coefficient		29	25	35	34	32	23	30	30	22	:	28	28

Source: CEC (2004)

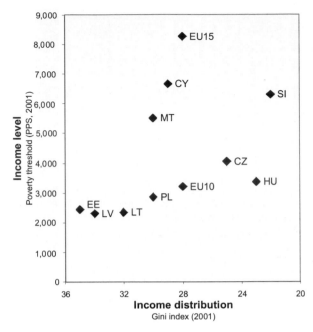

Data: CEC (2004)

Fig. 1: Income distribution and income level in the new member states[3]

Employment, Unemployment and Poverty

Employment and unemployment rates[4] vary considerably across the new member states (the "EU-10"). The overall employment rate for EU-10 is 55.9 percent, compared to 64.3 percent in the old EU-15; unemployment is very high, at 14.3 percent (EU-15: 8 percent).

---

[3] In this and the two following illustrations, movement from the bottom left toward the top right constitutes what is commonly associated with an improvement in social cohesion.

[4] The employment rate – also called the employment-to-population ratio – is the percentage of working-age people (aged 15 years and up) who have (full-time or part-time) jobs. The commonly used definition is usually that of the Labor Force Survey.

The unemployment rate is the share (percentage) of people in the labor force who are unemployed. The labor force includes all workers and the unemployed. However, in order to be considered unemployed, a person must satisfy several conditions. In particular, they must be currently available and looking for work.

Overall, Cyprus, the Czech Republic and Slovenia exhibit a satisfactory situation, with low or moderate levels of unemployment and employment rates at or well above the EU-15 level. While Malta and Hungary also have comparatively moderate levels of unemployment, labor force participation is rather low in both countries. The Baltic States, and Poland and Slovakia in particular, face severe labor market problems with particularly high levels of unemployment. As regards the integration of older workers in the labor market, Estonia and Cyprus above all have high participation rates. Slovakia, Slovenia, Poland, Hungary and Malta need to improve the employment prospects of older workers considerably if they are to keep up with demographic developments. Youth unemployment is a great concern in all new member states. Across the ten countries it is twice as high as in the old EU. Poland and Slovakia face a stiff challenge in trying to integrate young people in the labor market.

Employment also appears to be one, if not the main, determinant of (absence of) poverty and social exclusion. A high proportion of unemployed persons meet the poverty criteria[5]. Once again, significant differences exist between the new member states: Poverty is highest among the unemployed in Estonia and Malta, while Poland, with its high proportion of unemployed people, also demonstrates below-average performance on this indicator. On the other hand, the Czech Republic, Hungary, and in particular Cyprus present encouraging profiles: low unemployment rates and low unemployment poverty rates that are better than the average for the EU-10 and the EU-15.

---

[5] Unemployment poverty here represents the at-risk-of-poverty rate for unemployed persons, i.e. the percentage of unemployed persons who live in households with an equivalized disposable income (after transfers) below 60% of the median equivalized income of the country they live in (for a treatment of the limitations of this approach, cf. Guio 2004: 6ff.).

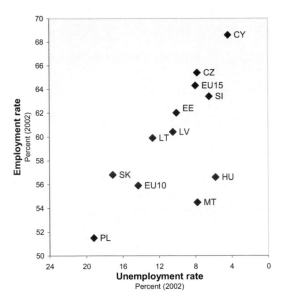

Data: CEC (2004)

Fig. 2a: Employment and unemployment rates in the new member states

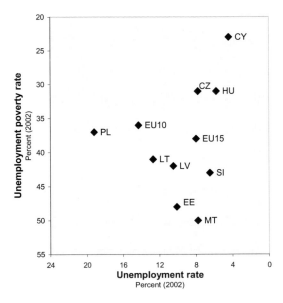

Data: CEC (2004)

Fig. 2b: Unemployment rates and unemployment poverty rates in the new member states

Table 3: Selected indicators of the employment situation in the new member states

All data refer to 2002	CY	CZ	EE	LV	LT	HU	MT	PL	SL	SK	EU10	EU15
Employment rate	68.6	65.4	62	60.4	59.9	56.6	54.5	51.5	63.4	56.8	55.9	64.3
Employment rate male	78.9	73.9	66.5	64.3	62.7	63.5	75.3	56.9	68.2	62.4	61.8	72.8
Employment rate female	59.1	57	57.9	56.8	57.2	50	33.6	46.2	58.6	51.4	50.2	55.6
Employment rate 55-64	49.4	40.8	51.6	41.7	41.6	26.6	30.3	26.1	24.5	22.8	30.4	38.8
Unemployment rate	4.4	7.8	10.1	10.5	12.7	5.8	7.8	19.2	6.5	17.1	14.3	8
Unemployment rate male	4	6.1	10.2	10.3	12.1	6	6.5	18.6	6.1	16.8	13.6	7.2
Unemployment rate female	5.1	9.9	10	10.7	13.3	5.5	10.5	20	7.1	17.4		8.9
Youth unemployment	9.7	16.9	17.7	24.6	21.4	11.9		41.7	15.3	37.3	31.9	15.1
Youth unemployment male	9.3	16.6	14.2	22.1	20.5	12.6		40.9	13.9	38.3	31.4	14.8
Youth unemployment female	10.1	17.2	22.9	27.8	22.6	11.0		47.7	17.2	36.1	32.7	15.5
Long-term unemployment	0.8	3.7	4.8	5.8	7.0	2.4	3.2	10.9	3.3	12.1	8.1	3.0
Long-term unemployment male	0.5	2.9	5.7	6.5	7.2	2.7	3.4	9.7	3.3	11.7	7.4	2.6
Long-term unemployment female	1.2	4.5	3.8	5.0	6.9	2.1	2.4	12.3	3.4	12.5	8.9	3.6

Source: CEC (2004)

Other Challenges

Education imparts human and cultural capital and is the key to employability and social participation. While no data is available on the poverty risks faced by poorly educated and/or skilled persons, these factors are usually empirically linked to worse chances for gainful employment and increased exclusion risks. Although adult literacy is high (above 97 percent) in all countries (except Malta, where the figure is 92 percent), disparities regarding the educational achievements of the labor force population persist, as do disparities in the prospective educational levels of the generations currently in school or higher education. In all countries, considerable shares of the population have no secondary education. These range from 12.4 percent in Cyprus to 34.2 percent in Hungary and 45 percent in Bulgaria (CEC 2003a: 212).

Little data is available on the association between household poverty and children's educational performance (CEC 2003a: 213). It may, however, be assumed that such relations exist, and that children from households that are affected by poverty and unemployment deserve special attention.

Many other particular challenges exist and are well documented in the Joint Inclusion Memoranda (JIM 2003). Rural/urban disparities need to be tackled in many of the new member states. Some countries need to integrate Roma minorities while other countries must focus on integrating non-national and ethnic minorities. Some countries have an especially strong need for improved housing conditions and affordable housing. Social capital is an issue that we emphasized above. The need to integrate people with special needs, the disabled and people with health problems in the labor market and in society in general are identified as problems in the Joint Inclusion Memoranda.

Conclusion

The core challenges with regard to social cohesion for the new member states can be condensed into two concepts: income gaps and unemployment rates. Generally, economic growth is pursued in order to bring standards of living into line with those of the EU-15 countries. Estonia, Latvia, Lithuania, Poland and Slovakia have large gaps to close, however. These countries also have the most uneven income distribution and the highest poverty rates.

At the same time, employment is desperately needed to fight poverty risks. Virtually all countries face challenges. Only Cyprus, the Czech Republic and Slovenia are in a somewhat better position. Unemployment is rampant in Poland and Slovakia. And unemployed persons face a very high poverty risk especially in Malta and Estonia – a problem they share with many EU-15 states.

3.2   Digital Divides: ICT Adoption in the New Member States

The rationale for conducting research into the digital divide is based on the assumption that the lack of access and potential for voluntary participation can cause disadvantages compound them where they already exist. Digital inclusion has to do with disparities in terms of citizens' participation in the information society. This participation may be conceptualized in the first instance as ICT access, levels of usage and patterns of usage, the main focus being on the Internet as the most ubiquitous and relevant tool of communication in the information society. Additional issues, such as the rationale for and sustainability of this participation, as well as related issues concerning access barriers, may also be considered to constitute digital inclusion. Recently, the emphasis in digital divide research has to some degree turned away from mere access figures to home in on disparities in ICT skills and the benefits derived from ICT (e.g. de Haan 2003). Some evidence has been found that, while access and usage (understood simplistically in binary yes-no categories) are tending toward a greater balance within and between countries, major gaps in skills and benefits still remain (de Haan 2003, Hüsing/Selhofer 2004).

Internet and computer uptake in the new member states[6] has not advanced as far as in the EU-15. About 29 percent of the adult (15+) population use computers and 21 percent use the Internet. But only 11 percent have Internet access at home. Internet adoption remains below EU-15 levels in all countries except Estonia. Hungary, Poland, Bulgaria and Romania in particular exhibit low usage and access rates.

The disparity between new and old member states is even greater when one examines home access rather than usage in general. This is because fewer users in the new member states have home access. Instead, they rely

---

[6] The following data refers to the SIBIS surveys carried out in eight of the new member states (all except Cyprus and Malta) and in Bulgaria and Romania. Data referred to here as the total for the Central and Eastern European countries (CEE) covers these countries.

on access elsewhere, especially at public Internet access points (PIAPs). PIAPs turn out to be of special importance in the poorer countries: Estonia, Latvia, Lithuania, Slovakia, Bulgaria and Romania. However, many of the disadvantaged parts of society cannot be reached with PIAPs (see box 1 *Who benefits from public Internet access points?*) Estonia nevertheless has the second-highest home access rate (27 percent), after Slovenia (34 percent). As home access is relatively scarce, so is the relative share of broadband. Only in Estonia (7 percent) has broadband access started to become more than a niche market for private households.

Table 4: Internet access and usage in Central and Eastern Europe (percentage figures for each country)

	CZ	EE	HU	LV	LT	PL	SK	SI	BG	RO	CEE	EU-15
Internet usage	33	52	18	28	30	20	24	37	21	13	21.3	46.4
Experienced users (2 years or more)	16	35	12	20	15	14	11	31	12	9	13.4	29.8
Internet access at home	19	27	11	7	10	13	9	34	9	4	11.4	44.1
Use of PIAPs	6	12	2	9	9	6	9	6	10	8	6.6	5.6
Broadband access	<1	7	1	<1	1	<1	<1	2	1	<1	0.4	7.5

Source: SIBIS survey data, 2003, the authors' calculations

ICT Adoption and GDP

Both national Internet access and usage rates can be expected to correlate to a country's economic performance. The more developed a country is in economic terms, the more people can afford ICT and the more they rely on these technologies in their daily business. Wealthier economies have experienced a shift from industrial goods production to a position as service economies, relying on the creation and processing of information and on knowledge workers who use ICT.

Empirically, however, this correlation is not so clear-cut, as the following illustration shows. Access and usage rates are compared with GDP per capita at purchasing power standards. A linear regression line[7] is included

---

[7] Unweighted, i.e. all countries have the same weighting. The regression line is only a rather inexact visualization of the effect. As access and use rates have a natural range of values between 0 and 100, an "S" curve would probably be more appropriate.

to assess the "performance" of Internet indicators against a GDP-induced trend.

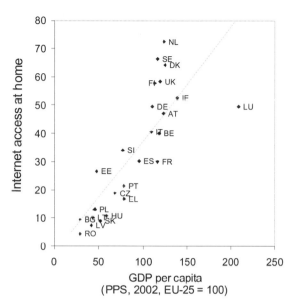

Data: CEC (2004) and SIBIS survey data (2003)

Fig. 3a: Internet access rates, by GDP per capita, across the EU-25

While there is an association between both variables overall, closer analysis reveals some important qualifications. Most strikingly, eleven Western European countries have a comparable GDP per capita level at around the EU-15 average but have Internet access rates varying between 30 percent (France) and 74 percent (Netherlands). Of the new member states, Estonia has a much higher penetration rate than Latvia, Lithuania, Poland and Slovakia, all of which also have comparable GDP per capita. This clearly illustrates that aggregate or macro-effects are not so pronounced.

As we will see later, however, an income/usage link does exist at the individual level. The fact that there is no simple correlation between the two at the macro-level reminds us that GDP per capita does not necessarily reflect individual propensities toward technology involvement, such as employment opportunities and skills. There is a national residual that may hinge on a whole bundle of factors. One of these factors is that redistributive access for all policies may have an effect, favoring the poor, the old, women, minorities, etc. The spread of English language skills appears to correlate with access and usage, as does the labor force participation rate. Smaller countries – i.e. more "open" or interlocking ones in economic and cultural terms – seem to be more advanced than larger ones. Cultural or mentality-related affinities have also often been raised in the discussion of differences, although these factors are more often than not used tautologically (as a last resort) to find explanations for unexplained residuals.

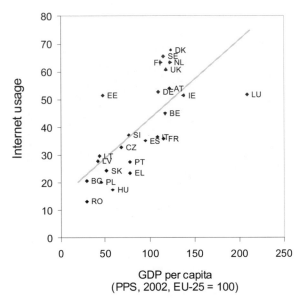

Data: CEC (2004) and SIBIS survey data (2003)

Fig. 3b: Internet usage rates by GDP per capita across the EU-25

With the exception of home access to the Internet, which obviously implies considerable expenses for equipment and access costs, Internet usage (wherever) may not depend so heavily on a household's revenues. This contention is supported by the empirical picture above. Internet usage is much more widespread than Internet home access in almost all new member states. Interestingly, there appears to be a usage/access differential that is virtually non-existent in the old member states. On this score, Estonia reaches a usage level equivalent to those in Germany, Austria, Ireland and Luxembourg. In Latvia, usage is four times the access level. In Lithuania, Romania and Slovakia, the ratio is about three to one.

It can thus be observed not only that there is no clear association between GDP per capita and ICT uptake, but also that different patterns exist in the Western and Eastern EU member states regarding the mode of Internet access. These differences permit a higher than predicted uptake in some of the poorer countries. This fact supports the view that there is genuine scope for different national developmental paths, and that strategies for access can make a real difference. It suggests that focused information society policies can have an impact.

ICT Adoption and Individual Pofiles

While the section above focuses on a country-level perspective, let us now turn to the micro-level correlation between ICT uptake and socioeconomic circumstances. The implicit assumption is that ICT uptake is much more significantly affected by individual patterns of education, labor status, income and socioeconomic status than by institutional or national economic conditions. Our work analyzes socioeconomic groups such as students, older people and the unemployed across national borders.

The first and most obvious finding is that, in the new member states, the Internet is currently very much a phenomenon for the younger generation and students. The fact of being a student is today the most decisive statistical predictor in explaining Internet usage. Severe disadvantages with regard to ICT usage can be observed for people with no tertiary education, the unemployed and the inactive, for people on low incomes, people with disabilities and older people. Farthest behind are those individuals with basic secondary education at best and those aged 65 and over. Less than 2 percent of either of these groups use the Internet.

With regard to age, the middle age cohorts already lag behind the younger cohort. Internet access at home in general follows the same trends, with the exception that the dominance of young people and students is not as significant. Rather, people with tertiary education tend to have highest home access rates.

The age effect between the young and middle-aged cohorts is not a statistical artifact caused by grouping age brackets together, as the following illustration depicts. People in their late twenties are already well behind the youngest cohorts in terms of Internet usage. The sharp decline in Internet usage rates as early as around 30 is nevertheless in large part caused by educational expansion. It appears that for cohorts aged 30 and older, higher secondary education was the norm.

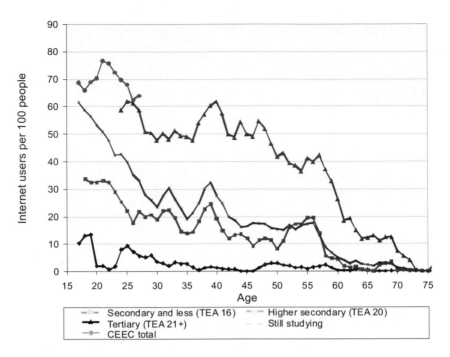

Source: SIBIS survey data, 2003, the authors' calculations. Floating 3-year averages. Weighted CEE totals

Fig. 4: Internet usage in CEE countries, by age and educational attainment

The overall Internet uptake rate curve for the total population is very similar to the uptake rate in groups with higher secondary education. For the younger cohorts, however, the total uptake curve is biased toward the student and tertiary education categories. This reflects the increasing importance of tertiary education and the impact of higher educational participation in younger cohorts.

Table 5: ICT adoption and usage in CEE countries (per category of population, percentages of the respective groups)

	Internet use	Computer use	Internet at home	Use of PIAPs	E-commerce use	Own mobile phone
Total CEE	21.3	28.7	11.4	6.6	2.1	43.7
Labor market participation						
Employed	31	44	18	5	4	64
Unemployed	11	16	7	5	<1	39
Not employed (other)	16	20	7	8	1	27
Income						
Three upper income quartiles	25	33	13	8	2	49
Low income quartile	6	10	3	2	1	23
Educational attainment						
Secondary and less (TEA 16)	1	3	1	<1	<1	15
Higher secondary (TEA 20)	15	23	9	3	1	48
Tertiary (TEA 21+)	42	54	25	7	6	63
Still studying	69	77	24	35	4	65
Age groups						
Up to 24	52	59	18	26	2	62
25 to 49	23	34	14	5	3	55
50 to 64	11	17	9	1	2	32
65 and over	1	2	1	<1	<1	12
Illness/disability status						
No illness/disability	26	34	13	8	2	51
Long-standing illness or disability	7	12	5	2	1	22

Source: SIBIS survey data, 2003, the author's calculations. Weighted CEEC totals

Box 1

Who benefits from public Internet access points in CEE countries?

As noted above, the gap between home access and Internet usage is much larger in the new member states than in the old EU-15, one reason being that many people who use the Internet cannot afford home access. So who are the PIAP users?

PIAP users are predominantly the younger age groups and students. Both these groups contain more PIAP users than people with home access. The unemployed and people with less education seldom use public access points. The core challenge therefore remains the same. Since disadvantaged groups hardly have the skills to use the Internet, they also do not know how to use the Internet in public places.

This argument is to some extent qualified by a comparison of national peculiarities, however. Different countries and national social groups exhibit huge differences regarding Internet usage in public places. While PIAPs seem to play no role in Hungary in particular, PIAPs do assume a significant role in providing disadvantaged population groups with access to the Internet in many of the countries surveyed. In Estonia, with its high usage level, the number of Internet users is twice as high as the number of people who have home access. In Lithuania and Latvia, both of which have a somewhat lower percentage, the ratio is as high as three to one. In Slovenia, on the other hand, home access and usage are more or less evenly balanced. In Estonia, public access peaks at 16 percent of the unemployed population. In the Czech Republic, Romania, Lithuania and Poland too, however, a small but significant proportion of the unemployed population also uses PIAPs.

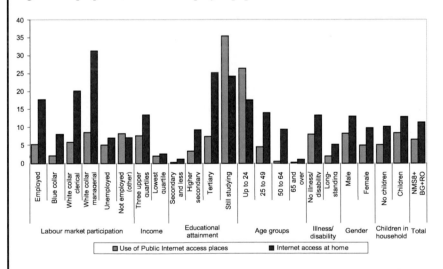

Source: SIBIS survey data, 2003, authors' calculations. Percentages of respective groups. Weighted CEE totals

Fig. 5: PIAP usage and home Internet access, by socioeconomic groups in the new member states

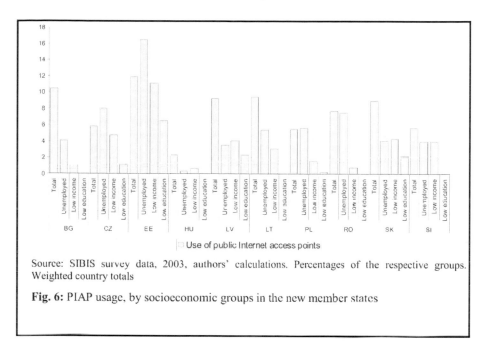

Source: SIBIS survey data, 2003, authors' calculations. Percentages of the respective groups. Weighted country totals

Fig. 6: PIAP usage, by socioeconomic groups in the new member states

ICT Skills and Individual Profiles

Access and usage in general are not beneficial *per se*. To gain economic advantages from ICT, a minimum skill level is required. Simply knowing how to use an Internet browser will not suffice. But which groups are knowledgeable about the Internet? SIBIS has developed a composite indicator that combines four types of skills at using the Internet into an overall "digital literacy" score[8].

A survey of the Internet skills distribution observed across social groups uncovers an even sharper picture of the digital divide than when looking at access and usage data alone (i.e. overall usage with whatever intensity and skills). In most of the economies observed, the Internet skills base is still

---

[8] The skills included are: communicating with others (by e-mail and other online methods), obtaining (or downloading) and installing software on a computer, questioning the source of information on the Internet, and searching for the required information using search engines. As defined here, "advanced skills" means that the respondent needs to score more than 50% of the scale maximum. In other words, they must feel very confident in at least two of these activities and fairly confident in at least one. "Basic skills" means that a respondent is fairly confident at least in one item. Non-users are assigned zero skills.

found in schools and universities. Excluding current students, the remaining population that is skilled in the use of the Internet tends to have a university degree and be in paid work. The Internet skills of the less well educated labor force are almost negligible, and are hardly existent among unemployed.

Table 6: Internet skills by activity status, level of education and age[9]

	Employed		Unemployed		Not employed (other)	
	Basic skills	Advanced skills	Basic skills	Advanced skills	Basic skills	Advanced skills
Education						
Secondary and less (TEA 16)	5	1	1	1	<1	<1
Higher secondary (TEA 20)	17	8	9	3	5	1
Tertiary (TEA 21+)	31	30	34	12	11	2
Still studying	30	44	-	-	49	29
Age groups						
Up to 24	30	23	25	10	44	26
25 to 49	20	13	8	3	10	3
50 to 64	17	10	6	1	3	<1
65 and over	:*	:*	:*	:*	1	<1

Source: SIBIS survey data, 2003, the authors' calculations. Weighted CEE totals

A glance at the middle age group (25-49 year–olds) reveals an especially sobering picture. ICT skills among these cohorts are inadequate. Astonishingly low skill levels are found among unemployed and inactive people in this age bracket. Yet only one third of people in paid employment have even a rudimentary knowledge of the Internet knowledge. Only 13 percent possess advanced skills.

---

[9] This indicator is a composite score of various items of self-reported capabilities concerning the use of the Internet. Percentages of the respective groups are not cumulative i.e. people with advanced skills are not included in basic skills. To identify the percentage of people with *at least* basic skills, both figures must be added up. An asterisk (*) signifies an insufficient number of cases for relevant statistical processing.

The middle age groups are hence a source of major concern, in terms of both access and their (lack of) ICT skills. The 25-49 year-old cohorts will supply a major part of the labor force in CEE economies for decades to come. They will be likely to face strong competition from younger age groups unless their IT user skills are cultivated rapidly. It is fair to assume that retrieving and processing information with ICT will become more and more important, i.e. that more and more jobs will include these activities as core routine or auxiliary tasks. The CEE economies cannot be expected to rely solely on their youngest cohorts to supply such capabilities. Neither will they be able to prosper in the years ahead without a labor force that has sufficient ICT skills.

Also for mobile phones, the relationship between GDP per capita and penetration is not very close. The gap between Poland and Estonia, which have similar levels of GDP per capita, is huge. Both Slovenia and the Czech Republic have much higher mobile phone access rates than Portugal, Greece and even countries with higher GDP per capita (such as Germany, France, Spain and even Denmark).

Mobile phone access is also somewhat more evenly distributed across the population in terms of higher access rates among disadvantaged groups. Socioeconomic and demographic variables (especially education and active participation) correlate strongly to mobile phone use, although not as strongly as Internet use. Especially the unemployed, low-income households and those with less formal education are more likely to own a mobile telephone than to use the Internet. While a total of 44 percent of the populations surveyed own a mobile phone, penetration is nevertheless lowest (12 percent) among over-65s, and is also low (15 percent) among those with at best basic secondary education. The unemployed are not as far behind on ownership of mobile phones as on Internet usage and access. Conversely, students are not as far ahead of the rest of society: Their mobile phone adoption figure is equivalent to that of people in employment.

The much higher uptake of mobile telephony gives rise to the question whether mobile phones offer social benefits to the same extent as the Internet. Some mobile applications may undoubtedly support e-learning, e-government, e-health and other mobile phone-based services to some degree. Using mobile phones will not have the side-effect of teaching people how to use computers and the Internet, however. If one takes the view that many of the concerns about the digital divide are not about easing some sort of social service delivery but about enabling people to attain the skills they need in the computerized economy, then the beneficial effect of mobile phone usage and "m-services" still remains to be verified.

Box 2

Are mobile phone adoption rates such a different matter?

Mobile telephony has penetrated much larger parts of the population than computers and the Internet. 44 percent of people in the countries observed own a mobile phone. The Czech Republic and Slovenia (76 percent each in 2003) are actually ahead of the EU-15 level (69 percent in 2002). Mobile phones have not yet achieved large market shares in Poland, Romania and Bulgaria.

Table 7: Mobile phone usage in CEE countries

	CZ	EE	HU	LV	LT	PL	SK	SI	BG	RO	CEEC	EU-15
Mobile phone usage	76	68	59	51	54	38	64	76	31	24	43.7	69.1
Text message usage	67	54	43	45	45	30	56	50	23	13	33.8	40.3

Source: SIBIS survey data, 2003. Country-specific percentages, the authors' calculations

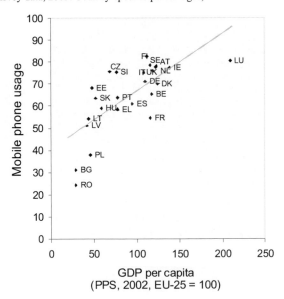

Fig. 7: Mobile phone access rates by GDP per capita

Conclusion

As regards general ICT adoption indicators throughout the population, all the new member states lag way behind the EU-15, with the exception of Estonia and, following at some distance, the Czech Republic and Slovenia. The digital divide between these countries is not solely attributable to their economic performance.

The unemployed and the less educated are well behind the average for the population as a whole concerning Internet and computer usage. Significant differences exist between the indicators "using the Internet" and "home access to the Internet" but do not correspond to patterns observed in the old EU-15. PIAPs seem to play a significant inclusive role in Estonia and in some other countries whose Internet usage is lower overall, such as Latvia and Lithuania.

An age gap is observable: Internet usage rates show a sharp decline for age cohorts upward of around 30 years. A breakdown of this decline by educational indicators again reveals the link between higher education and Internet uptake. The significantly higher usage rates in the youngest cohort can be seen mainly as a result of considerably higher rates of educational participation. This fact in turn makes the current threat of digital exclusion for middle-aged and older cohorts even more obvious. The middle age groups are a source of major concern, in terms of both access and ICT skills.

3.3   Social Divides: Can ICT Help?

ICT may well create inequalities, as it is not usually invented primarily to bridge social divides. Experience shows that technological progress tends to benefit the technology savvy and the highly skilled. It is thus prone to widen social gaps. As advanced users move ahead, non-users will most probably not keep pace in terms of life opportunities and jobs. Having neither access nor the skills and motivation to use ICT will entail serious disadvantages – all the more so as being IT savvy becomes a matter of course in the younger generations. Getting involved with ICT is therefore not just a new way to help the socially disadvantaged put up with a disagreeable situation. Ultimately, it is in fact a way to overcome insufficient economic chances. ICT will not reverse societal structure and suddenly create jobs for the unemployed and all the skills needed by the less well educated. However, digital exclusion will almost inevitably bring about the risk of decreasing social and economic chances for those excluded – and has already begun to do so.

Two mechanisms by which ICT is having a beneficial impact can nevertheless be distinguished. On the one hand, ICT can be used to support people and deliver services and subsidies. On the other hand, ICT has the potential to empower people's participation in the economic, social, political and cultural realms. The first mechanism refers to benefits deriving from the ability to draw on ICT-mediated interaction with government and public services. The second is about benefits deriving from the ability to use ICT, whether in a productive process, i.e. at work, or to participate in social, political and cultural life[10].

Sustainable support will probably be most valuable if it is used to foster the skills increasingly required by the labor market. As in the case of globalization, neither entire economies nor individual people have a truly viable option for opting out of the information economy and its rules of competition. This implies that policy should focus not only on delivering public services electronically but also on empowering people to develop the capability to participate in this economy. To put it bluntly: Participation in the (skilled) labor force is the key factor to help many people escape the poverty risk. The corresponding skills requirements will include a rising share of ICT skills in the years to come.

To answer the core question, "how can ICT bridge social divides?", one may revisit virtually the whole agenda of socioeconomic ICT research, be it ICT economics, research into e-government and e-work, ICT in education and life-long learning, e-inclusion or e-health. The following propositions constitute the hypothesis that underpins this paradigm:

a)   ICT skills significantly enhance employability. Unemployment affects low-skilled individuals to a large degree,

b)   ICT can significantly contribute to skills acquisition (both ICT and non-ICT skills),

c)   ICT can significantly enhance access to and the outcome of education and training,

d)   ICT can be used to give access to otherwise barred labor markets,

e)   ICT can be used to enhance labor market information and thus reduce frictional unemployment,

---

[10] Indirect benefits stemming from improved quality of public services due to internal process optimization, back-office integration and other coordination and delivery support activities are a third mechanism that is not taken into account in this context.

f)   ICT can be used to improve people's ability to draw on public services,
g)   ICT has the potential to improve access to the health system and thus improve preventive treatment and healthcare delivery,
h)   ICT can be used to sustain social networks, build communities and increase political participation.

While this paper does not have the aim to elaborate on all these propositions, we have tried to illustrate the relationship between employability and ICT below. Furthermore, some anecdotal evidence about the ability to draw on public services, on labor market information, e-health and social networking structures is presented (see box 3 *"What is ICT being used for?"*).

Internet Usage and Employability: Some Empirical Evidence from CEE

In the CEE countries, people in gainfully employment are much more likely to use ICT than are unemployed or inactive people. This observation is confirmed across educational and age groups and genders, as the following table indicates.

It is widely accepted that ICT skills significantly enhance employability. On the other hand, many learn most of their ICT skills through learning-by-doing processes at their workplace. Conversely, unemployment bars the jobless from accessing a major source of skills acquisition that would in turn help make them more employable. Employability and Internet usage appear to have a circular relationship. The arbitrariness of the viewpoint nevertheless already hints at a dilemma of causality here.

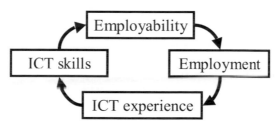

Fig. 8: ICT experience and employability – a virtuous/vicious cycle

Drawing on the survey data, we have calculated the unemployment rates of people with and without Internet skills. In none of the countries observed does the unemployment rate for people with more than basic skills (i.e. "advanced skills" in the sense defined above) exceed 4 percent. While the overall unemployment rate is 18 percent for people with no Internet skills, it drops to 8 percent for people with basic skills and to 3 percent for people with advanced Internet skills. In Estonia, however, the most advanced information society among these countries, basic skills no longer seem to suffice. They have become more common than in other countries and hence have lost some of their competitive advantage in the labor market[11].

To test whether Internet skills can contribute to employability, we analyzed a logistic regression model (see annex). Unemployment risks are statistically predicted based on the factors age, education, gender and health status.

Results show that the unemployment risk is significantly affected by all these factors. All other things being equal, women are 34 percent more likely to be unemployed than men. People with tertiary education run considerably less risk of being unemployed: their risk decreases by 76 percent[12]. On the other hand, disabled people face a 68 percent higher risk of unemployment.

---

[11] Although the same is true of Poland, the data here is less reliable due to the small number of observations of skilled Internet users.

[12] In terms of odds ratios. If exp(b) = .244, then the decreased risk is (1 - .244) = 76%.

Table 9: ICT usage in CEE countries, by labor force status across educational, age and gender groups

	Working			Unemployed			Other not working		
	Mobile phone	Internet usage	Computer usage	Mobile phone	Internet usage	Computer usage	Mobile phone	Internet usage	Computer usage
Education									
Secondary and less (TEA 16)	31	4	9	24	3	5	10	<1	1
Higher secondary (TEA 20)	63	22	35	39	10	15	29	5	8
Tertiary (TEA 21+)	78	57	73	65	33	41	27	12	16
Still studying	88	68	76	N/A	N/A	N/A	62	69	77
Age groups									
Up to 24	78	43	52	58	26	31	57	62	69
25 to 49	65	30	43	38	8	14	32	12	16
50 to 64	51	26	38	17	5	7	24	4	7
Gender									
Male	65	30	40	35	13	17	29	20	24
Female	62	31	47	43	9	15	26	13	17

Source: SIBIS survey data, 2003, the authors' calculations. Weighted CEE totals

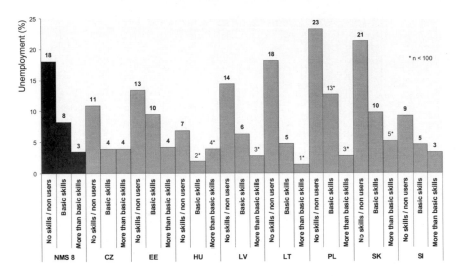

Source: SIBIS survey data 2003, the authors' calculations (respondents aged 15-64, re-weighted sample to fit official statistics unemployment totals)

Fig. 9: Unemployment rates, by Internet skills in CEE countries

While these are important findings, what is the effect of Internet usage? A second model suggests, that while all other effects remain valid, using the Internet adds considerably to the explanatory power of the model. Again, other factors (age, education, gender and health status) being equal, the simple fact of being an Internet user reduces the unemployment risk by 74 percent[13]. Hence employability significantly improves with ICT skills – and vice versa[14]. This finding strongly supports evidence for ICT's potential to overcome exclusion.

---

[13] As stated earlier, many people can only use the Internet because of their work. However, another model that tests the effect of home access still finds a highly significant effect (exp(b) = .399, alpha <.001). On the other hand, Internet usage may be strongly correlated with other explanatory variables not observed in this model. Notwithstanding, this admission does not change the empirical finding of a strong statistical link between Internet usage and employability.

[14] It is, however, not possible to trace trajectories or the durability of social positions at the individual level. A further avenue for research would thus be to analyze social structures and social mobility longitudinally (either via the panel approach or through retrospective interviews), including all "traditional", well-known factors and parameters, to add ICT information to these traditional variables, specifically including data about the use of ICT (which ICT, what skills

---

Box 3

What is ICT being used for in the CEE countries?

Some observers express the concern that ICT access alone is not enough to help disadvantaged groups experience social or economic benefits. The worry sometimes prevails that "unproductive" uses of ICT, like video gaming, dubious chat forums, pornography, spending money on useless mobile phone ring tones or owning equipment merely as a status symbol (for all of which cases there is no reason to believe that they would apply more to underprivileged users than to the better off) should not be encouraged by pro-access policies.

As a rough indicator of what it means to be disadvantaged, we have selected being unemployed (as opposed to being employed or self-employed). Among the activities less frequently performed by unemployed users are e-commerce (including information about products) and e-banking. This may easily be explained by the argument that they have little money to spend and, in many cases, probably have no bank account. Consequently, 46 percent of unemployed persons do not consider themselves well-informed in their capacity as consumers, against 63 percent of employed persons.

Conspicuously, e-mail is also used less by unemployed Internet users. This may support the interesting recent finding that the Internet is seldom embraced as a communication tool by novice low-income users (Jackson et al. 2004), simply because they do not have a sufficiently large social network that also uses the Internet. As regards Internet benefits, unemployed Internet users nevertheless see the same social benefits. Although fewer than average say it enhances contacts with friends, as many feel that the Internet enhances their social participation.

Unemployed Internet users use e-government as much as others do and do a little less health research online. 37 percent of unemployed Internet users use it as a job search tool.

---

level and what ICT use, etc.), and then to analyze the effects ICT may or may not have on individual social and economic transition processes.

Table 10: Internet activities of users, by labor force status (percentages based on all Internet users in the respective groups, weighted as CEE totals)

	E-mail	E-mail with at least half of friends, family	Information on products or services	Product or service orders	Online banking	Health information	Job searches	E-government
Employed	76	37	73	22	19	32	21	24
Unemployed	47	25	42	4	8	25	37	23
Not employed (other)	54	30	56	9	4	28	19	21

Source: SIBIS survey data 2003, the authors' calculations

Table 11: Users' perceived Internet benefits, by labor force status (percentages based on all Internet users in the respective groups, weighted as CEE totals)

	Would be less well informed as a consumer without Internet	Would feel socially excluded without Internet	Would have less contact with friends
Employed	63	35	58
Unemployed	46	34	46
Not employed (other)	50	34	61

Source: SIBIS survey data 2003, the authors' calculations

Conclusion

It can be argued that a circular relationship exists between labor force participation and the attainment of IT skills. For the time being, Internet skills are a major factor in reducing individual unemployment risks. This may be due to a current relative scarcity of IT skills. As long as this scarcity prevails, IT skills will be a significant competitive advantage in the labor market. Even if this competitive advantage is eroded as skills become more widespread in future, however, IT skills will still probably be a necessary basic condition of employability in many jobs.

3.4 National Social and Digital Divides: Match or Mismatch?

One research question asked at the beginning was to find out whether there are any cases of mismatches between social and digital divides. To examine the evidence for any such finding beyond the relationship between GDP and uptake, which we explored earlier, cases of social disparities in four countries have been investigated and correlated to ICT usage among the respective at-risk groups. This section outlines the economic and social problems of these four countries, building largely on the Joint Memoranda on Social Inclusion (JIM 2003). A case for challenges to social cohesion is made for these countries and mapped onto their respective national developments in relation to ICT and the digital divide.

Insights from Estonia: Unemployment and ICT Usage

Estonia, though still one of the poorest member states of the enlarged EU, but has experienced rapid growth since 1995. The average GDP growth rate in the period 1995-2002 was 5 percent per annum, peaking in 2001 and 2002 (at 6.5 and 6 percent respectively). GDP per capita in Estonia increased in the period 1995-2002 from 32 to 42 percent of the EU average and is expected to reach 50 percent of the EU average by 2010. Estonia is experiencing large inflows of FDI, mostly of Swedish and Finnish origin.

The Joint Inclusion Report (JIM 2003) emphasizes that, besides a persistently stable macroeconomic environment, continued foreign investment inflows will largely depend on Estonia's capacity to further develop a labor force with sufficient skills.

Unemployment increased sharply in the first half of the 1990s – from 1.5 percent in 1991 to 9.7 percent in 1995 – mainly due to workforce reductions in the course of economic and labor market restructuring. Unemployment stood at 10.3 percent in (the second quarter of) 2002. Although some sectors are performing relatively well, new jobs are still not being created nor unemployment cut to any significant degree. This is mainly because of structural unemployment: In spite of high unemployment, Estonia still suffers a lack of qualified labor. The education, skills and work experience acquired years ago are no longer competitive and do not meet the rapidly changing needs of the economy and the labor market. Long-term unemployment is running high, affecting some 6 percent of the labor force.

The JIM (2003) identifies the following risk groups

- Young people (the youth unemployment rate was 17.6 percent in 2002), who find it difficult to enter a labor market where high skills are demanded that can often only be gained from work experience and access to in-company training opportunities,
- The long-term unemployed (particularly in the 45+ age group and with a low level of education or obsolete qualifications), who accounted for 53 percent of the jobless total in 2002,
- People with disabilities and long-term health problems, whose employment rate is 25 percent, compared to 61 percent of the non-disabled population of working age,
- Non-Estonians, owing to the lack of Estonian language skills and their concentration in areas with high unemployment: In 2002, unemploy-

ment stood at 7.9 percent of Estonians and 14.9 percent of non-Estonians.

Since unemployment poses one of the major threats to social cohesion in Estonia, we sought to analyze how unemployed Estonians (as opposed to average users) use ICT, and to find out whether or not the social divide caused by unemployment mirrors a digital divide.

Unemployed persons in Estonia use ICT to a large extent compared to their peers in other countries. In fact, e-inclusion among the unemployed is much better than in the other CEE countries and equal to the average in EU-15. Almost half of the unemployed are computer users and almost one in four has access at home. Estonia obviously manages better to integrate the unemployed in the information society. PIAPs seem to play some integrative role here, as almost two in five unemployed Internet users rely on PIAPs at least as a secondary means of access.

In Estonia, exclusion from the labor market does not entail exclusion from the information society to the same degree. Even allowing for the fact that youth unemployment is high (17 percent), this level of jobless participation cannot only stem from the fact that younger generations of unemployed are keen Internet users[15]. On the other hand, it also indicates that basic e-skills do not seem to be a bottleneck in the Estonian labor market and hence do not suffice as door-opener, as has also been shown above.

One must nevertheless bear in mind that the unemployed population is a fairly heterogeneous group. Many young people may experience unemployment as a transient episode, whereas it has proved a more lasting condition for many who are perhaps less well versed in ICT.

---

[15] Breakdowns of the sample data by employment status, age and country can only give tentative answers because, despite national N=~1000, the number of observations soon becomes very low and statistical margins of uncertainty increase. Even so, although usage diminishes with age in Estonia too, more older unemployed persons here still tend to be Internet users.

Table 12: Unemployment and ICT usage in Estonia (percentage of users per group, CEE and EU-15 data weighted according to national population shares)

	Internet usage	Computer usage	Internet at home	Use of PIAPs	Mobile phone	E-government usage
Estonia						
Total percentage	52	55	27	12	68	29
Unemployed	43	46	23	16	66	17
Ratio (unemployed/ total)	83%	85%	86%	138%	97%	59%
CEE						
Total percentage	21.3	28.7	11.4	6.6	43.7	5.3
Unemployed	11.1	16.0	7.1	5.1	38.8	3.1
Ratio (unemployed/ total)	52%	56%	62%	77%	89%	58%
EU-15						
Total percentage	46.4	53.3	44.1	5.6	69.1	18.7
Unemployed	37.9	46.3	41.0	6.4	69.4	19.9
Ratio (unemployed/ total)	82%	87%	93%	114%	100%	106%

Source: SIBIS survey data 2003, the authors' calculations

Let us return to the initial question: Is there a mismatch between the social and digital divides? While the unemployed are of special concern in the context of social cohesion in Estonia, which has high unemployment rates and the highest degree of unemployment poverty, the country does not appear to have a digital divide that is specifically linked to unemployment.

Insights from Poland: Unemployment and ICT Usage

Compared to the enlarged EU, Poland is still a rather poor country in terms of GDP per capita. Also, Poland faces serious regional polarization as regards economic performance. Furthermore, the economic recovery of the

1990s has recently dwindled, with only low growth rates in 2001 and 2002.

Economic restructuring has hit agriculture and old industries hard. Both have shed significant volumes of labor. Since 1998, the Polish economy has been losing jobs continually. Total employment in 2002 was 10.2 percent lower than in 1998. In 2002, the unemployment rate reached 19.9 percent (20.9 percent for women and 19.1 percent for men).

Employment rates fell strongly, to 51.5 percent, in 2002. The figure is especially low among younger cohorts, more of whom (sometimes as a consequence of poor employment prospects) are now attending higher education than in previous generations in order to attain higher educational achievements.

The main challenges in Poland (cf. also JIM 2003) are:

- High youth unemployment: The youth unemployment rate (15-24) was 41.7 percent in 2002. Rising unemployment among school-leavers is of particular concern,
- Higher unemployment among the less well educated. Unemployed persons who have only basic vocational and lower education levels accounted for 60.9 percent of the total number of unemployed claimants registered with labor offices in 2002. The unemployment rate for this group was 24.8 percent,
- High and increasing long-term unemployment, which reached 10.9 percent in 2002. The long-term rate is higher for women (12.3 percent) than for men (9.7 percent). Long-term unemployment accounted for 54.4 percent of total unemployment,
- A low activity rate overall.

Poland's unemployed use the Internet much less than the national average. Unlike Estonia, Poland is less successful at getting large swathes of its unemployed to participate in the information society. Furthermore (subject to the necessary caveats because of the limited number of observations), those unemployed people who do use ICT in Poland tend to come from the 15-24 year cohort. Older unemployed people and even those in the middle age groups are excluded from ICT usage to a much greater extent than in Estonia.

It can thus be concluded Poland has a close match between the social and digital divides with regard to labor market participation.

Table 13: Unemployment and ICT usage in Poland[16] (percentage of users per group, CEE and EU-15 data weighted according to national population shares)

	Internet usage	Computer usage	Internet at home	Use of PIAPs	Mobile phone	E-government usage
Poland						
Total percentage	20	26	13	6	38	4
Unemployed	11	15	8	6	30	3
Ratio (unemployed/ total)	57%	58%	59%	102%	79%	75%
CEE						
Total percentage	21.3	28.7	11.4	6.6	43.7	5.3
Unemployed	11.1	16.0	7.1	5.1	38.8	3.1
Ratio (unemployed/ total)	52%	56%	62%	77%	89%	58%
EU-15						
Total percentage	46.4	53.3	44.1	5.6	69.1	18.7
Unemployed	37.9	46.3	41.0	6.4	69.4	19.9
Ratio (unemployed/ total)	82%	87%	93%	114%	100%	106%

Source: SIBIS survey data 2003, the authors' calculations

---

[16] Since ICT adoption has advanced to very different degrees in Poland and Estonia, it is difficult to judge whether the divide in one country is bigger than the one in the other. Assessing whether one gap or divide is smaller or larger than another, or whether it is closing or widening, is a delicate topic and it is often (mis)used in political argument (as described by Martin 2003). There is, however, no universally accepted, more or less objective measure by which to judge. In the absence of good time series data that permit an assessment of the time lag between two societies or strata (Sicherl 2003), any such evaluation must be taken with a pinch of salt. Both absolute percentage gaps and adoption ratios, as well as differences between ratios or odds ratios, depend on the overall adoption rate if one assumes "S" curve developments within different social groups (cf. Hüsing/Selhofer 2004, Martin 2003).

Insights from Hungary: Education and ICT Usage

Hungary has experienced steady economic growth since the second half of the 1990s. In the early 1990s, employment fell dramatically and unemployment increased sharply. In 2002, the employment rate was 56.6 percent – one of the lowest rates in the EU. Agriculture (6.2 percent) and industry (34.1 percent) have seen their share of employment erode. 59.7 percent of employed people today work in the service sector (compared to 68.8 percent in the EU-15). Increasing regional differences in unemployment, employment and sectoral activity can be observed. The low employment rate and high inactivity rate, as well as a mismatch of qualifications and skills in the labor force, are causing concern in certain regions.

Unemployment is slowly decreasing and stands today at the low level of 5.8 percent. Long-term unemployment stands at 2.4 percent. Youth unemployment too is among the lowest in the EU, at 11.9 percent. The youth activity rate is also deemed too low, however. As in several CEE countries, low employment levels among the younger cohorts are linked to higher educational participation.

The main challenges in Hungary (cf. also JIM 2003) are:

- The high inactivity rate/low employment rate,
- Regional disparities (the regions of Northern Hungary and the Northern Great Plain),
- Reforming the educational system to meet the needs of the labor market,
- Establishing equal opportunities for disadvantaged children in the educational system and reducing socioeconomic dependency on educational achievements,
- Integrating the Roma population in employment and education,
- Integrating the disabled and people with health problems in the labor market.

As social stratification appears to be a major concern with regard to educational outcomes and integration, we sought to analyze the social determination of and, especially, the educational impact on ICT usage in Hungary, and to identify the key factors that hinder ICT uptake.

Table 14: ICT usage in Hungary (percentage of users per group)

	Internet usage	Computer usage	Internet at home	Use of PIAPs	Mobile phone	E-government usage
Unemployed	12	19	8	<1	60	<1
Low income	4	4	1	<1	33	1
Low education	3	7	4	<1	34	<1
Age 65+	<1	<1	<1	<1	19	<1
Illness / disability	3	9	4	<1	31	<1
Total	18	28	11	2	59	4

Source: SIBIS survey data 2003, the authors' calculations

Hungary has a low level of ICT uptake overall. Such an early stage of development is usually dominated by early adopters who come from well educated and economically better off backgrounds. This is also the case in Hungary. Internet usage/access and computer usage are very low in all the disadvantaged groups observed here, though this statement is qualified to some extent by the uptake among the unemployed. Educational factors hinder the uptake of Internet and computers. While differences are sharp in this regard, they are also significant for mobile phones. Only 34 percent of people with at best secondary education own a mobile phone, compared with a national average of 59 percent.

It has been observed that the less well educated are excluded from the information society in many countries. How is the Hungarian situation to be assessed against this background? Is the Hungarian situation an exception? Or does it follow a generally observable pattern? To compare the influence of education, we compared the relative uptake in the four educational groups with the national average uptake. The number of students in Hungary who use the Internet is 4.4 times the Hungarian average. That is the highest figure in the EU-25, while people with at best secondary schooling are only 0.19 times as likely to use the Internet. 2.7 times as many people with a university education use the Internet – again the highest value observed. Altogether, Hungary has the fourth-highest variation coefficient, meaning that education is a greater determinant of Internet usage only in Romania, Poland and Lithuania.

Table 15: The educational variation in Internet uptake (Internet users per educational group as a percentage of the national average; total Internet usage: percentage of users per country)

	CZ	EE	HU	LV	LT	PL	SK	SI	BG	RO	BE	DK
Secondary and less (TEA 16)	19	25	**19**	14	7	1	15	4	3	0	21	44
Higher secondary (TEA 20)	81	78	**77**	67	46	53	81	85	83	50	89	93
Tertiary (TEA 21+)	187	129	**272**	130	129	217	192	145	216	197	134	111
Still studying	239	182	**440**	260	271	342	233	225	345	415	184	131
Total Internet usage	34%	52%	**18%**	28%	30%	20%	25%	38%	21%	13%	45%	69%
Variation coefficient	66	56	**82**	78	89	88	67	71	81	97	56	34

	DE	EL	ES	FR	IE	IT	LU	NL	AT	PT	FI	SE	UK
Secondary and less (TEA 16)	61	18	29	20	42	22	21	36	59	10	22	39	63
Higher secondary (TEA 20)	97	80	93	86	76	119	97	95	96	104	95	97	108
Tertiary (TEA 21+)	128	153	130	154	132	145	134	119	126	212	115	108	132
Still studying	165	216	227	209	165	207	175	147	172	271	145	142	151
Total Internet usage	53%	24%	35%	36%	52%	37%	52%	64%	54%	28%	63%	66%	61%
Variation coefficient	34	64	60	61	46	54	53	41	36	67	48	38	29

Source: SIBIS survey data 2003, the authors' calculations

The educational divide in Hungary thus does tend to be mirrored in ICT uptake. There is a significant and very considerable educational/digital divide. Referring back to our initial question, this country definitely evidences no "mismatch" between social exclusion and digital exclusion with regard to education.

Insights from Slovenia: The Aged Population and ICT Usage

Slovenia has the second highest GDP per capita and the most even income distribution of all ten new member states. Unemployment is the third lowest, at 6.5 percent. Slovenia is rapidly catching up in terms of economic development, with growth levels of between 2.9 and 5.2 percent in recent years. The at-risk-of-poverty level is below the EU-10 and EU-15 level overall, though it is higher for older people (65+) and the unemployed. The employment rate is almost on a par with that of the EU-15. Only old-age employment is significantly lower.

Agricultural and industrial activities are decreasing as a share of overall economic activity. The manufacturing sector has completed a positive re-structuring process, adding more value through capital-intensive, innova-tive and export-oriented activities (in chemicals, metals, engineering in-dustries and the production of electrical and optical equipment). At the same time, the proportion of labor-intensive activities (in the textile indus-try and footwear manufacturing) has dropped.

A slight gender gap is in evidence on the unemployment front. The annual unemployment rate is higher for women (6.4 percent) than for men (5.7 percent). The youth employment rate was 30.6 percent in 2002, lower than in the EU-15 (40.6 percent). This rate was particularly low for young women as a result of higher enrolment in secondary schools and universi-ties, but also due to higher unemployment among young women. At 24.5 percent, the employment rate for older persons (55-64) remains very low compared to the EU-15 average of 40.1 percent. People with a low educa-tional level are particularly hard hit by unemployment. Among the regis-tered unemployed, around 27 percent have no basic vocational training. Of these, 3 percent have no secondary education and 24 percent have no ele-mentary education. This also results in a high level of long-term unem-ployment. Unemployment and very low activity rates are a particular cause of concern among the Roma population.

The main challenges in Slovenia (cf. also JIM 2003) are:

- Employment chances for the older population,
- Labor participation among women,
- Labor participation for people with little schooling and no voca-tional training.

The research question thrown up by the Slovenian situation is this: Is the age/employment divide in Slovenia mirrored in a below-average ICT affin-ity among older Slovenians compared to the other countries?

Older people use the Internet much less than the national average. Al-though 26 percent of those aged 50-64 and 7 percent of those aged 65 and over have Internet access at home, less people (15 percent and 3 percent respectively) actually use it in either group. 28 percent of the 65+ age group own a mobile phone, as do 64 percent of the 50-64 age group.

Comparing these findings with the situation in other European countries nevertheless reveals that the influence of age on ICT uptake is not unusually pronounced in Slovenia. As regards the low Internet uptake among the oldest age group, Slovenia is no exception at all. Although there are good examples of comparatively smaller age divides (such as in Austria, the UK and Denmark), most other countries face the same challenges as Slovenia. Belgium, Greece, Spain, Portugal, France and Finland in the EU-15 and Estonia, Hungary, Lithuania and Poland among the newcomers do not even reach average Internet usage of 10 percent in this age group.

Table 16: ICT uptake in Slovenia, by age groups (percentage of users per age group)

Age group	Internet usage	Computer usage	Internet at home	Mobile phone
Up to 24	77	86	54	99
25 to 49	46	62	41	90
50 to 64	15	27	26	64
65 and over	3	5	7	28
Total	37	49	34	76

Source: SIBIS survey data 2003, the authors' calculations

Table 17: The age variation in Internet uptake (Internet users per age group as a percent of the national average; total Internet usage: percentage of users per country)

	CZ	EE	HU	LV	LT	PL	SK	SI	BG	RO	BE	DK
Up to 24	195	169	272	216	226	280	190	206	260	255	171	136
25 to 49	115	125	116	121	102	99	113	123	119	100	138	119
50 to 64	54	63	37	43	40	64	30	41	43	24	51	93
65 and over	13	8	<1	12	<1	5	10	7	3	4	7	30
Total	33%	52%	18%	28%	30%	20%	24%	37%	21%	13%	45%	68%
Variation co-efficient	72	67	98	81	93	92	84	82	92	103	71	42

	DE	EL	ES	FR	IE	IT	LU	NL	AT	PT	FI	SE	UK
Up to 24	159	225	209	174	160	197	165	146	175	240	145	142	143
25 to 49	130	113	103	127	105	131	109	114	116	113	128	123	123
50 to 64	76	28	48	52	68	52	79	98	63	28	70	100	83
65 and over	13	6	6	8	21	12	25	16	35	<1	7	24	32
Total	53%	24%	35%	36%	51%	37%	52%	63%	54%	28%	63%	66%	61%
Variation co-efficient	59	92	83	71	58	73	53	51	55	98	62	46	45

Source: SIBIS survey data 2003, the authors' calculations

Overall, the influence of age is weaker in the Czech Republic and Estonia, which are nevertheless comparable regarding the overall ICT uptake. However, a stronger influence is visible in Hungary, Lithuania and Poland, as well as in Bulgaria and Romania. Spain is the most similar country to Slovenia, with almost the same uptake rates by age group and in total. France and Italy, which are also comparable in terms of total Internet uptake, exhibit a slightly smaller age influence.

Evidently, the age divide in Slovenia is clearly reflected in lower ICT uptake. To summarize, however, Slovenia is no exception from the all-European rule in this regard.

3.5 Conclusions

All new member states (except Estonia) lag behind the EU-15 with regard to ICT adoption in the population at large. While digital divides appear to follow those dimensions of social structure that are associated with social inclusion or exclusion more or less everywhere, the size and shape of the digital divide varies considerably between countries. This reminds us that there is scope for policy to respond to digital divide challenges. And this fact alone supports the case for targeted national strategies.

After having analyzed the digital divides in the CEE countries, two major issues appear to be of concern to policy-makers: first, the correlation between IT skills, education and employability; and second, the unusual divide between the youngest generations and the next-oldest core workforce age groups.

Analysis bluntly shows that Internet experience and IT savvy have a very strong role to play in employability. At the same time, the unemployed and the less educated are way behind the national average in their Internet skills and the use of computers. Given the fact that gainful employment is one if not the major agent in acquiring ICT skills, and given the low level of ICT skills identified for the unemployed, the situation resembles a vicious cycle for those outside the production process and a virtuous cycle for those within. It has been shown that, today, people in the CEE countries who have Internet skills run virtually no risk of unemployment. In times of rampant unemployment in some of the countries, the unemployment rate for people with advanced Internet skills – i.e. people who use e-mail and search engines, download files and exhibit some other (by no means "geeky") skills – nowhere exceeds four percent. Further, analysis reveals that Internet usage has a surprisingly high and statistically significant effect on the risk of unemployment: Even after controlling for education, age, gender and health status, the likelihood of becoming unemployed is still three fourths lower for those who use the Internet.

Both IT savvy and employment are closely associated with education. Controlling for other variables, education is a very decisive predictor of Internet usage. There is a clear bias toward those with tertiary education compared to people who have less schooling. The main influence of education, however, still relates to those who are currently studying. The information society in the new member states – to a much larger extent than in the Western member states – so far remains a student and youth phenomenon.

The ICT skill base in the new member states is made up almost exclusively of the younger generation. Even among otherwise disadvantaged youngsters, IT skills are as widespread as among otherwise better-off older generations. This is not to say that the digital divide does not affect younger age groups. As these cohorts enter the labor market, special attention must be paid to those younger people who are still digitally excluded. They will face much harsher competition than the IT savvy majority of their age group, who will have better employment prospects.

At present, however, the middle age group of 25-49 year olds should be a special cause of concern. Considering that these cohorts will continue to constitute the core workforce for the decades to come, ICT skills are in very short supply. Exceptionally low skill levels are found among unemployed and inactive people in this age bracket. But the same is true of people in paid employment, only 13 percent of whom are in possession of advanced skills.

Younger cohorts have much greater ICT skills. This will affect productivity and competitiveness on the labor market, while the skills of the older and even the middle-aged generations are at risk of being devalued. In the medium to long term, this may entail changes to the social structure in the CEE countries. Occupational positions held by middle-aged cohorts are likely to be replaced earlier by subsequent generations. While this may bring about social advancement for some (otherwise disadvantaged) young people, it may also create the risk of a new generational divide, as well as the risk of shortages in the appropriately skilled labor force in the near future.

References

Commission of the European Communities, 2004 (CEC 2004): Commission Staff Working Paper: Social Inclusion in the New Member States. A Synthesis of the Joint Memoranda on Social Inclusion. SEC (2004)848.

Commission of the European Communities, 2003 (CEC 2003a): Social protection in the 13 candidate countries. A comparative analysis. Luxembourg.

Commission of the European Communities, 2003 (CEC 2003b): Joint report by the Commission and the Council on social inclusion. 6507/04 SOC 79 ECOFIN 55 EDUC 34 SAN 31 + COR 1 (de).

Commission of the European Communities, 2001 (CEC 2001): Draft Joint Report on Social Inclusion. 13926/01 SOC 447 ECOFIN 327 EDUC 136 SAN 147 REV 1.

Commission of the European Communities and National Governments, 2003 (JIM 2003): Joint Memoranda on Social Inclusion. Several issues.

Eurostat (2002): European Social Statistics. Income, poverty and exclusion. 2nd Report.

de Haan, Jos (2003): IT and Social Inequality in The Netherlands. IT & Society 1, Issue 4, pp. 27-45.

Guio, Anne-Catherine (2004): The Laeken Indicators: Some Results and Methodological Issues in Acceding and Candidate Countries. Background paper prepared for the workshop "Aligning the EU Social Inclusion Process and the Millennium Development Goals" April 26-27, 2004, Vilnius, Lithuania.

Hüsing, Tobias and Hannes Selhofer (2004): DIDIX: A Digital Divide Index for Measuring Inequality in IT Diffusion. IT&Society 1, Issue 7, Spring/Summer 2004, pp. 21-38.

Jackson et al. (2004): The Impact of Internet Use on the Other Side of the Digital Divide. pp. 43-47 in Communications of the ACM 47/7.

Jenson, Jane (2002): Identifying the Links: Social Cohesion and Culture. Canadian Journal of Communication 27, pp. 141-151.

Martin, Steven P (2003): Is the Digital Divide Really Closing? A Critique of Inequality Measurement in A Nation Online. IT&Society 1, Issue 4, pp. 1-13.

SIBIS consortium (2003): SIBIS 2003 NAS country reports. http://www.empirica.biz/sibis/reports/country.htm.

Sicherl, Pavle (2003): Different Statistical Measures Provide Different Perspectives on Digital Divide. Paper presented at 6th ESA Conference, Murcia 2003. (http://www.sicenter.si/pub/Sicherl_Digital_divide_Murcia.pdf).

Vranken, Jan, et al. (2001): Non-monetary Indicators of Social Exclusion and Social Inclusion: What Does Exist and What Do We Need? Research Report, University of Antwerp.

Annex: Logistic Regression Analysis of Unemployment

We used the data of all ten countries and examined only the 15-64 age groups and those in (self-) employment or unemployment, thus excluding people in education and other inactive persons. To analyze the impact of different demographic and socioeconomic variables on the risk of being unemployed, we used binary logistic regression. The dependent variable is dichotomous (subjects are either unemployed or employed). The independent variables are coded at the categorical level. Interpretation is based on the effect coefficient exp(b), which is the effect of the independent variable on the odds ratio of being unemployed.

Table: Logistic regression of unemployment

	Model 1			Model 2		
	Exp(B)	Std.Dev.	Sig.	Exp(B)	Std.Dev.	Sig.
Gender: female	**1.341**	.066	.000	**1.315**	.068	.000
Education: Reference: Secondary and less			.000			.000
Higher secondary	**.422**	.089	.000	**.507**	.091	.000
Tertiary	**.244**	.113	.000	**.413**	.118	.000
Age: Reference: up to 24			.000			.000
25-49	**.427**	.094	.000	**.370**	.098	.000
50-64	**.377**	.116	.000	**.305**	.120	.000
Presence of long standing illness or disability	**1.676**	.094	.000	**1.643**	.095	.000
Internet usage				**.259**	.098	.000
Constant term	1.084	.116	.487	1.368	.120	.009
-2 log likelihood			5740.3			5507.0
Cox & Snell R²			.050			.087
Nagelkerke R²			.077			.135
Number of observations			5809			5809

Source: SIBIS survey data, 2003, unweighted data, the authors' calculations

Calculations are made using the binary logistic regression procedure in SPSS.

4 The Role of European Governments in the Digital Economy

Arnoud De Meyer, INSEAD

What is the role of government in the digital economy? It is not our intention to go into an in-depth ideological debate on whether governments should intervene in the business sector. We will try to adopt a pragmatic approach and explore what already happens in practice. It is up to the reader to make a judgment to what extent the governments should be involved in the ICT sector. There is enough indication that, due to network externality effects, governments need to take on an active role in stimulating an e-environment to jump-start the move toward a higher level of e-readiness.

In this chapter, we will argue that the government can play an important role in at least four areas: stimulating the enhancement of the infrastructure that enables e-Europe; investing in improved services (e-government); stimulating an e-friendly business environment; and creating an all-inclusive information society. For each of these areas we will provide insights into how the government can play an effective role[1].

4.1 Stimulating the Infrastructure that Enables a Vigorous e-World

An effective e-Europe needs to have a basic infrastructure in place in order to reach out to its citizens or to provide a robust network over which business can operate. Waiting for the private sector to build this infrastructure all alone will not work, or will suffer from serious delays because of the network externalities that create a serious hurdle for any private firm wanting to start with investments in the ICT infrastructure.

An important focal point of the successful IT policies in Sweden, Denmark and Belgium, for example, has been the establishment of dense broadband

---

[1] This chapter is partially based on De Meyer, A. and Loh, C., (2004), *Impact of ICT on government innovation policy: an international comparison,* International Journal of Internet and Entreprise Management, vol 2, no 1.

telecommunications networks linking the entire country. The principle is that the government is responsible for ensuring that this infrastructure is available throughout the country, while broadband expansion should be left primarily to market players.

This basic infrastructure also needs to be accessible at reasonable rates. The study reported in this book shows clearly that a country's e-readiness is to a large extent determined by the combination of broadband penetration (DSL and other forms of broadband) and low access costs.

A good infrastructure needs more than the hard component, however: There is also a soft side to it. This soft side involves stimulating creative research and development in the field of ICT. It also requires the construction of networks between research institutes, universities, and industry players, where each supports the others in the technological innovation process, as well as the creation of an information and communications infrastructure. As Valtonen[2] puts it, the ability to transfer new and existing knowledge to the right place at the right time in order to transform it into a marketable product or service is one of the key issues for the business world in today's technology-savvy and knowledge-intensive environment. Networks play a very important role in enabling this transfer.

Research and the presence of technological networks between the business community, universities, and research and information centers can facilitate the technological innovation process by building on the strengths of each and creating synergies. From the examples provided by what countries like Finland and Ireland do, networks operate mainly on two levels: (a) a more *micro* level, where collaboration may be in specific sectors or industries; and (b) a more *macro* level, where complementary resources are pooled for a designated area.

An example of the second form of collaboration are the Finnish centers of expertise. These centers of expertise pooled complementary research resources in designated areas and became catalysts in the innovation process. Launched by the Finnish Ministry of the Interior in 1994, the objective of Finland's centers of expertise program was to improve the conditions that enable the location and development of internationally competitive, knowledge-intensive business enterprises. Instead of supporting weak ar-

---

[2] Valtonen, M. (1999), *The Role of the Regional Centres of Expertise in Business Networks*, editors: Gerd Schienstock and Osmo Kuusi, Transformation Towards A Learning Economy: The Challenge for the Finnish Innovation System, SITRA, pp. 284-91.

eas, the strategy is to focus on and further develop regional strengths. The 11 regional centers of expertise thus act as a catalyst in enhancing the links and cooperation between universities, research institutions, enterprises and regional authorities.

Another example of how one can create such networks, this time perhaps more at the micro level, is the establishment of *virtual* information centers such as the Swedish site *itsweden.com*. This website focuses on the IT sector in Sweden, including the country's venture capital and e-learning industries[3].

4.2   Investing in Improved Services: e-Government

Having stimulated the development of infrastructure, governments need to improve the services they provide to citizens and business by going online. As Leitner[4] points out in her evaluation of e-government in Europe based on the *e*Europe Awards Program, e-government has reached a turning point in Europe. The question is no longer simply whether to go online or not. Data sharing and back-office integration already offer substantial benefits to governments all over Europe. Now, however, e-government is increasingly being regarded as a key enabler for citizen-centric, cooperative, seamless and polycentric modern government.

Since the government has the one of the largest client bases, and all citizens and businesses are at some point customers of the government, the public sector can serve as a leveraging platform to demonstrate how ICT can improve living standards. In doing so, it can create a *demand* for ICT. At the same time, the development of electronic government can also create a *market* for ICT applications developed by private-sector firms and thereby stimulate the development of the ICT industry.

However, in order to become a truly meaningful agent of modernization and change, governments will have to replace the still-prevalent technology bias with a focus on socio-cultural transformation.

---

[3] This website was set up jointly by the Ministry of Foreign Affairs Sweden, the Swedish Trade Council, the Association of the Swedish IT and Telecom Industry, the Invest in Sweden Agency, and the Swedish Office of Science and Technology. See http://www.itsweden.com/.

[4] Leitner, C. 2004, eGovernment in Europe: the State of Affairs, Eipascope, www.eipa.nl.

Being still a relatively new concept, e-government is often something of a misnomer insofar as people believe an agency has an e-government strategy if it has a government website. As with business IT strategies, it entails much more than that. In essence, e-government is really about examining the entire government strategy model to see how government agencies can work together more effectively and efficiently, using ICT to add value to customer relations with the government. This process has been explicitly outlined by the World Bank, which defines an e-government as one that *leverages the use of ICT to transform relations* with citizens, businesses and other government agencies. Better delivery of government services to citizens, improved interaction with businesses, citizen empowerment through increased access to information, and more efficient government management lead directly to the potential rewards of e-government: reduced corruption, greater transparency and convenience, revenue growth and/or cost reductions. These rewards will accrue not only to businesses and citizens but also to the overall government sector.

In general, the development of an e-government can be categorized into two main thrusts. The first is to move information and appropriate services online, the objective of which is to create a "24/7 government" and enable greater convenience in citizen-government or business-government communications. This typically progresses from posting information online to fostering greater interactivity to implementing transactional capabilities. The sequence, in other words, is *publish* → *interact* → *transact*[5], where the value created increases exponentially. This publish–interact–transact model is similar to the ICDT model developed by Angehrn[6], where I-C-D-T stood for Information, Communication, Distribution and Transaction. This ICDT model is generic and can be used in a variety of sectors.

The second thrust is to develop an ICT-enabled public sector workforce that can work efficiently in the new knowledge-intensive environment. This entails strong top leadership commitment to the development of an e-government. At the rank and file level, public sector workers should be equipped with knowledge management and ICT skills, as the strategy of maximizing automation will minimize direct face-to-face contact and will shift their roles from labor-intensive to knowledge-intensive.

---

[5] Accenture (2001), Rhetoric vs Reality: Closing the Gap, e*Government Leadership*, April.

[6] Angehrn, A.A. (1997), "Designing Mature Internet Strategies: The ICDT Model," *European Management Journal*, vol. 15, no. 4, pp. 335-474.

We have identified the crucial pillars of an e-government strategy as: (a) a clear e-government vision and prompt installation of delivery mechanisms; (b) putting in place interactive capabilities, moving from mainly *publishing* information to creating a portal that provides integrated and client-centric services (*"interact"*); (c) developing and enhancing secure transactional capabilities through public key infrastructures (PKIs), to progress from one-way informational flows to bilateral and transactional flows (*"transact"*); and (d) cultivating knowledge workers in the public sector. These four aspects, as illustrated in figure 1 (see below), form the structure of the discussion that follows.

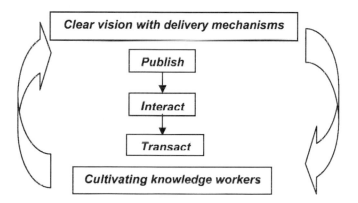

Fig. 1: E-government strategy

4.2.1 The Vision of e-Government and Its Implementation

The first step in an e-government strategy is to develop a broad e-government vision and put in place responsibility centers and mechanisms to ensure delivery accountability. Leading e-governments have, in their e-government visions, articulated the role of the public sector as a *catalyst* in creating an information economy and the need for seamless one-stop access to citizen-centric government services. In particular, leading e-governments such as those in Denmark, the United Kingdom and Finland have stressed the importance of four focal areas: service to *individuals*; service to *businesses*; *intergovernmental affairs*; and *internal efficiency and effectiveness*. At the same time, it is also vital that government leaders pass down their e-government vision to the middle management and ensure that the general public sector workforce understands the "why" and "what" of change.

Implementation mechanisms include the formulation of a well-defined action plan. This often requires the creation of an *intergovernmental* agency or a strong coordinator to oversee the implementation process. As articulated in the e-Norway Action Plan, an e-government action plan should be a clearly defined operational plan that describes *where* the country is at, *what* needs to be done, *who* is responsible and by *when* actions are to be implemented. Also, an e-government strategy should be an *agency-based* one. This means that the relevant government agencies should be made responsible for identifying which services are "appropriate" for electronic delivery and in what sequence and manner. To help agencies decide, it is also useful to provide some guidelines on the criteria that should be used. However, the important thing is for agencies to ensure that the major back-end systems and processes are in place to fully realize the benefits of going online.

Having a vision does not mean that everything has to be feasible. E-government programs are expensive and their financial returns have thus far been limited. Funding such partnerships is therefore a demanding task. Public-private partnerships may offer an opportunity for funding as well as for collaborative development. Pooling resources across different agencies is an important tool for allocating funds effectively. The Belgian Crossroads Bank for Social Security that ties together public institutions at different government levels with the private sector is an interesting example of this integration and pooling of resources[7]. This e-government approach in the Belgian social security sector is mentioned as best practice in the most recent benchmarking study ordered by the European Commission. Let us look at it as a short case study, because it illustrates well some of the points we made earlier about vision, the pooling of resources and the need for a coordinating agency.

Like many social security systems throughout Europe, Belgian social security is a complex mechanism. It consists of three types of insured groups (employees, self-employed persons and civil servants). It covers a maximum of seven different social risks, e.g. incapacity for work, industrial accidents, occupational diseases, unemployment, etc. And it spans four assistance systems, e.g. subsidies for the handicapped, guaranteed family allowances, minimum incomes and income guarantees for the elderly. In total, about 2,000 institutions are responsible for implementing the Belgian social security system. Close to 10,000,000 socially insured persons and 200,000 employers have very regular contacts with these institutions.

---

[7] http://ksz-bcss.fgov.be. Crossroads Bank for Social Security.

15 years ago, an in-depth analysis of the operations of this system showed that the business processes of the social security institutions was not customer-oriented and was certainly not harmonized across the different social security institutions. Each institution had its own set of paper forms with accompanying instructions. The institutions very often asked insured persons and their employers for information that was already available on paper at another social security institution. The customers therefore had to retrieve and supply this paper, instead of having the institutions exchange this information directly between themselves.

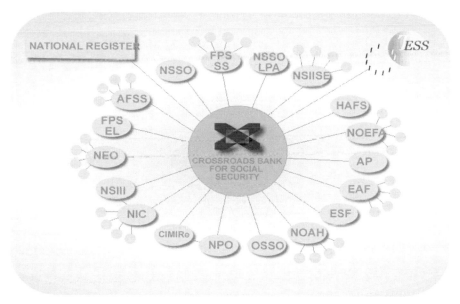

Fig. 2: The Belgian Crossroads Bank for Social Security (source: CBSS website)

To improve service delivery to socially insured individuals and companies, and to resolve the above mentioned shortcomings, the Crossroads Bank for Social Security (CBSS) was created 14 years ago (figure 2).

The mission of the CBSS was to be the engine of e-government in the social security sector. Based on a common vision, the actors in the Belgian social security sector benefited from new technologies that let them improve and radically reorganize their mutual relationships and processes, and this in such a way that privacy was absolutely guaranteed.

The introduction of this system is regarded as a considerable success. In the past, insured persons or their employers had to get about 170 paper certificates from one social security institution, only to hand them over to another social security institution. These paper certificates have now been eliminated and replaced by direct electronic data exchange between the relevant social security institutions. In 2003, 339 million such items of data were exchanged electronically. Some 50 types of forms previously required by the social security system have been eliminated. Insured persons and their employers can now submit all their social security data on the basis of a single form and uniform set of instructions. They only have to report each item of data once to the entire social security apparatus. The number of contacts between insured persons and their employers on the one hand and social security on the other has been reduced drastically. Hospitals and pharmacists no longer have to encode about 100 million paper certificates a year concerning insurance statuses in the healthcare sector. Now, they can read this information electronically on the social security card.

The quantitative benefits in this case are considerable, which is not always the case. In determining a successful e-government strategy any agency will have to determine its priorities. Since e-government is so expensive, cost/benefit analyses will become a prerequisite. In these analyses, qualitative criteria such as the range of channels through which a service can be accessed, the variety of services offered, a reduction in the actual or perceived wait time for users, better accountability, greater openness, transparency, and improvements in the quality of life of vulnerable user groups may still play an important role.

4.2.2   Putting in Place Interactive Capabilities: From Publishing to Interaction

The second step in an e-government strategy is to progress from a passive online government information directory ("*publish*") to the creation of a web *portal* that operates as a "one-stop shop" that provides *interactive*, *user-centric* and *integrated* government services ("*interact*").

At the *publish* level, government websites should have a logical and systematic structure (see figure 3). Like corporate websites, two key success factors are a single point of "official" access and a coordinated framework for linking the available information. Specifically, the structure should encompass (a) a master government home page for accessing all government information that is available online; (b) consistent formats, links and functions; (c) a logical structure that users can click through easily to obtain the required information; and (d) quality assurance for the information available and for all organizations and agencies linked to the site.

Example of an *unstructured* website

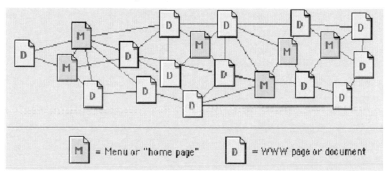

Example of a *highly structured* website

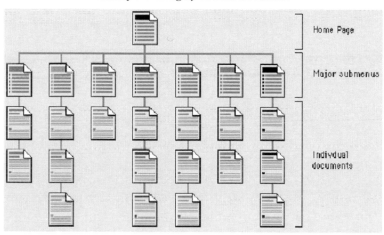

Fig. 3: DeConti, L. (1998), "Planning and Creating a Government Web Site: Learning from the Experience of U.S. States", *Information Systems for Public Sector Management*, Working Paper Series, paper no. 2, July, Institute for Development for Policy and Management, University of Manchester, UK http://www.man.ac.uk/idpm/idpm_dp.htm - isps_wp

In the area of integrated and citizen-centric online deliverables, the Irish government's OASIS portal and the site operated by the Flemish government in Belgium are good examples of citizen-centric and integrated G-to-C services. Based on the "life events" approach, information and services are integrated into *multi-agency* packages and organized around a typical citizen's needs from birth to death, such as "Register Birth", "Move House" and "Get Married"[8].

In delivering G-to-B services, the sharing of information is an essential underpinning element to allow the "one-stop shop" concept to be implemented across all government agencies. It is important for governments to realize that, in the information economy, it is very inefficient to make businesses provide the same information to various agencies. They must therefore identify *which* agencies need *what* information and *in what order* to accomplish basic tasks. Businesses do not distinguish between government agencies: They see agencies collectively as "the government". The aim of a G-to-B portal should therefore be to create a seamless and "intelligent" web portal, where a business need not know which agencies are responsible for a given transaction. It should only have to submit basic information once, whereupon all the affected state agencies' records will be updated.

The Irish G-to-B portal, known as BASIS (Business Access to State Information and Services)[9], provides business-centric government services based on the key "life events" of a typical business. On this site, key business activities are grouped into twelve main "events" based on growth (lifecycle) phases, key functional categories, and service categories. The virtual customs office of the Swedish government[10] offers another interesting example of a site that is organized along the logic that a business user would follow in approaching a customs officer.

Another aspect of integrated government deliverables is the development of a "single identifier", which, as articulated by the Irish government, identifies and verifies users and streamlines all their dealings with the government. Identifiers range from more "offline" processes that are relatively easy to implement, such as the Irish Personal Public Service Number developed as a single citizen identifier, to more "online" processes that can more effectively ensure security and safeguard authentication of user identity through the implementation of a PKI framework.

---

[8] See www.gov.oasis.ie and www.vlaanderen.be.
[9] www.basis.ie.
[10] www.tullverket.se.

4.2.3 Enhancing Transactional Capabilities

A common problem among many e-government applications is that, of the services that are currently available online, a large proportion involve the provision of relatively static and *one-way* information flows. Because most information transmitted via ICT to government agencies is private and confidential, and because online transactions with the government often require some form of authentication and integrity checks, the government web portal must continuously improve secure transactional capabilities to encourage bilateral informational flows.

To do so, a form of public key infrastructure (PKI) has been implemented by most European government agencies. This requires a mature e-commerce platform that addresses the four key elements of a PKI: authentication, non-repudiation, confidentiality and integrity.

Among the key success factors of PKI implementation, the most important is that it remains a collaborative effort with the private sector. Also, the diffusion of information about PKIs and the level of public awareness about them should be emphasized. The latter aspect is especially important, as it determines public confidence in the security of online transactions with the government.

This becomes very important in the implementation of online tax returns, for example. A recent survey of e-government in Europe[11] reported that the usage of such a service in Europe ranged from 5-10 percent up to 35 percent for the leading governments. It is interesting to observe that the average user reported a saving of 71 minutes, representing more than seven million hours in 2003. According to service providers, the maximum take-up could be as high as 80-90 percent, indicating a potential benefit of more than 100 million hours per year for EU citizens. However, this will work only if citizens trust the service and consider it to be user-friendly. This will require a reliable system of providing electronic certificates that enable secure authentication, for instance. An excellent example of an integrated portal for e-government transactions, security and legally binding electronic signatures is the Bremen Online Service in Germany, another 2003 eEurope Awards winner.

As a backbone, the creation of a secure and predictable environment for online transactions between the government and its clients requires a

---

[11] Ramboll Management, 2004, Top of the Web, User satisfaction and usage survey of eGovernment services, www.europa.eu.int/eeurope.

strong supporting legal framework. The *directive on electronic signatures* is now in force in the EU and is gradually being implemented by the various member countries.

4.2.4 Equipping Knowledge Workers

E-government requires public sector employees to become knowledge workers in the digital economy. Since ICT is merely a tool for the government to improve its relationships with its clients, public sector employees must be equipped with both management skills and the skills to use ICT if they are to fully exploit their potential. Putting computers on the desks of civil servants will not make a country a thinking society if the people in front of the computers keep on thinking in the same old way. The challenge is therefore to have a workforce that is capable of using ICT to design, develop, and deliver citizen-centric government services. What is also needed is a leadership that can set an example by applying ICT to respond to the needs of citizens and businesses. The continued development of knowledge workers in the public sector will be the backbone of the whole e-government strategy. At the 2003 European e-government conference in Como, Italy[12], many speakers stressed that (re)training staff, changing approaches to management and redefining tasks and practices are essential to the successful implementation of e-government. This will require a significant investment in the reorganization of the public sector and in the skills of its employees.

4.2.5 Lessons Already Learned

In her analysis of the 2003 *e*Europe Awards, Leitner[13] made a number of interesting observations on what we have already learned about the implementation of e-government. It is good to celebrate successes from time to time. The lessons learned can be summarized as follows:

- The 357 cases she studied show a society that is undergoing a true revolution and evolution in basic government structures, cutting through red tape and bureaucracy. Modernization and good governance are the order of the day,

---

[12] http://europa.eu.int/information_society/egovconf.
[13] Leitner C., 2004, op.cit.

- There is a clear trend to remove command and control from the top and replace it with people-centric, responsive and flexible structures that meet the real needs of society,
- There are vast differences across Europe in terms of capabilities, but also in terms of the needs of citizens. E-government is sometimes about highly localized and specific solutions,
- In the process of implementing e-government, governments have learned a lot about change management,
- Collaboration between the private sector and the different levels of government is increasing. This paves the way to more integrated solutions,
- There is a growing interest in cross-border and pan-European co-operation and service provision. Many projects are delivered in multiple languages, sometimes particularly targeting visitors, sometimes reflecting the multicultural aspects of cities and regions, sometimes simply reflecting the trend toward mobility in Europe.

4.3 Creating an e-Friendly Business Environment

In the internationalizing knowledge-based economy, tax incentives and subsidies are no longer a very effective way for countries to encourage technological innovation and attract hi-tech and knowledge-intensive firms to their shores. More than ever, these decisions are increasingly based on a complex mix of soft factors (such as knowledge resources, work ethics and the regulatory environment) and hard physical infrastructure, such as technology and communications. Based on the "best practices" of leading innovative countries such as the United States, Sweden, Finland, Singapore, Israel and Japan, we have developed a framework to assess how public policy can be designed to encourage technological innovation and facilitate knowledge transfer in the private sector. The six strategic thrusts of our framework are identified in figure 4. We apply them to show how an e-friendly business environment can be created.

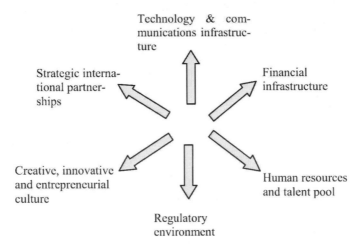

Fig. 4: Components of a government's innovation policy

4.3.1   Technology and Communications Infrastructure

We have already referred to the need to stimulate the creation of an effective infrastructure, both hard and soft. Such a high-performance, accessible technical infrastructure is a *sine qua non* to be successful.

4.3.2   Financial Infrastructure

A well-developed financial infrastructure is critical to the creation of an enterprise ecosystem. Integral aspects include a deregulated financial industry, a mature stock exchange and a vibrant venture capital (VC) industry.

The stock exchange serves as an important source of capital for companies and investors. To serve its purposes, policies should ease listing and administrative requirements to make it easier for companies to raise capital. At the same time, they must ensure that regulatory checks, such as in the area of financial reporting, are in place such that quality is not compromised and investors are protected.

The vibrancy of the VC industry depends in part on the profile of the venture capitalists, i.e. whether there is a good mix of ex-entrepreneurs, business operators and ex-financiers, as each looks at different aspects of the business. The venture capital industry in Sweden is a melting pot with a variety of players catering to different needs: business angels who often work behind the scenes; senior entrepreneurs who have left the board rooms of the old economy and entered into new partnerships with each other; new venture capitalists who form venture capital companies based on the classic model; and foreign capital interests investing in the Swedish market. The experiences of several European countries indicates that the best way to encourage greater corporate venturing is not so much to institute new programs but to reduce the tax and regulatory barriers, as these are the main obstacles to the corporate venturing scene.

4.3.3 *Developing a Skilled Workforce and a Critical Mass of Talent*

This strategic thrust deals with two important aspects: (a) developing a professional workforce skilled in ICT and knowledge management; and (b) building a critical mass of engineers, investment bankers, financial analysts, accountants and lawyers, as each plays a vital role in the innovation process. This is important because, unless countries develop the human expertise needed to manage knowledge, they will lose their strong competitive edge as their proven business models will not continue indefinitely.

Let us take an example from outside Europe where a comprehensive program was developed to increase the pool of ICT-savvy human resources. In Singapore, an *Infocomm Training Framework* was established in June 2001 to improve the ICT competence of the professional working community. The infocomm training needs of professionals are sieved into three levels of programs (see Figure 5), namely

(a) the **E-Business Savvy** *program*, which offers classes catering specially to executives, managers and operators of SMEs *outside* the infocomm industry;

(b) **Conversion** *programs*, to grow infocomm manpower in strategic infocomm industries, such as the *Strategic Manpower Conversion Program in Infocomm*, and the *Strategic Manpower Conversion Program in E-Learning*, designed to train a pool of skilled manpower for the e-learning industry, specifically in the area of instructional design; and

(c) **Infocomm Specialization** *programs*, targeted at infocomm professionals, such as the *Critical Infocomm Technology Resource Program* to provide training in the areas of e-commerce, infocomm convergence, project management and business management, and the *Specialist Manpower Program* to provide training in the areas of telecommunications, wireless communications, software development and networking. Training in innovation strategy, transfer and marketing is also provided for leaders of established SMEs through the existing Initiatives in New Technology (INTECH) scheme.

Similar frameworks have been developed throughout the European Union, but rarely in the same comprehensive manner as described above.

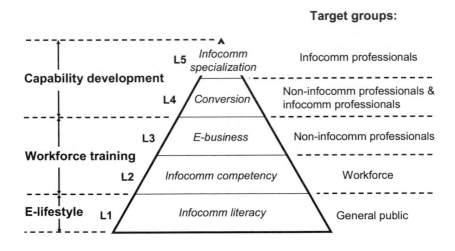

Fig. 5: Infocomm Training Framework (ITF) in Singapore

4.3.4   *Regulatory Framework*

A strict and enforceable regulatory framework is an essential pillar of the information society. As deregulation and liberalization become the buzzwords for the new economy, a good balance between the regulator's dual roles – i.e. to encourage greater technology and knowledge-intensive activities while ensuring that industry players play by the rules – becomes more important than ever. Two main aspects of this are discussed here, namely the creation of a strong and independent regulatory body for the telecommunications industry, and the need to institutionalize a regulatory framework for the knowledge and e-commerce industry, focusing on intellectual property protection, the reliability of electronic signatures and records, and the international compatibility of national laws governing electronic commerce.

A regulatory body for the ICT industry that is separate and distinct from the government is important to prevent a conflict of interests and to carry out "pro-competitive" reforms.

To enable the healthy development of the knowledge and e-commerce industry, the government has a role to play in regulating the industry. According to the International Chamber of Commerce, governments should concentrate on the areas they alone can handle, namely in providing a clear legal framework, law enforcement, intellectual property protection, healthy competition policy rules and a level international playing field[14]. With the use of ICT, new business models and methods are generated every day whose ideas become more abstract and conceptual. At the same time, the use of Internet domain names as source identifiers has rapidly achieved popularity. The realization that the misuse of a domain name could significantly infringe, dilute, and weaken valuable trademark rights has thus led to the need to attribute intellectual property rights to them[15]. The protection of such intellectual property is still relatively new. But it is important that governments recognize the significance of what is at stake.

In regulating the authentication of electronic signatures and records, countries have generally adopted one of three approaches: the *minimalist* approach, which focuses mainly on the removal of existing legal obstacles; the *prescriptive* approach, which prescribes a specific protocol or technology; or a *synthesis* of the two, i.e. a "two-tier" approach. Because of these divergent approaches adopted by different countries, policy-makers should, as far as possible, take steps to ensure that they are internationally compatible and coordinated. Ill-coordinated government regulation is perhaps the single biggest obstacle to the development of the e-business and knowledge industry. Because internationally incompatible national laws will ultimately cause a fragmented global market, they may rob the Internet of its instant global reach, which is its most precious asset. Therefore, the Internet Law and Policy Forum has devised a set of International Consensus Principles on Electronic Authentication. These principles are as follows: (a) Remove legal barriers to electronic authentication. (b) Respect freedom of contract and parties' ability to set provisions by agreement. (c)

---

[14] International Herald Tribune (IHT) (2001),"Keeping E-Commerce Regulation-Free", November 8.

[15] White House (1997), A Framework for Global Electronic Commerce, The White House, July 1, see http://www.ecommerce.gov/framewrk.htm.

Make laws governing electronic authentication consistent across jurisdictions. (d) Avoid discrimination and the erection of non-tariff barriers. (e) Allow the use of current and future means of electronic authentication. (f) Promote market-driven standards. Adopting standards in these areas will thus cut common ground and create a predictable legal environment for the further development of e-commerce.

4.3.5 Creative, Innovative and Entrepreneurial Culture

Innovation, creativity, and an entrepreneurial spirit are essential ingredients to generate sustained growth in the knowledge-based economy. Societies based on innovation attach high priority to creativity (in the form of new ideas, concepts, knowledge, theories and business models). They also make full use of the creative talents in individuals organized in networks to come up with new ideas for technologies, products, systems and businesses. The importance of an environment that encourages creativity and innovation in the knowledge-based economy cannot be overstated. Policies can focus on three main areas: (a) reducing the social stigma of failure; (b) assisting the entrepreneurial and innovative process; and (c) rewarding creative, innovative and entrepreneurial behavior through awards and role models.

To encourage more entrepreneurial and innovative pursuits, an important step is to alleviate the social stigma attached to failure. No amount of policies can help if people are not willing to take risks. This is one of the most difficult areas, as it requires a shift in mindsets and a willingness to accept failure as part of the learning process. The government can play a role by revising institutional arrangements and regulations. Several European governments have adapted their bankruptcy laws to create a climate where business failures need not result in bankruptcy, and where those who become bankrupt through misfortune are treated differently to those who go bankrupt through mismanagement.

One area where governments can play an effective role is to reward creative, innovative, and entrepreneurial behavior in the private sector. As far as possible, make it known to the public that innovation and invention is a good thing. This can be done by creating role models and giving prestigious awards at all levels to reward such behavior. The eEurope Awards program discussed earlier is a good example of such a program.

4.3.6   *Strategic International Partnerships*

Finally, in today's information society, countries have increasingly forged value-adding partnerships with other knowledge-intensive countries that possess complementary capabilities. This creates synergies and enables national innovation programs to take full advantage of the global innovation system. Besides individual countries' *bilateral* cooperation with one another, international collaboration can also be *multilateral*. One example is the recent establishment of the Digital Opportunity Task Force (DOT Force) by the G8 countries to help developing and emerging economies in embracing ICT.

One country that has stood out in this area is Israel. Israel has developed rapidly as a high-tech powerhouse, and the formation of international partnerships has played an important role in its development. As expressed by the Israeli Ministry of Science, international partnerships should display the following traits: (a) steady, working relationships with countries that are leaders in the science and technology arena; (b) access to special (mostly very expensive) technology that is not available in Israel; and (c) access to foreign funding sources. Over the years, strategic partnerships have been developed with a host of leading industrialized countries such as Canada, the European Union (EU), Germany, Singapore and the United States. The *U.S.-Israeli Bilateral Industrial R&D* (BIRD) initiative is the first and most prominent bilateral initiative that Israel has formed with another country. Since its inception in 1977, its success and popularity has stimulated a number of similar bilateral initiatives with, for instance, Germany in 1986 (the *German-Israeli Foundation for Scientific R&D*), Canada in 1993 (the *Canada-Israel Industrial R&D Foundation*), and Singapore in 1997 (the *Singapore-Israel Industrial R&D Foundation*).

Israel was also the first non-European country accepted as an Associate Member of the EU Framework Program. The EU Framework Programs emphasize "pre-competitive research", whose definition closely coincides with the "strategic (or generic-strategic) research" that is the cornerstone of the current efforts of the Israeli Ministry of Science. Collaboration allows Israeli research entities in academia and industry to apply for the projects funded under the program on the same basis as legal entities in member states. Other than the provision of funds with ownership of intellectual property rights (IPR) and no payback, potential leverage also exists in the form of new technology, market intelligence and entry to new markets. Other forms of Israeli-EU collaboration also include participation in the EUREKA European network for market-oriented R&D, the Israeli Innovation Relay Center (IRC), and the German-Israeli Cooperation in Science and Technology Programs.

Another common form of international collaboration is the establishment of physical information centers in partnering countries. Examples include the nine *Euro Info Centers* (EICs) in Sweden to provide companies with local access to a range of specialist information and advisory services, as well as direct links to the European Commission in Brussels and a business support network comprising 240 EICs across Europe, plus 19 Euro Info Correspondence Centers in Central and Eastern European countries and around the Mediterranean. The EIC network thus serves as "first-stop shops" for Swedish companies to obtain information and advice on business and EU matters.

4.3.7   *Where to Go From Here*

By examining the policies implemented by leading innovative countries in these strategic areas, the six-pronged strategy illustrated in figure 4 provides a systematic approach to fostering technological innovation in the private sector. Due to each country's limited resources and unique conditions, the important issue for policy-makers is to first identify, in their own countries, barriers to technological innovation in the private sector. Strengths should be further reinforced and international collaboration actively pursued with countries that possess complementary capabilities to improve in areas of weakness. This framework should thus enable policy-makers to take stock of where their country stands in the global innovation process and guide them in designing new innovation policies and evaluating existing ones.

4.4   Building an All-Inclusive Information Society

To exploit the full benefits of ICT in communication, innovation and learning, citizens – the *change agents* – must first be willing and able to use ICT. One critical pillar of government innovation policies is therefore to equip people by first increasing their access to ICT and encouraging citizens to use them creatively in their learning and communication process. In this section, we look at what the government in Singapore has done to build an all-inclusive information society. Other chapters in this book analyze in much more detail some aspects of what we call the inclusive information society but what others refer to as the digital divide. We will also briefly outline some important regulatory issues as ICT becomes a way of life.

The strategy of developing an all-inclusive information society is to first transform non-ICT users into passive ICT users by providing greater access to ICT and skills training, followed by measures to transform them into active ICT users for whom ICT becomes a way of life (see figure 6). This is the vision of the Swedish Technology Foresight Project, which describes a future scenario where the boundaries between work, education and leisure become less clear, and more people are engaged in knowledge-intensive activities[16]. ICT can be used to tailor education and existing knowledge to the needs of the individual and, thereby, to support the process of life-long learning.

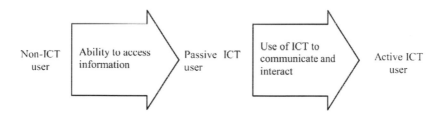

Fig. 6: Building an all-inclusive information society

4.4.1   Ability to Access Information

Policies to enable greater access to information through ICT involve (1) making ICT products and services more affordable, (2) making ICT hardware and support infrastructures more widely available, and (3) applying ICT in education and training programs.

4.4.1.1   Affordability of ICT Products and Services

One barrier to citizens' access to ICT may be the high cost of access and the expense of ICT products and services. High communication costs re-

---

[16] Ministry of Industry, Employment, and Communications (Regeringskansliet) (2000), *An Information Society For All: A Publication for the Swedish IT Policy*, December,
http://www.naring.regeringen.se/pressinfo/infomaterial/pdf/n2000_57.pdf.

main a major obstacle to the widespread use of the Internet. Although this is not the *only* factor, countries with relatively inexpensive Internet access do tend to have a higher Internet host density. The data from the extensive study reproduced in the eEurope 2005 index very clearly shows that there is a definite relationship between communication costs and Internet usage.

According to the Ministry of Transport and Communications in Finland, the most important factor influencing the price of mobile telephony is the level of competition[17]. Therefore, to make ICT products and services more affordable, policy-makers can actively liberalize the ICT industry to enhance greater competition. Finland has indeed been at the forefront in liberalizing the telecommunications industry, as evidenced in its Telecommunications Market Act. For example, by stating that third-generation (3G) mobile operators were allowed to roam on GSM networks on terms defined by the authorities, the law prevented existing operators from abusing their strong market position to hamper the business of 3G operators that did not have their own GSM networks. Similarly, in several European countries, providers of basic public telecommunication services are required to work with all IASPs in a non-discriminatory and non-exclusive manner, to prevent them from leveraging existing relationships with telco parents and engaging in anti-competitive practices. Over time, these measures, which are aimed at increasing competitive market forces in the ICT industry, will lower the cost of access and hence make ICT more affordable to the general population.

4.4.1.2 Availability of ICT Hardware and Support Infrastructures

To make ICT hardware and services more widely available, the strategy adopted by Singapore, Finland and Sweden is to locate them in easily accessible places. In Finland, public libraries are heavily frequented. Therefore, as part of the strategy, 80 percent of public libraries have access to the Internet. These public libraries are being developed into learning centers where users will have extensive computer hardware, information search facilities, printed and electronic information resources, workspaces, expert guidance and information services at their disposal.

To support the creation of an efficient and appropriate infrastructure for information transfer in education, the Foundation for Knowledge and Competence Development has given a total of around SEK 250 million to al-

---

[17] Ministry of Transport and Communications (2001), *Economic Effects of Mobile Telecommunications in Finland*, February 1, http://www.mintc.fi.

most all universities and colleges to promote the broad use of ICT. Colleges and universities will serve as engines in the expansion of IT-based regional interactive networks that cover colleges, SMEs and high schools. This is part of the strategy of transforming Swedish students into leading ICT users and thereby to establish the country as a technology-savvy society. Edu.Stockholm, an advanced school data network introduced at the end of 2001 in the Stockholm region, provides 175 schools, 86,000 students, and 14,000 teachers with gigabyte access to a network.

4.4.1.3 Applying ICT in Education and Training Programs

It is critical for policy-makers to realize that making ICT more affordable and accessible is essential, but that it is not sufficient to encourage the broader use of ICT by citizens. These only constitute supply-side measures. To increase citizens' demand for ICT, however, they must be taught the skills to use this technology. To enable all citizens to have a basic level of ICT competence, policy initiatives are mainly targeted at three levels: (a) ICT in schools; (b) equipping senior citizens with basic ICT skills; and (c) raising the ICT competency of the general workforce through training.

(a) ICT in Schools

National ICT programs for schools have increasingly focused on providing schools with computers and Internet access, and equipping teachers with the skills to use ICT as an educational tool. The Swedish National Action Plan for IT in Schools, for example, is the most extensive investment in the use of ICT in Swedish schools. Aimed at stimulating the use of ICT as an educational tool in primary and secondary education across municipalities, this government initiative is installing computers on a wide scale in public schools. Teachers are being trained in how ICT can be used to its fullest potential as an educational tool. State grants are also provided to increase schools' Internet access, provide e-mail addresses to all teachers and students, develop the Swedish and European Schoolnet (showing teachers how they can integrate ICT in their teaching), and design special IT programs for students with disabilities.

(b) Equipping Senior Citizens with Basic ICT Skills

In Sweden, one-fifth of the surfing population, and also the fastest-growing Internet user group, is aged 50 to 79. These figures signal the success of SeniorNet, a national non-profit organization aimed at facilitating the use of IT among adults aged 55 and above, and to introduce them to the available opportunities. The aim of the association is to enhance the quality of life of this target group by using the opportunities afforded by Internet use to prevent generational and social divisions and isolation. Activities conducted by SeniorNet Sweden include a website where senior citizens can share their experience, a short SeniorNet introduction course on IT and the Internet (so far attended by a total of around 35,000 senior citizens), and SeniorSurf Sweden, an event organized for the first time in September 1999, where more than 30,000 senior citizens visited some 350 participating libraries that are staffed with librarians and tutors to help them surf the Internet.

In many European countries, such as Belgium, France and the Netherlands, senior citizens are currently the fastest-growing group of ICT users. This was already the case in northern Europe in the late 1990s and the early part of this decade. Now, however, the trend has become pervasive throughout Western Europe.

(c)   ICT Training for the General Workforce

Taking students, senior citizens and the workforce as a whole, probably the greatest challenge to policy-makers today is to raise the IT competency of the general workforce – especially those who do not need to use ICT in their work. Irrelevance and the lack of time and any real incentive to do so is often the largest obstacle to government initiatives in this area. To alleviate this problem, government agencies can collaborate with private-sector firms to: (a) provide a central source of information on ICT training programs; (b) provide financial incentives to encourage more private-sector firms to train their staff; (c) facilitate greater exchanges of information between high-tech firms and the education and training community in order to develop more appropriate programs that meet the needs of industry; and (d) make training more accessible to workers. Collaboration will be most successful when employers clearly define and communicate their requirements, employees have an up-front stake in learning new skills and training providers are attuned to market demand.

To make training programs more accessible to the workforce, existing worker training programs should be tailored for convenience. This will entail more evening classes, weekend classes and distance learning, as well as skills taught on a job-specific, on-site and just-in-time basis. To encourage more employers to invest in computers for their staff, one of the initiatives implemented by the Swedish government is to give special tax reductions to all companies that supply employees with personal computers, regardless of whether these are required for their work. Under recent tax reforms, benefits reaped by employees from using company computer equipment for private use are also tax-exempt.

4.4.2 ICT as a Means of Communication and Interaction

More important than having access to ICT is the ability to use it creatively to communicate and enhance learning. The trend in education today is shifting away from books and classroom-based teaching toward a greater focus on customized teaching, hands-on experience, and outdoor teaching in the form of field trips, internships, science exploration programs, and so on. All of these methods have the potential to be empowered by ICT.

As ICT becomes a way of life, issues pertaining to the protection of privacy and ownership of information in the information society will become more relevant and crucial. Like a new business model where the do's and don'ts are not yet clearly defined, policy-makers will have to strike a delicate balance between encouraging citizens and businesses to make use of ICT while ensuring that institutional capabilities and legislative checks are in place to minimize the inherent risks.

However, as the 9/11 terrorist attacks have shown, the ability to protect private information that flows over the Internet may be abused by specific interest groups. The attacks demonstrated the potential dangers in a "borderless" information society – especially the shift of power away from traditional sources toward those who have access to ICT and possess the skills to exploit it. Regulatory issues such as these will represent one of the most sensitive trade-offs in public policy in the next few years.

Another important regulatory issue in the information society is the control and ownership of personal information. With advanced ICT, personal data nowadays can easily be converted into "public" information that can be exchanged, bought or sold for secondary use without the originator's knowledge or consent. The growing challenge for regulators is to institutionalize a legal framework that makes the "middleman" legally liable for disseminating personal information to third parties without prior consent from the originator of the information.

4.5 Conclusion

Recognizing the critical role of technological innovation and knowledge management for sustained growth and wealth creation in the digital economy, European policy-makers have attached increasing importance to the use and diffusion of ICT on a wide scale. The data provided in this book shows that European governments have achieved very different levels of e-readiness, and that all of them still have a long way to go.

Public policy must increasingly focus on stimulating broad-based demand for ICT, facilitating technological innovation on a broad scale and creating an all-inclusive information society in which no-one is left out. Since governments have the largest client base, the public sector can play an important catalytic role by demonstrating the extra value that ICT can add to existing relationships with the government. This can create a "market" for ICT applications developed by the private sector, strengthening the growth of the ICT industry.

To facilitate technological innovation on a broad scale, policy-makers should concentrate on developing the enabling structures and links that can apply to all agents in the innovation process. Countries should focus on developing their strengths, while actively tapping into the global innovation system to share knowledge by forging international alliances in S&T. Finally, since the rate at which the use of new and existing technologies can lead to broad-based productivity gains depends on the development of human capital, public policy should focus on making ICT more affordable and accessible to *all* citizens, and on giving everyone the skills to participate in the information society. Progress toward the information society creates new risks. European policy-makers must therefore pay closer attention to ICT-related issues such as privacy, the ownership of information and the shift in the power base from traditional sources to those who have access to ICT and possess the skills to exploit it.

This chapter provides a framework and highlights "best practices" that show what governments can achieve in the digital economy. The balanced approach emphasized herein is designed to give readers a helpful resource and guiding framework so that governments can systematically evaluate their policies and plot their next stage of development toward an e-Europe. In light of limited resources, governments should carefully weigh the needs of businesses and their citizens, implementing those strategies that will add most value for both and thereby exploiting the strengths of each economy to the full.

5 Value-Based Information Management in European ICT Strategies

Kai Bender, Julia Hoerauf and Gérard Richter
Roland Berger Strategy Consultants

5.1 Introduction

The eEurope 2005 study focuses on the unique situation facing the 10 new EU member states, some of which are still struggling with the transformation from centrally planned to market economies, their new sovereign status and the development of their national economies. The stages of development reached by these countries vary considerably.

Market forecasts nevertheless predict that Eastern Europe's populations, economies and IT markets will expand at more than three times the current rates in Western Europe, putting this region on a par with other growth markets such as Latin America and Asia.[1] As this trend unfolds, information and communication technology (ICT) will serve to boost productivity and improve quality of life. Especially in the new EU member countries, companies will increasingly invest to improve performance, become more transparent and create more value. ICT is a catalyst that will enable firms to realize these goals.

If information technology is to be leveraged effectively, a company's overall business strategy must be linked to its IT strategy. Every aspect of IT strategy – IT governance, IT processes, application architecture roadmaps and so on – must be derived from the overall business strategy. The challenge is not primarily a technological one. Rather, it is the need to craft an effective IT strategy on the basis of appropriate information management. Companies must fully understand the industry-specific links between business drivers, emerging customer needs and technology requirements, and must translate this understanding into suitable information management strategies.

Roland Berger Strategy Consultants strongly believes in the strategic business value of using IT to help clients maximize the value of their business.

---

[1] Gartner Dataquest 2003.

In our view, successful information management demands action in four specific areas. IT strategy must be aligned with business strategy. Performance must be improved by rigorously managing complex IT implementation projects. An appropriate IT organization must be built. And IT costs must be managed effectively.

The sections that follow draw on recent examples from the Roland Berger project portfolio to explain this approach.

5.2   Information Management

5.2.1   Implementing Value-Based IT Strategies

IT can be leveraged to address business challenges and create real business value. Accordingly, it should not be regarded purely as a technological "commodity" – as so many lines of code, say – but as a measurable contribution to the value of the company. The practice of defining, updating and implementing IT strategy must be anchored in the company's objectives with the aim of increasing the return on investment, reducing costs and minimizing overall risk. IT strategy should be a subset of the general strategy development process. Performance indicators have to be defined in order to evaluate the specific benefits of IT. The whole IT team must then be attuned to these performance objectives. Compliance must be monitored on a permanent basis. The decisive factor is not whether IT projects deliver outcomes on time and on budget, but how much value they add by reducing process times, slashing process costs and raising quality. Companies should also define rules governing collaboration between user organizations and IT departments.

Companies can use existing IT structures and emerging innovations to exploit revenue potential and cut costs. To do so, however, they have to know what opportunities innovative technologies have to offer. State-of-the-art IT solutions can help them get to know their customers better and tailor products and services to the specific needs of their business. To help companies cut costs too, technology-based platforms are useful to optimize their processes both within the company and in their industry-specific value chain.

To make their IT departments more effective and efficient across the board, companies have to boost transparency in these departments and in IT-related business areas. They must harmonize and consolidate their IT organization on a global scale, with a well-defined IT roadmap and organizational structure, optimized IT processes, and a consistent architecture for their IT infrastructure and applications.

Figure 1 outlines one possible approach to information management strategy projects. The approach breaks down into four phases: The first consists of assessing and analyzing the existing strategy. Building on business strategy and identified IT performance needs, the second phase involves defining a new information management strategy. The third step is to draw up an improvement roadmap. Finally, the selected improvement actions must be implemented.

A four-phase approach can develop a portfolio of integrated actions to better align IM support with business strategy

Overview of IM strategy project

Fig. 1: Overview of one approach to information management strategy projects

Two of Roland Berger's most challenging projects to date involved building an organizational structure and defining a culture of collaboration between users and technology experts. The client was able to implement innovative solutions within an ambitious timeframe. Bringing both sides together into one group and getting them to work side by side on pilot applications helped to bridge the gap between them. The projects were nevertheless a constant battle against inherited traditions – in terms of both technology and attitudes.

5.2.2 Managing Large IT Implementation Projects

Good information management means better project performance. Companies are gradually waking up to the fact that IT is one of the most important vehicles for reliable strategy implementation. Practically all strategy implementation projects therefore spawn one or more IT implementation projects. Managing complex IT projects is, however, a very challenging task that is fraught with pitfalls.

Top management must set clear priorities to ensure that business value is genuinely created. In mission-critical projects, it is not always possible to give equal weighting to quality, punctuality and budget compliance. Closely monitoring progress and critical key performance indicators helps companies to stay focused on core decisions. Rigorous project planning and monitoring are likewise essential to keep IT projects on track.

Changing requirements can be a major pitfall in any IT project. One key to successful projects is therefore to assess requirements rigorously in advance. At the same time, actively managing internal and external risks will help companies to prepare for changing circumstances. "Commodity" processes such as error handling often turn out to be major drivers of project complexity. In such cases, experienced experts and transparent reporting are needed to counteract this trend.

Our experience shows that most initial project plans make no provision for fallback options, changing business requirements and all the related cost categories. The screening of typical project-related business cases often reveals that project costs were underestimated by as much as 50 percent. This risk can be mitigated by focusing on realistic business assumptions and involving all relevant stakeholders as early as possible.

In two high-profile cases, we managed to get projects involving more than 300 staff firmly back on track. By combining our business, IT and project management skills, we were able to address all mission-critical risks one by one. We brought users, developers, operators and suppliers to one table and provided all parties with consistent information. Another major challenge was external communication with the media, which we managed successfully.

5.2.3 Developing an IT Organization

Many companies have never consciously shaped their IT landscapes, but have simply let them evolve unsystematically over time. Many companies focus almost exclusively on applications and infrastructure. Yet topics such as IT governance, striking the right balance between centralized and decentralized organization, and molding efficient structures and processes within the IT department are critical drivers of overall business value. Developing the best possible IT organization to ensure both top quality and low cost is the key challenge posed by our projects in this field.

There is no perfect blueprint for IT organizations for each and every company. The "optimal" solution depends on many different factors, such as the varied nature of the business units, the degree of autonomy that each enjoys, the depth of their IT expertise, and the corporate culture. Each company must therefore begin by analyzing their business and IT strategy. From there, they can go on to develop the IT organization that best suits their individual situation.

There are definite success factors for an efficient and effective IT organization. Responsibility for IT must rest with senior management. Companies must determine the degree of centralization that fits their structures. They must institutionalize processes for enhancing IT efficiency and properly managing human capital in IT. All of which will help put the information management organization back on track.

Streamlining the IT organization and implementing a precise IT governance strategy will help companies to raise efficiency and reduce both operating costs and overhead resources in the plan, build and operate phases. Experience shows that this can shave 15 to 20 percent off existing IT budgets.

Outsourcing, including offshoring and on-demand computing, is back in fashion. The really challenging question, however, is not "whether" to outsource, but "what". Accordingly, suitable outsourcing strategies must be assessed and defined by comparing the outsourcing option with the optimized internal solution. This exercise must be performed for every single case. It gives the management a solid basis on which to decide whether to outsource, say, application development, IT infrastructure operation or user support. It is then important to pick the right service provider. Fair contract design is equally vital. Contracts must cover all critical issues, reducing the risk of future disappointments for both parties.

Well-managed outsourcing deals can help companies reduce the total cost of ownership by up to 20 percent. More efficient IT can also make a substantial contribution. In one particular project, our client saw revenues increase by 47 percent and operating profits by 238 percent over a four-year period. Caution is nevertheless in order when considering such numbers. It is no secret that outsourcing deals often fail to live up to defined expectations. Additional transaction costs, vaguely formulated service level agreements and unexpected rework expenses can easily eat into notional savings potential.

Experience shows that soft skills are very important in IT organization projects. In most cases, at least one of the parties involved will have to cede a measure of responsibility, competencies, headcount or budget. As everyone is fully aware of this, it is important to communicate frankly right from the beginning of the project and to involve all relevant stakeholders. Companies should not expect radical organizational changes overnight, but should instead look for an attractive, feasible transition path.

5.2.4 Managing IT Costs

With IT budgets having constantly been in the spotlight in recent years, IT cost management remains a key issue on every CIO's and CFO's agenda. The issue takes on even greater significance when one considers the relatively high "hidden" cost of IT as a percentage of revenue across different industries. For example, an average of 8.7 percent of revenues in the telecommunications sector was spent on IT in 2003. Of this figure, 0.7 percent can be regarded as hidden IT spending[2].

The most powerful lever is usually to examine the corporate project portfolio and skip less important projects. At the same time, it is important to define short-term (up to one-year) and medium-term (up to two-year) levers to reduce IT costs without threatening service levels. Dividing IT costs into five categories – application development, application maintenance, data center operations, networks, and desktop/end-user support – enables potential "savings levers" to be identified in each category:

- Application development: Short-term levers can, for example, include managing demand, improving project management and renegotiating existing contracts. Medium-term levers could include managing the software development life cycle and the improvement of development tools,
- Application maintenance: Capturing resources, reducing process overheads and, again, renegotiating existing contracts all rank as short-term levers. Improving documentation and consolidating the application landscape can be seen as medium-term levers,

---

[2] Source: Gartner.

- Data center operations: Streamlining and de-layering support organizations, reducing service levels and skipping a generation in the systems upgrade roadmap can be regarded as short-term levers, while outsourcing, consolidating and automating monitoring activities must be classed as medium-term levers,
- Networks: Here, short-term levers include consolidating and renegotiating contracts, analyzing network usage and managing demand. One medium-term lever would be to consolidate private networks,
- Desktop and end user support: In the short term, savings can be realized by outsourcing services and help desk support, managing demand and rigorously enforcing defined policies. In the medium-term, useful levers can include optimizing asset management, implementing desktop replacement policies, standardizing desktop profiles and running the help desk as a call center.

Substantial savings can be realized by applying these levers. The exact figure usually varies between 5 and as much as 50 percent of the IT budget (see figure 2).

Standard IT cost ratios (e.g. IT cost over revenue) give companies only a rough estimate of what target IT costs should really be. Many companies with relatively high IT spending are actually among the top companies in terms of overall corporate performance in their respective industries. The key question is therefore not how much should be spent on IT, but what exactly it should be used for.

There are good reasons why some IT cost reduction projects succeed and others do not. Many organizations tend to hide IT budgets in departmental budgets. Any IT cost management project must therefore start by creating a valid baseline. Successful IT cost management projects do not merely define actions. They also make provision for consistent implementation monitoring.

In order to keep IT costs at an acceptable level once they have initially been reduced, information management must clearly assign responsibility for budget targets to named individuals. Where necessary, budget compliance must be enforced. Companies should adopt a process perspective, defining process owners who are responsible for both IT costs and process quality.

It is useful to combine a structural perspective with a process-oriented view of IT costs. We have substantially reduced IT costs at companies in virtually all industries. Clients benefit in particular from our rigorous approach to implementation monitoring. We help clients identify their hidden IT spend – a constant but manageable challenge.

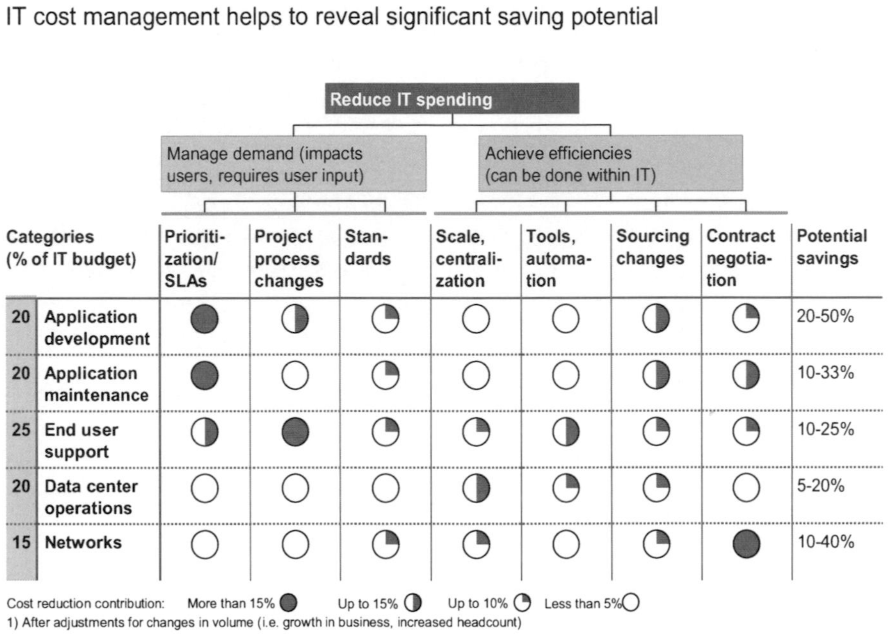

IT cost management helps to reveal significant saving potential

Categories (% of IT budget)	Manage demand (impacts users, requires user input)			Achieve efficiencies (can be done within IT)				Potential savings
	Prioritization/ SLAs	Project process changes	Standards	Scale, centralization	Tools, automation	Sourcing changes	Contract negotiation	
20 Application development	●	◐	◔	○	○	◐	◔	20-50%
20 Application maintenance	●	○	◔	○	○	◐	◔	10-33%
25 End user support	◐	●	◔	◔	◐	◔	◔	10-25%
20 Data center operations	○	○	○	◐	◔	◔	○	5-20%
15 Networks	○	○	◔	◔	○	◔	●	10-40%

Cost reduction contribution: More than 15% ●   Up to 15% ◐   Up to 10% ◔   Less than 5% ○
1) After adjustments for changes in volume (i.e. growth in business, increased headcount)

Fig. 2: Overview of potential savings thanks to IT cost management[3]

5.2.5   Implications and Challenges for the New EU Member States

The expansion of the European Union to include ten new member states will not generate sudden changes in the Western European business world. Major enterprises such as IBM and HP, for instance, have been present on the Czech market for a long time. Companies such as Germany's gedas and EDS have followed their clients to the Czech Republic and now rank among the leading IT service providers. Also, companies such as Accenture and LogicaCMG, which offer BPO services in addition to IT services in the Czech Republic, have increased their presence in recent years. Further expansion is on their agenda.

---

[3] Sources: PSM database, Gartner, Salary.com.

Scandinavian countries discovered the Baltic states quite some time ago because of their highly-qualified workforce, low wages and cultural similarities. Attractive subsidies and low taxes are further good reasons for Western European companies to practice "nearshoring" in the new EU member states. In Slovakia, Hungary and the Baltic states, for example, the average tax rate is considerably below 20 percent.

The new membership of the ten states will create more favorable conditions for business cooperation within the EU. This will in turn encourage further investment. In the past, lack of capital and investment security in particular were obstacles to the progress of business cooperation. Furthermore, the new member states can now also expect significant financial support from Brussels.

While EU expansion is improving basic conditions, however, it will also lead to increased costs (e.g. through increasing wages) in the new member states. Therefore, the challenge to companies based in the new member states is now to sharpen their competitive advantage – high-quality work at low cost – and leverage their proximity to Western European countries in order to protect and grow their business in future.

Companies in the new member states can only continue to offer competitive prices and meet demands for greater efficiency if they improve their IT systems and exploit the potential that value-based IT strategies offer. Companies in Eastern Europe can make targeted use of information management to improve their own performance, thus making themselves more attractive to foreign companies and increasing cooperation opportunities. Especially through joint ventures with Western partners, Eastern European companies can acquire additional expertise and experience, enabling them to boost both their national and their international business.

In this context, the implementation of a value-based IT strategy provides companies in new member states with a framework to enter the market successfully and add substantial value internally. An IT strategy that is aligned with the business strategy can further enhance the already prized quality of their work while reducing process time and costs.

Moreover, companies in the ten new member states should focus attention on developing their ability to manage large IT projects, as the offshoring business necessitates cross-border project management. To generate real business value and avoid pitfalls, balanced project plans must be developed and their implementation controlled. Complex development tasks should not be thwarted by communication problems. Nor should high internal planning and monitoring costs erode cost advantages.

Appropriate IT structures should be developed to ensure effective interfacing with parent companies, most of which are likely to be based in Western Europe. Furthermore, this is also necessary to the success of outsourcing deals and to support clients as they move toward signing such deals. The goal of contractual negotiations must be to reduce the client's total cost of ownership as far as possible while honoring defined service level agreements. To do this effectively and efficiently, companies need appropriate internal IT structures. The latter also helps both Eastern European IT service providers and their parent companies alike to acquire new client groups for outsourcing projects.

Finally, Eastern European companies can further reduce IT costs and expose hidden costs by means of targeted IT cost management. This not only increases their cost advantage over Western European companies, but also frees up capital for new innovation projects.

5.3   Case Study Merging Large-Scale IT Organizations

CEE countries are likely to become even more important as preferred IT outsourcing locations. As the IT industry matures, a consolidation process will be initiated, forcing organizations to merge large-scale IT organizations in very short time without threatening service levels. It is therefore reasonable to examine IT consolidation projects in Western European countries in order to learn lessons in preparation for forthcoming issues in CEE.

The company in question was one of Europe's leading banks. Unlike a number of its competitors, it had managed both to stay profitable and, by virtue of successive acquisitions, to grow so strongly that there appeared to be no threat to its position among the top five European banks for a long time to come.

After its last merger with another large bank in the same country, the management board initially focused on building up Retail/Corporate Banking and Investment Banking, its principal business divisions. Within Retail/Corporate Banking, this gave rise to an IT unit totaling some 4,000 people, of whom over half were external service providers. The total budget for this unit came to around EUR 2 billion.

The following structural units were anchored at the very top level:

- User Support,
- Operations,

- Systems Integration,
- Business System Development,
- Distributed System Development,
- Systems Engineering,
- Architecture and Service Management.

When the IT management was told to make sustainable cost cuts, the CIO decided to design a new IT organization. One fundamental assumption he had to consider was the need to uphold the strict organizational separation between Retail/Corporate Banking on the one hand and Investment Banking on the other.

The entire IT unit at Retail/Corporate Banking was subjected to an IT function analysis whose aim was to clearly define the tasks assigned to all IT staff. The analysis was supported by a department set up specially for this purpose within the unit. A database tool was used to process and analyze the structural data.

Since the possibility of merging with the IT functions of the Investment Banking arm had been ruled out from the word go, it was only possible to look at a reorganization within the Retail/Corporate Banking division. The tasks of the former Systems Engineering unit were split between the Distributed System Development and Operations units. Across-the-board functions spread across all departments were bundled together to form a new structural unit. The Architecture unit was downsized significantly, while User Support was optimized based on a new process model. Potential savings totaling EUR 300 million per annum were identified, and concrete measures to tap this potential were put in place.

Some of the key lessons learned from this example were as follows:

- The success of IT systems must always be measurable in terms of quality or efficiency gains in the business processes they are intended to support. A high service level makes sense in all cases where a business process can be measurably improved,
- IT organizations have to learn to see themselves as service providers who must adapt what they supply to what their customers demand. Internal issues – i.e. the way in which the IT unit is organized and structured – must be subordinated to this principle,
- IT managers must know those aspects of IT in which their organization has the edge in terms of knowledge or experience, and must consciously cultivate this lead internally,

- IT efficiency cannot be achieved by sophisticated allocation and controlling methods, but by learning to handle IT resources efficiently and intelligently,
- Having a "mastery" of technology does not only mean understanding how to use equipment and software. It also (and especially) means the ability to quantify the economic potential of a technology,
- IT organizations must be forward-looking – but they must also be able to work sensibly with aging technologies. "Application retirement" is not always a viable option,
- IT architectures are merely a means to an end – the end being support for business processes and IT efficiency.

6 Finland – A Prototypical Knowledge Economy?

Petri Rouvinen and Pekka Ylä-Anttila
ETLA, the Research Institute of the Finnish Economy

Acknowledgements

This chapter is in part based on ETLA's prior work on the subject (Dahlman & Routti, forthcoming in 2005; Hyytinen, Paija, Rouvinen, & Ylä-Anttila, forthcoming in 2005/6; Rouvinen & Ylä-Anttila, 2003). This research is a part of the "Locational Advantage in a Global Digital Economy" collaborative research program operated jointly by BRIE, the Berkeley Roundtable on the International Economy at the University of California at Berkeley, and ETLA, the Research Institute of the Finnish Economy. This work was conducted while Rouvinen was a Jean Monnet Fellow at the European University Institute in Florence, Italy. He gratefully acknowledges the hospitality of the Robert Schuman Centre for Advanced Studies and the financial support of the Academy of Finland and the Yrjö Jahnsson Foundation.

6.1 Introduction

In the early 1990s, Finland was on the brink of bankruptcy. It seemed that the country would cease to exist unless the rapid downward slide could be stopped. The era of relatively successful resource- and investment-driven growth had come to an end. Its economy and business activities were simply not sufficiently extensive and competitive to support the current standard of living.

Fortunately, Finland was able to achieve a quick turnaround. In the new millennium, it has, on several occasions, held the top position in the World Economic Forum's global competitiveness rankings of over one hundred national economies. Manuel Castells – arguably one of the leading thinkers of our time on the subject – has portrayed Finland as the most promising prototype of the future network society, a society based on the intense generation, sharing and use of knowledge.

This chapter outlines the Finnish path toward becoming a knowledge economy. It also briefly considers the elements of locational advantage in a global digital economy in light of recent Finnish experience. Section 2 discusses the current developmental stage in the Finnish knowledge economy. Section 3 provides a general examination of the developments that preceded this stage. Section 4 focuses on the historical development of Finland's ICT cluster, focusing especially on its core: the mobile communications equipment industry and Nokia. Section 5 identifies some of the factors underlying the Finnish success in ICT provisioning. Section 6 discusses current challenges to the sector before section 7 sums up.

6.2   Finland as a Knowledge Economy: The Four Pillars

The World Bank (http://info.worldbank.org/kam/) identifies four main pillars of a knowledge economy: economic incentives, innovation, education and information infrastructure. A knowledge economy is the sum of its constituent parts and should be reasonably well balanced. For example, it might not be a lack of technological infrastructure or skilled engineers that restrains economic growth. It might equally well be a lack of entrepreneurs or proper economic incentives and opportunities. Various elements of the Finnish knowledge-based economy are discussed below in light of the World Bank's knowledge economy index (KEI), which uses over 70 indicators to rank more than 120 countries worldwide. Figure 1 shows selected countries by overall KEI ranking. Finland scores highly on all four pillars.

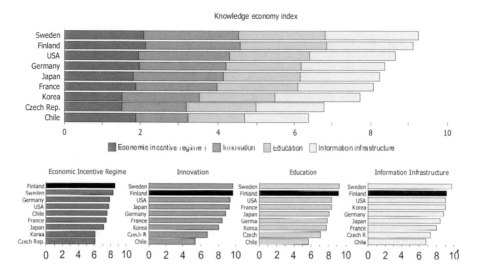

Source: The World Bank (http://info.worldbank.org/kam/).
Note: Refers to the most recent values available in January 2005.

Fig. 1: The World Bank's knowledge economy index (selected countries)

6.2.1 Economic Incentive Regime

The economic incentives pillar is the weakest one for Finland. Arguably, its relative weakness here is a flip side of the Nordic welfare state, which is based on egalitarian values, advanced social security and, consequently, high and progressive taxes. Incentives for entrepreneurship are insufficient. Hence entrepreneurs account for a relatively low proportion of total employment. This might be a hindrance to the rapid adoption and diffusion of new technologies, as well as to industrial renewal, thereby posing a risk to longer-term economic growth.

The "new economy" boom in the late 1990s seemed to offer both enhanced incentives and opportunities, particularly in ICT-related fields. While there were abundant examples of students and graduates of technical universities establishing new firms, for instance, the effects on overall entrepreneurial activity appear to have been disappointingly low (Koski & Sierimo, 2003).

Politicians and civil servants agree that the lack of entrepreneurial dynamics is perhaps the single most important problem in the Finnish economic landscape. Major efforts are thus being undertaken to address this issue.

Company taxation was reformed at the beginning of 2005 to make the tax system more internationally competitive. The aim of the reform is to promote corporate investment, encourage growth and spur entrepreneurship. The corporate income tax rate has been reduced considerably. Traditionally, only weak tax incentives have existed for small and medium-sized enterprises and the entrepreneurs that run them. The reform is likely to improve this situation to some degree.

6.2.2 Innovation

According to the European Community Innovation Survey conducted in 2004 (http://www.cordis.lu/), Finland ranks second among the EU countries in overall innovativeness. The country does superbly on technical innovation, but seems to be underperforming in organizational innovation and commercialization. A recent evaluation of the Finnish national innovation system (Georghiou, Smith, Toivanen, & Ylä-Anttila, 2003) has also suggested that – while standing out as a relatively fine-tuned "machine" in other respects – the system has deficiencies in its non-technical dimensions.

Finland has been quite innovative in its technology policy. It was the first country in the world to introduce the concept of a national innovation system as the basic frame of reference in policy formulation. As far back as the 1980s, collaboration between the private and public sectors and between industry and the research community was emphasized in policymaking. Gradually, policy emphasis has shifted from a "science push" to an "industry pull" mentality. National technology programs were adopted as a main instrument of technology policies in the 1980s.

Technology policy started to emphasize ICT in the early 1980s, i.e. well before the boom in the mid-1990s. Extensive programs in this field contributed to the country's later success and paved the way to today's knowledge-based economy.

6.2.3 Education: The Quest for Equity and High Quality

Education is a key element of a knowledge-based economy, as it affects both the supply of and demand for innovation. Human capital, embodied in skilled labor, complements new technologies by aiding their development, adoption and diffusion.

In the recent OECD's Program for International Student Assessment (PISA), Finland came top in terms of learning skills among 15-year olds in all three areas: mathematics, science and reading literacy. Finland also exhibited exceptionally low variation among schools and students. Even the country's "low performers" were above the mean of the forty countries studied.

Similarly, the OECD's International Adult Literacy Survey (IALS) suggests that Finland's 16 to 59 year-olds are top performers in terms of prose, documented and quantitative literacy. To some extent, the high, even performance of both young people and adults reflects the egalitarian values of Finnish society.

While internationally compatible data is much less readily available on higher education performance, this is one area where the Finnish system is arguably only a mediocre performer. Resources are perhaps spread too thinly to enable the relevant institutions to conduct education and research at the global forefront. The policy of aiming for equal opportunities and outcomes may hold back the most gifted. While there is only anecdotal evidence of a "brain drain" problem, the country is certainly not enjoying any significant "brain gain" in terms of foreign students or skilled labor.

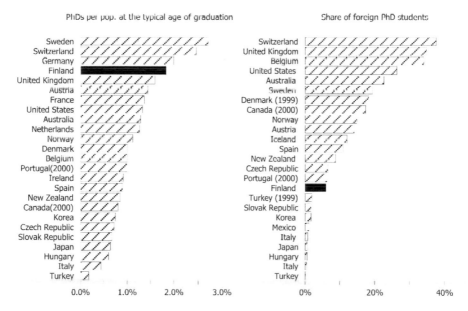

Source: OECD (2004b)
Notes: Both charts refer to 2002 (or the latest year for which data is available in early 2005). See the original source for additional notes.

Fig. 2: Doctoral degrees in the population at the typical age of graduation (left) and the share of foreign PhD students (right)

6.2.4   Information Infrastructure

A highly developed information and communication infrastructure is a necessary – albeit not sufficient – condition of a knowledge-based economy. The spread of PCs and Internet access across homes and offices is perhaps the most important prerequisite if a knowledge society is to blossom. In Finland, however, mobile telephony has led the way. After the mid-1990s, the country became renowned as a "mobile wonderland" due to the rapid diffusion of mobile communications. It is plausible to argue that this development also boosted ICT diffusion more generally. Internet diffusion in Finland is nevertheless not much higher than the OECD average, and the spread of broadband access has until recently been sluggish.

Again, official policies have created deficiencies in ICT diffusion. Recent tighter policies have increased competition in broadband access provision and subscriptions have risen. The choice of particular technologies *per se* is, however, left to market participants.

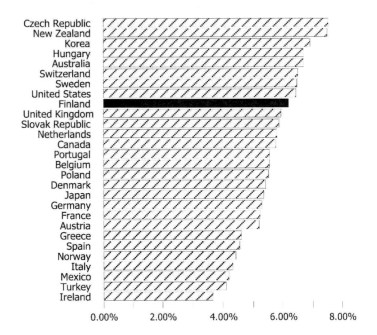

Source: OECD (2004a)
Note: Refers to the year 2003. ICT intensity is defined as ICT market size relative to GDP.

Fig. 3: Intensity of ICT usage

6.3   Laying the Foundations

6.3.1   Historical Backdrop

High social cohesion, a consistent and predictable policy environment, a sound basic infrastructure, and a just and efficient legislative and juridical environment are often emphasized as the necessary foundations for a knowledge economy. In Finland, these attributes have been built over the course of several centuries. The country can be accurately characterized as an open but small Nordic welfare state with relatively even income distribution and minimal class distinctions.

Finland's most important (and virtually only) endowment of natural resources – forests – proved to be the decisive factor in the take-off phase of industrial growth. Swift advances in prosperity toward the end of the 1800s and in the early 20th century were based on rapidly growing exports of forestry products: first timber and, later, pulp and paper. From the late 1950s to the late 1970s, the Finnish forestry industry invested massively, gradually transforming itself into a global technology leader with the most modern and efficient production capacity in the world (Raumolin, 1992). By the late 1980s, the forestry sector had developed into a globally competitive industrial cluster that today provides high value-added paper grades, as well as forestry technologies and consulting services (Hernesniemi, Lammi, & Ylä-Anttila, 1996; Rouvinen & Ylä-Anttila, 1999).

Numerous structural transitions characterize the history of the Finnish economy. The rise of the manufacturing industries as the engine of growth during the 19th and early 20th century and changes in the relative importance of the different manufacturing industries over time are prime examples of this, as are the industrial changes that World War II and the associated war reparations to the former Soviet Union induced in Finland. The structural change that preceded the economy's emergence as a global wireless player, was, however, unusually profound.

Between 1990 and 1993, Finland ran into an unprecedented economic crisis, induced by a number of coincidental and structural factors. These included: a downturn in the forestry-related industries that were vital to the national economy; disruption to the country's sizable eastward trade due to the collapse of the Soviet Union; a speculative bubble in the domestic securities and real estate markets, fueled by uncontrolled credit expansion and favorable terms of trade; and mismanaged financial liberalization, which eventually led to a credit crunch and excessive private sector indebtedness (Kiander & Vartia, 1996). In addition to these immediate reasons for the recession, rigidities in economic and political systems as well as corporatist structures pushed the country into an economic dead-end.

6.3.2 *Structural Transformation*

The deep recession initiated a structural transformation. Widespread corporate restructuring and bankruptcies modified the economy's industrial structure. Also, the banking crisis that coincided with economic recession triggered a fundamental change in the structure of the Finnish banking system (Hyytinen, Kuosa, & Takalo, 2003).

The transition in the structure of Finland's industry and exports in the 1990s was unique both nationally and internationally. In less than a decade, electronics became the most important single industry in terms of production and exports. Finnish industry shifted from a raw materials, capital, energy and scale-intensive focus to a knowledge-intensive focus.

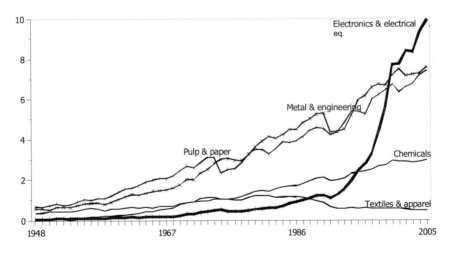

Sources: ETLA/Maury, based on Hjerppe et al. (1976) and Statistics Finland

Fig. 4: Finnish manufacturing production volume (billions of euros, at 2000 prices)

The recession also led to a clear shift in policy thinking. Greater emphasis was put on long-term microeconomic as opposed to short-term macroeconomic policies, in recognition of the fact that the foundations of sustained national competitiveness are largely created at the micro level – in firms, financial institutions and various innovative policy agencies.

Networking and cooperation in society in general, and in the business sector in particular, were acknowledged as important factors in knowledge generation and use. To advance this goal, the government assumed the role of facilitator and coordinator. Industrial policy goals were set in a context of intensive and informal communication between government, industry, academia and the labor market. The objective was to build and enhance businesses' operating and framework conditions, and not to provide heavy subsidies or other direct government support. A number of forums had been founded to promote interaction between different interest groups, the most prominent of which is the Science and Technology Policy Council. The Council is chaired by the prime minister, and its membership consists of seven other ministers (including the minister of finance). Industrial associations, acting as influential intermediaries between industry and the public sector, have also played a salient role in the Finnish policy arena.

The recession of the early 1990s proved to be a watershed between the investment and knowledge-driven stages of national development. Today, Finland's relative R&D intensity – gross domestic research and development expenditure (GERD) as a proportion of GDP – is among the highest in the world (3.4 percent in 2003). If intensity were defined in terms of human effort, Finland would clearly top the world in this respect.

The European integration process fueled the shift in policy that the economic crisis of the early 1990s had initiated. Finland joined the European Union in 1995 and, unlike other Scandinavian countries, adopted the euro from the outset. For Finland, integration meant, among other things, that the scope for national macroeconomic policies was considerably reduced.

One key factor behind the emerging knowledge economy is a strong commitment to education. Due to increased investments in the education system, younger generations of Finns were, by the late 1980s, among the best educated in the world. Education that would enhance technological change was prioritized in the policies of the 1960s and 1970s. Among the OECD countries, the Finnish educational system trails only the Korean and German systems in terms of its relative emphasis on natural sciences and engineering.

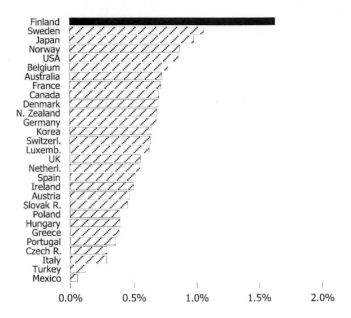

Source: OECD (2004b)
Notes: Refers to 2002 or the latest year for which data is available. See the original source for additional notes.

Fig. 5: Share of researchers in total employment

During the most intensive ICT-driven growth period, the supply of skilled labor ran short in face of the industry's requirements. The government responded by increasing the number of openings in higher education institutions. From 1993 through 1998 the total intake nearly doubled at universities and nearly tripled at polytechnics. In early 1998, the government adopted a program aimed at further increasing ICT education between 1998 and 2002. Resources allocated to universities did not, however, match the sizeable growth in enrollment. As discussed above, basic education nevertheless continues to be the focal point of the Finnish educational system.

6.4   The Finnish ICT Cluster

6.4.1   Origins of the Telecommunications Sector

The origins of the Finnish ICT sector and its peculiarities can be traced back to the Telephony Decree of the Finnish Senate in 1886, which distributed numerous private operator licenses in order to circumvent Russian telegraph regulations. When the country gained independence in 1917, an additional public telephony operator (PTO) and regulator was established to operate the telegraph and military telephone network left behind by the Russians. In the 1930s, there were hundreds of private telecommunications operators in Finland. Even today there are still some 40 significant operators.

From the outset, the Finnish telecommunications equipment markets were open to foreign suppliers. Unlike in countries with an equipment manufacturing monopoly, e.g., France, Germany and Sweden, there was no public interest in protecting domestic supply in Finland. As independent operators were free to choose between different suppliers, the domestic providers that slowly emerged were kept under constant competitive pressure.

Private operators' interest in state-of-the-art technology was fueled by the threat of being taken over by the PTO regulator in the event of underperformance. The tension between the public and private "camps", originating from the early days of telephony, was hence an important source of industry dynamism. This long tradition of a "dual" market structure later provided a basis for balanced competition.

Anticipating worldwide deregulation in telecommunications and, in particular, the liberalization efforts of the EU, the development of the Finnish market culminated in the early deregulation of the telecom market at the turn of the 1990s. When deregulation began, Finland already had a relatively competitive and diverse telecommunications operators and equipment markets. The deregulation process was therefore relatively smooth. There was, for example, no need for extensive government intervention to induce equitable competition between the incumbent(s) and the entrants.

6.4.2 Emergence of the ICT Cluster

Finnish telecommunications equipment manufacturing was initiated around 1920 in three separate organizations that were finally merged in 1987 under the management of one company, Nokia. The original companies had somewhat different focus areas at the outset: Salora concentrated on the resale of radio and TV sets; Suomen Kaapelitehdas focused on cables and electricity production; and the radio laboratory controlled by the Ministry of Defense, later named Televa, started out with military radio systems.

In 1963, a call for tenders issued by the Finnish army for a battlefield radio spurred companies to give physical expression to their accumulated expertise. Ultimately, the army did not have the resources to purchase the system. But the prototypes served as the forerunners of commercial portable phones. Also, state agencies, including the telecommunications administrator, the state railways and the coastguard, with their demanding communications requirements, had a major influence on companies' product development efforts[1].

The Auto Radio Puhelin (ARP, car radio phone) network was introduced in 1971 as the first mobile telephone network in the country to provide nationwide service. It provided good geographical coverage but was not technologically sophisticated. In the mid-1970s, the service had some ten thousand subscribers. Finnish radio phone manufacturing gained a substantial market share across the Nordic countries. Although ARP did not turn mobile communications into a major business, it provided experience and customer interfaces for companies such as Nokia, Salora and Televa. It also indicated that there was commercial potential in mobile services.

In network systems, development was intensive and progressive but yielded little sales revenue. In fact, it was other electronics applications, such as TV sets, computers and industrial process control systems, that dominated Finnish commercial electronics up until the late 1980s. The adoption of semiconductor technology in the 1960s served as the basis for electronics development. Coupled with pioneering product development in digital transmission and digital signal processing, it generated knowledge that proved pivotal for Finland's later success in digital telecommunications.

The development of the analog Nordisk Mobil Telefon (NMT, Nordic Mobile Telephone) standard in the 1970s was one very valuable outcome of the traditional cooperation between Nordic telecommunications administrators and industry. It aimed at creating a Nordic market for mobile telephony and inducing competition. The standard development project was open to third-country suppliers as well. Openness promoted competition with regard to network equipment and handsets. Advanced features such as roaming were included and, fortunately, the diffusion-promoting "caller pays" practice was also adopted.

---

[1] Important additional demand, in terms of both learning and sales revenue, came from Soviet authorities, which valued not only Finnish technical innovativeness and flexibility, but also the country's political neutrality.

In the early 1980s, the Nordic countries constituted the largest mobile communication market worldwide in terms of the number of subscribers. Mobira, a joint venture of Nokia and Salora, supplied the first NMT portable phones[2]. In contrast, Finnish companies were neither ready nor willing to supply network technology in the early phase of the NMT project. Eventually, under pressure from the PTO, which was keen to curb the market power of Sweden's Ericsson and rein in equipment prices in general, Mobira, and later Tele-Nokia, started to manufacture network equipment (Palmberg, 2002).

Table 1: Share of the market for NMT handsets in 1985 (83,525 units in total)

Mobira	Finland	25.70%
Ericsson	Sweden	16.90%
Panasonic	Japan	8.90%
Storno	US, until 1977 Denmark	7.10%
Dancall	Denmark	6.50%
Mitsubishi	Japan	6.10%
NEC	Japan	6.00%
Siemens	Germany	5.60%
Motorola	US	5.60%
Simonsen	Norway	2.30%

Source: Nokia Mobile Phones (as cited in Häikiö, 2001)

In 1988, the telecommunication authorities in the European Community published the Groupe Spécial Mobile standard (GSM, digital global system for mobile communication). The technological challenges surrounding GSM related primarily to the digitization of radio transmissions and to the exponential increase in the complexity of the signaling and control software. These were fields in which Nokia had accumulated competencies working with its customers in the advanced banking sector. Consequently, this expertise gave it an entry ticket to the standard development project (Palmberg & Martikainen, 2003).

---

[2] Weighing approximately five kilograms, the original NMT terminals were not quite the handsets we know today.

At the same time, Nokia reorganized its telecom divisions to cater to the envisioned GSM-based growth in cellular systems, and to help meet the deadline for the inauguration of the GSM Service in Europe in 1991. The tight deadline was met in Finland when the world's first GSM call was placed in June 1991, even though the pan-European launch of the service was delayed due to technical problems. Nokia and Ericsson were among the first companies to adopt GSM, which eventually became almost universally accepted – with the notable exceptions of the United States, Canada and leading Latin American countries. Recently, GSM has also been gaining ground in these markets.

On the operator side, the PTO had a monopoly of the NMT service. Owing to the lucrative nature of the mobile market, the private camp applied for a second license, but without success. In 1988, it decided, on the basis of a regulatory loophole, to construct a mobile network without a national license. This private venture chose the newly developed GSM standard, which was not yet in commercial use anywhere in the world. In 1990, a license was finally granted to a newly established company, Radiolinja, after an intensive political debate on the viability of parallel networks in a small country. The digital mobile service was commercialized the following year by Nokia, which thus made its global GSM debut with Radiolinja's network. The PTO followed suit in a partnership with Ericsson.

The mobile market entrant started to erode mobile service pricing. Soon, Finnish mobile services were the least expensive in the world. Fueled by more affordable portable phones, which were gradually replacing common auto phones, mobile communications was adopted by the masses.

Although the foundations of domestic equipment manufacturing were laid in the 1920s, foreign manufacturers dominated the market up until the 1980s. During the 1970s and 1980s, Finland made rapid advances in digital and mobile technologies. Nokia participated in these developments and, since the 1970s, has become a central force in the consolidation of the industry. By the late 1980s, a fair part of the Finnish telecommunications equipment industry had merged under the aegis of Nokia.

6.4.3 Nokia, the Engine

The merger of Nokia (originally a timber-grinding mill), Suomen Kaapelitehdas (Finnish Cable Works) and Suomen Gummitehdas (Finnish Rubber Works) in 1967 can be regarded as the birth of the Nokia Corporation that exists today. Although the forestry-based company lent the name, the cable company provided the core knowledge base for the new entity. In

1960, this unit had established an electronics department reselling computers, providing computing services, and also manufacturing some of its own electronic devices. It also assumed an important role in educating its own staff – and Finns in generally – in the area of digital technologies.

Nokia was still pursuing a conglomerate strategy in the 1980s and made several sizable acquisitions in consumer electronics (e.g. televisions, such as Sweden's Luxor in 1984 and the German Standard Elektrik Lorenz in 1987), information systems (e.g., the Swedish Ericsson Information Systems in 1988) and other fields not directly related to telecommunications. Indeed, Nokia was the biggest manufacturer of personal computers and color TV sets in the Nordic countries and ranked among the top 10 in Europe. This conglomerate strategy thus explains, at least in part, Nokia's role in merging the various businesses of Salora, Suomen Kaapelitehdas and Televa.

The conglomerate strategy was, however, not a success story. Exacerbated by managerial and ownership problems and the early 1990s recession, it plunged the company into a deep crisis. Nokia almost went bankrupt in the early 1990s, primarily as a consequence of its overly ambitious and costly acquisition and internationalization strategy. In 1992, Jorma Ollila became the CEO. Under his leadership, the course changed and activities outside mobile communications were divested. This process was completed by the late 1990s.

With the exception of UK-based Technophone, Europe's second-largest mobile phone manufacturer at the time (in 1991), Nokia has effected no major foreign acquisitions in communications. In fact, it retreated from its acquisition strategy almost completely after the early 1990s. Alliances were nevertheless important from early on. In handsets, Nokia established joint ventures with America's Tandy and engaged in private labeling with Tandy-owned Radio Shack, AT&T and others. On the network side, it initially partnered with Alcatel (France) and AEG (Germany) to provide GSM solutions.

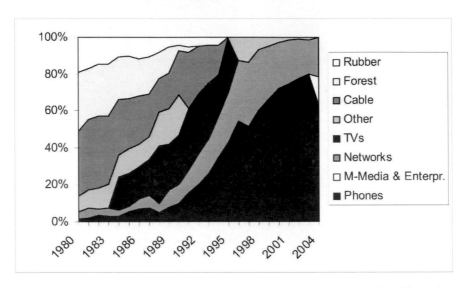

Sources: Derived by the authors from an earlier version by Paija (2001), with additional
information from Häikiö (2001) and *Nokia*'s annual reports
Note: "M-Media & Enterpr." refers to the combined share of two new business units –
Multimedia and *Enterprise Solutions* – formed at the beginning of 2004.

Fig. 6: Nokia's sales by industry: from conglomerate to mobile communications
company

With a share of about 30 percent, Nokia is the market leader in mobile
handsets and also one of the dominant players in mobile network infrastructure equipment. It has been riding the wave of exploding global mobile telecommunication markets, fueled by worldwide deregulation in telecommunications. Thanks to its narrowly defined and globally-orientated
strategy, it has been able to meet the market challenge somewhat better
than its closest competitors. Furthermore, management has been able to
build an innovation-driven culture and supportive organizational structure,
flexibly exploiting both internal and external networking – yet retaining, in
contrast to its main competitors, most of its manufacturing in-house.

In the 1990s, Nokia's challenge was to manage rapid organic growth. In
the new millennium, the challenge has been to manage its end. Nokia's
growth was clearly aided by its agility and lack of bureaucracy. Although
the company has Finnish roots and its executive board is mainly populated
by Finns, Nokia's orientation has been distinctively global. While Nokia
has had its share of problems and challenges as well, what seems to set
Nokia apart from many other gigantic corporations is its ability to react
quickly and improvise in times of crisis. The company's most recent crisis

nonetheless suggests that it has – at least temporarily – abandoned some of its core values.

In late 2003 and early 2004, Nokia's market share dropped rapidly by some five percentage points to about 30 percent – way off the announced target of 40 percent. For outside observers, it seemed that three things came together at once: First, the company implemented a major organizational change at a time of exceptional market turbulence. Second, it was stubbornly trying to educate the market, i.e. it apparently refused to offer the increasingly popular clamshell designs, was slow to include cameras in its mid-range models, and introduced its models for the next generation mobile networks surprisingly late. And third, it chose to fight the operators by not letting them adapt the phones to their customers' needs and introduce co-branding. Price cuts in early 2004 and new product roll-outs later in the year nevertheless enabled the company to secure its market position. The company has also become more responsive to the requests of operators and quickly diversified its product portfolio to better meet changing consumer tastes.

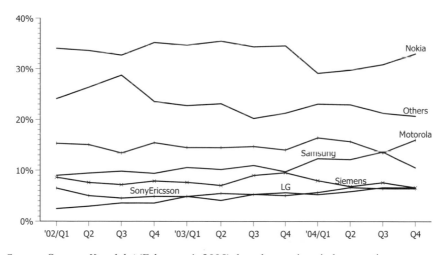

Source: *Suomen Kuvalehti* (February 4, 2005), based on various industry estimates

Fig. 7: Market shares of major mobile phone manufacturers: *Nokia* remains the leader

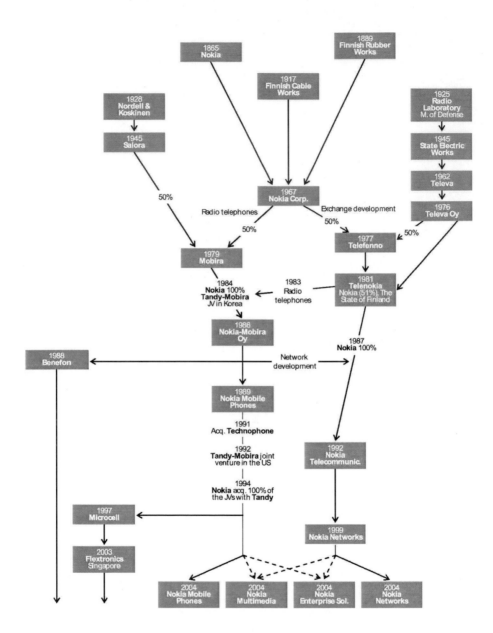

Source: Derived by the authors from an earlier version by Paija (2001)

Fig. 8: The evolution of the Finnish mobile communications industry

6.4.4   Other ICT Firms

While Nokia's central role cannot probably be overemphasized, the emergence of the Finnish ICT cluster is not entirely driven by this one company. The Finnish ICT sector – or cluster – comprises 4,000 to 6,000 firms (depending on the definition employed), including some 300 first-tier suppliers of Nokia (Ali-Yrkkö, 2003). There is hence more to the Finnish ICT cluster than one highly successful company.

Table 2: Top 20 ICT companies in Finland in 2003

Company	Line of Business	Sales 2003 (MEUR)
Nokia	Communications equipment	29455
TeliaSonera Finland	Network service / maintenance	1939
Elisa	Network service / maintenance	1538
Tietoenator	IT service	1374
GNT Finland	Equipment wholesales	532
IBM	IT equipment	452
Hewlett-Packard	IT equipment	422
Siemens	Communications equipment	418
WM-Data Novo	IT service	369
Finnet	Network service / maintenance	352
Eltel Networks	Network service / maintenance	287
Tellabs	Communications equipment	272
Fujitsu Services	IT service	255
Tech Data Finland	Equipment wholesales	225
Scribona Distribution	Equipment wholesales	210
Canon North-East	Equipment wholesales	208
Elektrobit Group	Communications equipment (ODM)	148
L M Ericsson	Communications equipment	148
YIT Primatel	Network service / maintenance	129
Atea Finland	IT service and equipment resale	127

Sources: Tietoviikko (the 2004 special issue: the 250 biggest ICT companies)

Although other Finnish ICT companies are gaining ground in global markets, there have been no major breakthroughs in broader ICT market segments. Given the substance and sophistication of Nokia's computer-related activities, coupled with the fact that Finnish universities have been hatcheries of several ground-breaking Internet-based inventions, the weak commercial success of the Finnish ICT sector outside wireless communications is somewhat disappointing. However, ethical and social, rather than commercial motives have characterized some of the best-known Finnish innovations in the Internet realm[3].

Firms such as Ericsson, Fujitsu, IBM, HP and Siemens have established R&D units in Finland, which has been interpreted as a sign of the viability of the country's ICT cluster. However, there have been recent indications that other locations, such as South Korea, are challenging Finland's leading position as a pioneering ICT market and, thus, as an inspiring environment in which to develop technology.

6.5   Success Factors in ICT

6.5.1   The Desperate Need for Something New

For Finland, the recession of the early 1990s provided a decisive break with the past. It fostered a pragmatic and straightforward culture in both politics and business. Faced with deep recession, the Finns simply could not afford inflexibility or bureaucracy. Thanks to the country's stable political environment and social cohesion, political institutions remained

---

[3] The best-known example of non-commercial pursuits is the open source software Linux that today challenges the predominance of Microsoft. This revolutionary operating system, which today includes contributions from thousands of programmers, was initiated by 22 year-old student Linus Torvalds in 1991. Torvalds' original objective was to understand task-switching operation. In the following year, Linux was combined with US-based open software GNU to produce a complete, free operating system. Another widespread Internet application, the real-time chat environment (Internet Relay Chat, IRC), also originated from a Finnish university classroom. Furthermore, the first Internet information browser to feature a graphical user interface was created by a group of Finnish students in 1992 – a year before Mosaic was released by the National Center for Supercomputing Applications at the University of Illinois, USA. The students, however, shelved the software due to the lack of business interest. Another invention in the category of "missed Internet business opportunities" includes the router, which connects local and general networks. Nokia's engineers created a router in 1983, before Cisco, but gave precedence to modem development and so neglected it. Some student-initiated inventions have grown into viable businesses, particularly in the area of secure network solutions (e.g. SSH Communications Security and F-Secure). Even the most successful companies that have an international reach are still classed as small and medium-sized enterprises, however.

functional. The necessary policy adjustments could therefore be made even during the crisis.

Vast unemployment in the 1990s gave the emerging ICT cluster the large recruitment pool it needed for its expansion. The public educational system also responded to ICT-related needs. Furthermore, the collapse of eastward trade freed up resources that firms could then channel into developing ICT (including GSM) and pursuing the subsequent expansion.

6.5.2   Relaxed Capital Constraints

The liberalization of global markets for goods, services, capital and technology, triggered by developments in the United Kingdom and the United States in the late 1970s, led to a globalization boom in the mid-1980s. As a result of this globalization and concurrent Europe-wide liberalization efforts, Finnish companies gained access to new markets and became increasingly exposed to global competition.

Lack of capital was long regarded as the Achilles' heel of the Finnish economy. This realization was instrumental to the liberalization of capital markets in the 1980s and to relaxed capital constraints in the early 1990s. After deregulation and Finland's accession to the European Economic Area (EEA) and the EU, larger Finnish companies in particular gained direct access to foreign investors. A huge influx of capital to Finland followed in the mid-1990s and, for a couple of years, the Helsinki Stock Exchange was the most international one in the world, measured by the share of market value held by foreigners.

The Finnish financial system moved away from a bank-centric system in the mid-1990s, when the stock market grew and intermediated debt finance contracted as a result of the banking crisis in the early 1990s. Greater availability of venture capital has been especially important to small Finnish ICT firms, which apparently have a need to maintain conservative leverage ratios (Hyytinen & Pajarinen, 2005).

6.5.3   Technological Opportunity

Digitization was a major technological breakthrough in voice and data storage, processing and transmission. This was important for Finland, as it provided an opportunity for new players with neither experience nor vested interests in computing or communication. Finland had sufficient expertise in digital technologies in general and in telecommunications in particular, both of which were vital to the big GSM breakthrough.

Radio technology, in addition to a profound understanding of telecommunications, was one of the prerequisites for building a mobile telephone system. University-level education in radio technology had started in the early 1920s. It "lurked in the shadows" in many Finnish firms well before being channeled into commercial applications.

6.5.4 Winning Standards

Telecommunications standardization in the Nordic and European contexts may be the single biggest factor that explains the Finnish ICT success story. Finland was an early adopter of first NMT and then GSM, both of which eventually proved to be the "winning technologies" in their eras.

Early on, NMT provided critical mass and relatively high penetration rates, leading to early recovery of development costs as well as the accumulation of hands-on knowledge and scale economies. Many types of network benefits in both production and consumption also accumulated.

When the transition to digital technologies came, Nokia bet heavily on GSM as the second-generation (2G) standard. Eventually, this technology commanded three-quarters of the worldwide user base. Nokia managed to capitalize on its early lead in both GSM networks and handsets.

6.5.5 Sophisticated Demand

During and prior to the Cold War era, telecommunications operation was considered a natural monopoly and equipment manufacturing was largely kept nationalized for strategic reasons. Since then, both operation and equipment markets have been almost completely deregulated and liberalized. Finnish ICT firms, unlike many of their international competitors, had ample experience operating in a competitive environment with diverse customer needs. Besides having a history of telecommunications competition that dated back over a hundred years, Finland was also some three years ahead of other industrialized countries in taking the final steps toward completely deregulating communications markets.

In mobile telecommunications in particular, deregulation gave rise to eager "second-tier" operators and service providers that wanted to deploy new networks rapidly and with a minimum of technical problems. Former monopoly operators were forced to respond by upgrading their networks. Competition, and the resultant lower prices, fueled demand, which in turn led to further investments. Thus, the industry indeed experienced a virtuous demand cycle in the 1990s.

Scandinavians seem to be accustomed and therefore quite willing to test new technologies. In the early years of mobile telecommunications, new generations of phones always caused quite a stir and "forced" many users to shop for an upgrade. Fortunately, customer needs in these markets preceded those elsewhere, thus giving something of a first-mover advantage to Scandinavian firms. Finland and Sweden are also leaders in certain types of ICT usage, such as online banking and mobile payments. The Scandinavian market was therefore a rather happy marriage of technological competence in both production and use.

6.5.6 Cooperation and Visionary Management

Competition encourages efficient and lean organization. Somewhat paradoxically, cooperation has been equally important to the success of ICT in Finland. Indeed, international comparisons suggest that intensive inter-organizational cooperation is one of the essential features of the Finnish national innovation system.

As we saw earlier, a diverse array – but by no means all – of Finnish communications expertise was eventually merged into Nokia. In the 1980s, the corporation was relatively similar to some other Finnish conglomerates. In the 1990s, however, it transformed itself into something exceptional. Despite its roots, Nokia was able to give up its forestry-related activities and realized early on that Soviet trade was best treated as a "cash cow" to finance developments elsewhere. Focusing on mobile communications was a bold move on Nokia's part in the early 1990s, but one that paid off handsomely.

6.5.7 Supporting Policies

The institutionalization and strengthening of science and technology policies began in the early 1960s. Important changes that contributed to the knowledge-driven growth and expansion of the ICT sector took place throughout the decades that followed. The main aim of these policies was to strengthen industry's science and technology base (Lemola, 2002).

At the start of the 1980s, technology policy became increasingly target-oriented and systematic. The National Technology Agency (Tekes) was established in 1982 to coordinate public R&D support and related efforts, such as national technology programs. Technology transfer and the commercialization of research results were emphasized. Tekes and its programs became important instruments for implementing policies. The focus of the new agency's operations was information technology. In fact, two extensive information technology programs had already been initiated before Tekes was established.

Toward the end of the 1980s, a more systemic view of policy-making was adopted. Then, in the early 1990s, the deep recession fostered the relative importance of microeconomic policies. In the 1990s, the Science and Technology Policy Council also introduced the national innovation system as a basic framework for policy-making. Innovation was seen as being of a systemic nature, contrary to the traditional linear innovation model. This enhanced cooperation between various policy agencies and improved possibilities for making use of emerging, complex ICT. The systemic view also highlighted the role of education in adopting, diffusing and utilizing new technologies (Georghiou et al., 2003).

6.6   Challenges in the ICT Sector

6.6.1   An Emerging All-IP World

One of the key challenges for the Finnish ICT cluster is the ongoing convergence of voice and data communications, information systems, consumer electronics, and the digital content that is being tailored for these various channels and devices. Mobile Internet – perhaps more appropriately referred to as "anytime, anywhere, anyway" Internet services – will introduce a new playing field with a diverse array of players. Indeed, participants in the respective industries are already competing in both handsets and networks, and this tendency will only strengthen as the Internet Protocol (IP) increasingly forms the basis for all electronic communication. Over time, the focus on equipment weakens as it becomes more diffused, shifting to applications and content.

With a view to the all-IP future, Finland has two major weaknesses. First, it has little clout outside mobile telecommunications equipment. Thus, it cannot to a significant extent leverage market power in other areas as the industry transforms itself. Second, the all-IP world is not likely to favor the integrated and closed architectures and business models of the telecommunications world. The first problem can be addressed by acquiring a broader set of competencies and forming alliances with the leaders of the respective industries. The second problem can only be addressed by actually competing in the ever more open and fragmented operating environment.

6.6.2   Winning Standards in Future Network Generations?

Another challenge relates to the uncertainty over the next generation of mobile networks. In the mid-1980s, the International Telecommunications Union (ITU) assumed an active role in the introduction of third-generation (3G) standards. Although the ITU pushed for one worldwide standard, three were eventually accepted in the International Mobile Telecommunications (IMT-2000) guidelines: W-CDMA (better known as UMTS, the Universal Mobile Telecommunication System), CDMA2000 (promoted in particular by America's Qualcomm) and the Chinese TD-SCDMA variant. Originally, ITU's decision was considered a victory for the Nokia-Ericsson camp, which promoted UMTS. Early market developments nevertheless seem to suggest that CDMA2000 is also showing some strength.

The main benefit of the first-generation digital (as opposed to analog) system was improved voice quality. The key promise of 3G is improved data communication. This shift is indeed taking place, albeit somewhat unexpectedly from the European point of view. Whereas Europeans seem to have assumed that the mobile Internet would be an extension of mobile telecommunications, the American approach – extending wireline data communications architectures into wireless local area networks – appears to have an early market lead.

Arguably, a combination of WLAN and an intermediate-generation (2.5G, e.g. GPRS, general packet radio service) mobile telecommunications system with "always-on" capability could be used to reach the goals of 3G. WLAN nevertheless still faces a number of unsolved problems, such as controls for login and access rights, payment, and coverage, that have already been solved for 3G. It is too early to say how the market will unfold. Most likely, 3G and WLAN will coexist with in-between roaming.

6.6.3   Mobile Culture?

In a sense, the discussion of 3G versus WLAN is also about how the wireless culture will evolve. Will typical users eventually require broadband access at all times and locations for streaming video and similar applications, or are they going to be happy having hotspots in areas of peak demand and limited communication ability elsewhere? Perhaps more importantly, how much are they willing to pay, and for what?

For the majority of us, the office or home desktop computer remains the most important means for storing the flow of our lives. A number of small electronic appliances, mobile phones, along with personal digital assistants, electronic organizers, laptops and palmtops, are trying to take over from the personal computer in this respect and become all-encompassing "trusted personal devices", perhaps even replacing our wallets and passports.

Early experience with the Wireless Application Protocol (WAP) suggests that, in addition to how well the technology works, service pricing can matter a great deal. If the technology does not fully meet customers' expectations, demand is likely to be price-elastic (Gao, Hyytinen, & Toivanen, 2005).

Depending on the actual configuration, Finland may stay on the cutting edge and continue to serve as a useful testing ground for new applications, or it may have to play catch-up with respect to some other lead-user concentrations such as South Korea, China, India and some US regions. Individuals, both as consumers and business representatives, will ultimately decide who wins in the market place.

6.7   Locational Advantage in a Global Digital Economy

Concentrating on the ICT sector and Nokia obscures the fact that the knowledge-intensity of the Finnish economy has been changing in virtually all major industries. The transformation taking place within individual industries is as important as the one taking place between industries. In the past, the Finnish economy has mostly rested on its "wooden leg". In the 1990s, however, the ICT cluster raised a challenge to forestry-related activities in terms of national importance. While the ICT cluster comprises thousands of companies, Nokia's leadership is undisputable.

Today, Finland is both the most forestry-dependent *and* ICT-dependent country in the world (ICT commands the highest shares of business employment and value added in Finland according to OECD, 2004a). In both sectors, Finland has traditionally been an important location for manufacturing activities. In the new millennium, however, the country has increasingly been concentrating on R&D. While production in these sectors is migrating to more cost-competitive locations and/or closer to key markets, Finnish exports are picking up in niches within several traditional sectors. While this will keep the country's prospects relatively bright in the short and medium term, further specialization toward knowledge creation would certainly require some progress in new knowledge-intensive fields and/or altogether new approaches in old industries by exploiting expertise in the nano, bio, information and/or cognitive (NBIC) technologies, for example.

Table 3: The roles played by forestry, ICT and Nokia in the Finnish economy

	Forestry	ICT (including Nokia)	Nokia
Number of firms	5,576	5,063	1
Share of GDP	3.9%	9.9%	3.7%
Share of employment	2.9%	5.2%	1.1%
Share of manuf. employment	15.4%	8.0%	5.0%
Share of manuf. exports	25.3%	19.6%	21.0%
Share of business R&D (BERD)	2.8%	58.0%	42.5%
Share of market capitalization	12.4%	51.5%	34.2%

Sources: ETLA calculations based on Statistics Finland, OECD/ANBERD and own estimates

Notes: With the exceptions of total R&D (2001), total market capitalization (end of 2004) and other Nokia data (2002), the figures refer to 2003. Forestry is defined as the sum of two manufacturing industries (NACE rev. 3: 20; 21). ICT is defined as the sum of two manufacturing and two service industries (NACE rev. 3: 30, 32; 64; 72). It should be noted that forestry (or the concept of the forestry industry cluster or forestry-related industries) is rather more narrowly defined than ICT, as it neither includes related services nor machinery and equipment. "Share of market capitalization" refers to the shares of the total market valuation of the main list of the Helsinki Stock Exchange at the end of 2004.

For a peripheral high-cost country such as Finland, the knowledge-intensive strategy certainly poses risks. On the other hand, it is arguably the only viable strategy to attain a high and growing standard of living in the current economic climate. While it was hard to reach top position among the knowledge-intensive economies, maintaining it might prove even harder.

In the past, technological advance was largely the preserve of developed countries. In the new millennium emerging markets and developing regions have become increasingly important targets for and sources of technology. Ever more value-added activities are being off-shored. As suggested by export patterns in areas such as mobile phone manufacturing, this shift has been rapid indeed.

Location certainly matters. It is just that, in relative terms, regions outside traditional "hotspots" have become much more attractive for all types of business activities. So far, developed countries and regions have been the main beneficiaries of economic globalization. Now, the fruits are being distributed more equally. Adjustments will take place in all countries. While final outcomes are unforeseeable, it is nevertheless clear that the most adaptive and agile will gain the most or lose the least. It seems likely that countries will increasingly specialize in line with their accumulated knowledge stocks. The role of basic factors of production will diminish, but will not disappear altogether.

The Finnish example shows that it is possible to make a rapid transition from a resource- and investment-driven economy to one driven by knowledge without sacrificing society's core values. It should be noted, however, that the foundations of the quick turnaround were laid over several decades, and that a number of special circumstances came together at once.

Public policy played a curious role in the Finnish developments. Seemingly it became less important as the focus shifted away from acute business and industry needs. On the other hand, in a Nordic welfare state, the basic foundations of a knowledge society are mostly cultivated by the public sector. Acknowledging some of the causes leading to the recession in the early 1990s, greater emphasis was put on longer-term microeconomic – as opposed to shorter-term macroeconomic – policies. The change in policy thinking manifested itself as information society programs and as a shift in industrial policies toward knowledge creation and innovation. A previously resource and investment-driven economy took a huge step toward a knowledge economy, a step enabled by the generation and adoption of new knowledge created by scientific research and technological development. Commitment to education, quick adoption of best practices and openness to the global economy were the crucial building blocks of this transition.

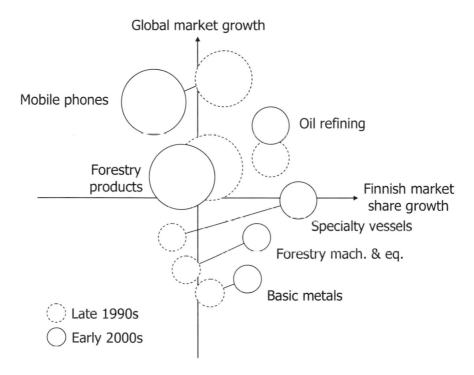

Source: The authors' estimates

Fig. 9: Stylized global market growth and Finnish market shares in some key products

To advance the nation's knowledge base and enhance its industrial structure, Finland did not, like Taiwan, rely on tax holidays or similar incentives. It did not, like Ireland, attract the business activities of multinational enterprises. It did not, like Japan, protect its domestic markets in order to nurture infant industries and technologies. And it did not, like South Korea, concentrate its efforts on a few national champions. Yet all these countries rank among the great success stories of postwar economic history, not least thanks to the policies exercised. This suggests that very different strategies for economic development can work. Countries are thus well-advised to imitate sound policy-making and provide world-class framework conditions, but not to try to replicate out of context particular approaches or decisions that have been taken by others.

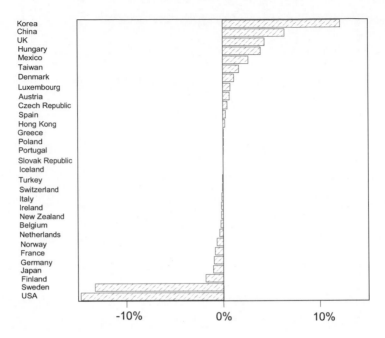

Source: ETLA calculations based on OECD International Trade by Commodities Statistics
Notes: Percentage points. Here, "mobile phones" data is based on the International Trade
by Commodity Statistics (HS96) code 852520 (transmission apparatus for radiotelephony,
incorporating reception apparatus). The total global export market is defined as the sum of
the above 31 countries. The difference in shares is calculated from nominal US dollar values in 1996 and 2002. Export statistics unavoidably include some through-traffic. Caution
must therefore be exercised in interpreting them.

Fig. 10: 1996–2002 change in countries' global mobile phone export market
shares: manufacturing moves to cost-competitive locations

The Finnish case is, in many aspects, unique. Unlike any of the afore-
mentioned countries, Finland had for decades benefited from an "exclu-
sive" technology-hungry export market in the former Soviet Union. The
Finns themselves have also been and remain exceptionally technology
savvy: The country was instrumental in giving birth to two successive generations of winning standards. Almost by coincidence, the country found
itself well-positioned on the eve of a major technological discontinuity and
the global liberalization of key sectors. Besides these aspects, closer in-
spection reveals countless other both planned and coincidental factors that
turned to the country's advantage. Therefore, while the Finnish case holds
many lessons, the idiosyncrasies of the situation may make replication difficult.

References

Ali-Yrkkö, J. (2003). Nokia – A Giant in the Finnish Innovation System. In G. Schienstock (Ed.), *Catching Up and Forging Ahead: The Finnish Success Story*. Albershot, Hants, UK: Edward Elgar.

Dahlman, C., & Routti, J. (Eds.). (forthcoming in 2005). *Finland as a Knowledge Economy – Elements of Success and Lessons Learned*. Washington D.C.: The World Bank.

Gao, M., Hyytinen, A., & Toivanen, O. (2005). Demand for Mobile Internet: Evidence from a Real-World Pricing Experiment. *ETLA Discussion Paper, 964*.

Georghiou, L., Smith, K., Toivanen, O., & Ylä-Anttila, P. (2003). *Evaluation of the Finnish Innovation Support System*. Helsinki: Ministry of Trade and Industry (Publications 5/2003).

Häikiö, M. (2001). *Nokia Oyj:n historia*. Helsinki: Edita Oyj.

Hernesniemi, H., Lammi, M., & Ylä-Anttila, P. (1996). *Advantage Finland: The Future of Finnish Industries*. Helsinki: Taloustieto (ETLA B 113, Sitra 149).

Hjerppe, R., Hjerppe, R., Mannermaa, K., Niitamo, O. E., & Siltari, K. (1976). *Suomen teollisuus ja teollinen käsityö 1900–1965*. Helsinki: Bank of Finland.

Hyytinen, A., Kuosa, I., & Takalo, T. (2003). Law or Finance: Evidence from Finland. *European Journal of Law and Economics, 16*(1), 59-89.

Hyytinen, A., Paija, L., Rouvinen, P., & Ylä-Anttila, P. (forthcoming in 2005/6). Finland's Emergence as a Global ICT Player: Lessons from the Finnish Wireless Cluster. In J. Zysman & A. Newman (Eds.), How Revolutionary was the Revolution? National Responses, Market Transitions, and Global Technology in the Digital Era: A BRIE/ETLA/Helsinki Project. Stanford, CA: Stanford University Press.

Hyytinen, A., & Pajarinen, M. (2005). Financing of Technology-Intensive Small Businesses: Some Evidence of the Uniqueness of the ICT Industry. *Information Economics and Policy, 17*(1), 115-132.

Kiander, J., & Vartia, P. (1996). The Great Depression of the 1990s in Finland. *Finnish Economic Papers, 9*(1), 72-88.

Koski, H., & Sierimo, C. (2003). Industrial Entry and Exit Patterns: ICT vs. Other Sectors. *ETLA Discussion Paper 847*.

Lemola, T. (2002). Convergence of National Science and Technology Policies: The Case of Finland. *Research Policy, 31*(8-9), 1481-1490.

OECD. (2004a). *Information Technology Outlook*. Paris: Organization for Economic Co-Operation and Development.

OECD. (2004b). *Science, Technology and Industry Outlook*. Paris: Organization for Economic Co-Operation and Development.

Paija, L. (2001). The ICT Cluster in Finland – Can We Explain It? In L. Paija (Ed.), *Finnish ICT Cluster in the Digital Economy* (pp. 9-70). Helsinki: Taloustieto (ETLA B 176).

Palmberg, C. (2002). Technological Systems and Competent Procurers – The Transformation of Nokia and the Finnish Telecom Industry Revised? *Telecommunications Policy, 26*(3-4), 129-148.

Palmberg, C., & Martikainen, O. (2003). Overcoming a Technological Discontinuity – The Case of the Finnish Telecom Industry and the GSM. *ETLA Discussion Papers, 855*.

Raumolin, J. (1992). The Diffusion of Technology in the Forest and Mining Sector in Finland. In S. Vuori & P. Ylä-Anttila (Eds.), *Mastering Technology Diffusion – The Finnish Experience* (pp. 321-378). Helsinki: Taloustieto (ETLA B 82).

Rouvinen, P., & Ylä-Anttila, P. (1999). Finnish Clusters and New Industrial Policy Making. In OECD (Ed.), *Boosting Innovation: The Cluster Approach* (pp. 361-380). Paris: Organization for Economic Co-Operation and Development.

Rouvinen, P., & Ylä-Anttila, P. (2003). Case Study: Little Finland's Transformation to a Wireless Giant. In S. Dutta, B. Lanvin & F. Paua (Eds.), *The Global Information Technology Report 2003-2004* (pp. 87-108). New York: Oxford University Press (for the World Economic Forum).

7 Data Analysis and Index Computation: Methodology

Amit Jain, INSEAD

The eEurope 2005 Index was developed based on the eEurope benchmarking framework proposed by the European Commission[1]. Examining a country's overall index gives an idea of how that country compares to other EU countries, in particular with respect to the incumbent EU-15 countries. In calculating this *index*, the overriding aim was to provide the most scientific and credible interpretation of reality. The process included selecting relevant quality variables, estimating missing data, condensing the data into factors relevant to each component index, and calculating the index by averaging the five component index scores. The data analysis methodology can be divided into three different phases: data preparation, data validation and index computation.

7.1 Data Preparation

The main steps to prepare data for analysis are shown in figure 1 and explained in greater detail below.

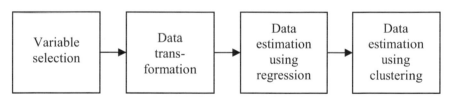

Fig. 1: Steps in data preparation

---

[1] The eEurope 2005 Action Plan has been recommended for implementation in the Council Resolution of 18 February 2003 as seen in the Official Journal of the European Union pages C48/2 to C46/8.

Variable Selection

The first step in the study was to collect the most complete and high-quality set of data possible about information and communication technology in general and the Internet in particular with respect to the eEurope 2005 benchmarking framework. The variables selected were required to have a minimum of 65 percent country coverage. At the outset, 78 variables were short-listed based on their qualitative relevance to the eEurope 2005 Index. Twenty nine of these seventy eight variables were dropped due to their failure to pass the observation threshold of 65 percent. The remaining forty nine variables were then divided into five component indexes: Internet indicators, modern online public services, dynamic e-business environment, secure information infrastructure and broadband.

Two types of variables were short-listed: soft data and hard data variables. For the purposes of this study, the subjective data gathered from survey questionnaires is termed "soft" data and statistical data collected by independent agencies is termed "hard" data. The soft data initially selected for the study was extracted from the 2004 Global Competitiveness Report (GCR; also referred to as the Executive Opinion Survey (EOS)). The hard data was extracted from six different sources: SIBIS, World Development Indicators (WDI), the World Information Technology and Service Alliance (WITSA), the International Telecommunication Union (ITU), Pyramid, and the World Economic Forum. While soft data is critical in identifying the opinions of the decision-makers and opinion leaders who are intimately familiar with a particular economy, hard data captures fundamental elements related to the development of infrastructure, human capital and e-commerce.

Selecting the Countries

The main criteria used in selecting countries were the scope and reliability of the data available. Limitations in the availability of reliable data led us to accept 25 countries for the study out of the 28 countries in total (the EU-15 countries, the ten new member states and the three candidate countries). Three countries – Cyprus, Malta and Turkey – could not be included in the study due to limitations of data availability. Table 1 lists the countries covered by this research.

Table 1: Countries included in the research

	Country	Type
1	Austria	EU-15
2	Belgium	EU-15
3	Bulgaria	Candidate
4	Czech Republic	NMS
5	Denmark	EU-15
6	Estonia	NMS
7	Finland	EU-15
8	France	EU-15
9	Germany	EU-15
10	Greece	EU-15
11	Hungary	NMS
12	Ireland	EU-15
13	Italy	EU-15
14	Latvia	NMS
15	Lithuania	NMS
15	Luxembourg	EU-15
17	Netherlands	EU-15
18	Poland	NMS
19	Portugal	EU-15
20	Romania	Candidate
21	Slovak Republic	NMS
22	Slovenia	NMS
23	Spain	EU-15
24	Sweden	EU-15
25	United Kingdom	EU-15

Countries not included in the study

26	Cyprus	NMS
27	Malta	NMS
28	Turkey	Candidate

A number of the 25 countries included in the study are not covered by some of the data collection agencies in their research. Where data was missing for some countries, it was therefore necessary to use several estimation techniques to derive appropriate data points. As a result, some caution is warranted when interpreting the results for those countries whose index scores are very close.

Data Transformation: Making the Data Comparable

In order to compare the data across the 25 selected countries, a number of variables that could not be used in their absolute form to calculate the NRI were transformed. These variables were identified and then weighted against an external variable such as GDP, population or GDP per capita (PPP) to make them comparable across the countries. Table 2 lists the transformed variables:

Table 2: Transforming variables to make them comparable

Variable no.	Variable	Denominator
3.01	Residential telephone connection charge	GDP per capita
3.02	Business telephone monthly subscription	GDP per capita
3.03	Business telephone connection charge	GDP per capita
10.01	DSL broadband access	Population

Soft data such as that of EOS 2004 and that drawn from SIBIS did not require transformation. Other hard data variables retained in the index and not listed above also required no transformation, as the data had already been weighted by the data collection agencies (either as a percentage or by a common denominator such as population).

Estimating Data Using Regression

Despite reducing the number of variables from 78 to 49 as described in the section above ("Variable selection"), a number of observations were still missing and had to be estimated. It was decided to estimate the missing data rather than leave it blank, because missing values would have led to a bias in calculating the index and would have limited the ability to make comparisons across the countries. Different approaches were used to estimate the missing data.

In the first approach, the missing values were estimated using regression analysis. The process involved picking a variable (X) that correlated closely to another variable (Y) with the missing values. X was then used as the independent variable to estimate the dependent variable (Y) in the linear regression $Y = a + bX$.

In a more extensive form, a bivariate correlation analysis of the 49 short-listed variables and three external variables was conducted as a first step. The three external variables chosen were Gross Domestic Product (GDP), GDP per capita (PPP) and population. Where more than one closely correlated variable existed, the variable with all 25 observations and the highest coefficient of correlation was chosen as the independent variable (X). Where there was no closely correlated variable that had all 25 observations, the most closely correlated independent variable that had data for the countries with missing observations was used.

Table 3 lists the variables retained for index computation for which data was estimated using this approach. Even so, this method was not sufficient to estimate all the missing values. A second approach was therefore used in the study to estimate the rest of the missing data.

Table 3: Estimating missing data by correlations

Var. no.	Variable estimated	Observations estimated	Estimated by	Coefficient of correlation
1.07	ISDN subscribers	1	GDP per capita	0.5628
1.11	Households online	3	Regular and occasional Internet usage	0.7984
3.02	Business telephone monthly subscription	5	Average cost of local telephone call	0.6850
6.02	Internet use by the disabled	5	Health related online search	0.8757
7.02	B2C e-commerce	4	Internet access from home	0.8900

Estimating Data Using Clustering

The variables that could not be estimated using the regression method were estimated using a clustering technique. The need to use the clustering approach arose for two main reasons. First, not all the variables requiring estimation of missing data correlated closely to other variables in the data set. Second, in some cases where a closely correlated variable existed for a given variable, data values were still missing even for the closely correlated partner variable. For instance, residential telephone connection charges correlated closely to business telephone connection charges, but both variables lacked data for the same countries in some cases.

Countries were clustered or grouped according to their Gross Domestic Product per capita. Estimates were made by averaging the available non-estimated data values for countries with a GDP per capita in the range of +/-20 percent of the country in question.

Special care was taken never to estimate data on the basis of other estimated data.

Table 4: Estimating data by clustering

Variable no.	Variable description	No. of observations estimated
2.03	Teleworking usage	1
3.01	Residential telephone connection charge	5
3.03	Business telephone connection charge	5
6.01	Online health searches	1

In all, 30 observations (i.e. 3.6 percent) were estimated out of a total of 950 observations used to compute the eEurope 2005 Index.

7.2   Data Validation / Reduction

Up to this point, the data had been attributed to different component indices within the eEurope 2005 framework based on qualitative judgments on the data. A method was now needed to ensure:

1. *Consistency:* The data in each component index had to be a true measure of the given effect in a statistically significant way,
2. *Reduction:* The data needs to be aggregated to a higher-level construct corresponding to the component index.

To meet these two objectives, the three-step data validation process shown in figure 2 was performed.

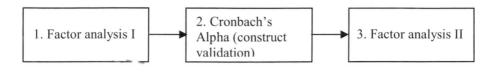

Fig. 2: Steps in data validation and reduction

7.2.1   Factor Analysis I

Factor analysis based on the principle component analysis technique was conducted on each component/sub-index, taking into consideration all the variables allocated to the sub-index. Care was taken during this phase to ensure the significance of Bartlett's test of sphericity and the Kaiser-Meyer-Olkin measure of sampling adequacy. In addition, it was ensured that only eigenvalues greater than one were considered. Rotation based on the Varimax method was also performed where more than one factor existed.

Factor analysis performed in this way for each component index thus permitted the identification of a number of different factors into which data for each component index could be reduced. Based on the communalities of each variable resulting from this analysis, variables were divided among the factors comprising each component index.

7.2.2   Cronbach's Alpha

Next, each of the identified factors in the constructs was analyzed for reliability using Cronbach's alpha method. Items were deleted where necessary to achieve an alpha of at least 0.6 and, preferably, greater than 0.7. However, the alpha value for three factors – e-government factor 2, e-learning and broadband – was found to be below the 0.6 threshold. This problem can only be solved by a richer set of data and therefore constitutes one of the limitations of this research.

As a result of the first two steps in the data validation process, a total of 12 variables were further eliminated from the set of variables used to compute the NRI index. This reduced the number of variables used for index computation from 49 to 37.

7.2.3 Factor Analysis II: Computation of Factor Scores

The factor scores for each factor in the sub-indexes were computed after finalizing the variables that make up the sub-indexes. Once again, it was ensured that all the conditions that apply to factor analysis were used (such as the significance of Bartlett's test of sphericity and the Kaiser-Meyer-Olkin measure of sampling adequacy). Moreover, it was verified that the eigenvalues were above the cutoff limit of 1.

Table 5: Results of factor analysis step 1 and Cronbach's Alpha analysis

S.no.	Variables included	Variables dropped	Cronbach's alpha	Variance explained
I. Internet indicators				
	Citizens' approach to and use of the Internet		0.9608	82.2%
1.01	Home Internet access	1. Cable modem subscribers		
1.02	Internet usage			
1.03	Internet usage intensity			
1.04	E-mail			
1.05	Internet users			
1.06	DSL Internet subscribers			
1.07	ISDN subcribers			
1.08	Home Internet usage			
1.09	Internet usage at work			
1.10	Internet access in schools			
1.11	Households online			
1.12	Personal computers			
	Enterprise access to and use of ICT		0.8566	79.2%
2.01	Employees with Internet access	2. Competition in the ICT sector		
2.02	Business PC	3. ICT market value relative to GDP at current market prices		
2.03	Teleworking usage	4. Internet hosts per 10,000 inhabitants		
2.04	Teleworking intensity			
	Internet access costs		0.7429	74.5%
3.01	Residential telephone connection charge	5. Total Internet per 20 hours of use		
3.02	Business telephone monthly subscription	6. Residential monthly telephone subscription charge		
3.03	Business telephone connection charge			

Table 5 (continued)

S.no.	Variables included	Variables dropped	Cronbach's alpha	Variance explained
II. Modern online public services				
	E-Government factor 1		0.8185	63.4%
4.01	Government online presence	7. Internet usage for job search		
4.02	Government online services			
	E-Government factor 2		0.4386	84.7%
4.03	Online book service	8. Internet usage for documents (passports, driving licenses, other personal documents)		
4.04	Government prioritization of ICT			
4.05	Online tax rerturns			
4.06	Government ICT promotion			
	E-learning		0.5584	64.8%
5.01	Internet access in schools	9. Personal computers installed in education		
5.02	Online learning			
5.03	Offline electronic learning			
	E-health		0.8455	96.8%
6.01	Online health searches	10. Telephone mainlines per employee		
6.02	Internet use by the disabled			
III. Dynamic e-business environment				
	Buying and selling online		0.6028	97.8%
7.01	Online purchases	11. B2B e-commerce		
7.02	B2C e-commerce			
	E-business readiness			
8.01	Laws relating to IT			
IV. Secure information infrastructure				
9.01	Online privacy		0.7644	81.9%
9.02	Secure online commerce			
V. Broadband				
10.01	DSL broadband access	12. Internet bandwidth per inhabitant	0.5841	81.9%
10.02	Broadband subscribers			

7.3   Index Computation

The final step was to calculate the eEurope Index. First, each sub-index was calculated by taking an average of all the *factor scores* in each block. Next, the average of the sub-indexes was taken to calculate the five component indices, namely Internet indicators, modern online public services, dynamic e-business environment, secure information infrastructure and broadband. The following computations were performed:

$$Internet\ indicators = \frac{\left(\begin{array}{l} Citizens'\ access\ to\ and\ use\ of\ the\ Internet \\ +\ Enterprise\ access\ to\ and\ use\ of\ the\ Internet \\ +\ Internet\ access\ \text{costs} \end{array}\right)}{3}$$

$$Modern\ online\ public\ services = \frac{\left(\begin{array}{l} \left(\begin{array}{l} e-government\ factor\ 1 \\ +\ e-government\ factor\ 2 \end{array}\right)\Big/2 \\ +\ e-learning + e-health \end{array}\right)}{3}$$

$$Dynamic\ e-business\ environment = \frac{(Buying\ and\ selling\ online + e-business\ readiness)}{2}$$

$$eEurope\ 2005\ Index = \frac{\left(\begin{array}{l} Internet\ indicators \\ +\ Modern\ online\ public\ services \\ +\ Dynamic\ e-business\ environment \\ +\ Secure\ information\ infrastructure \\ +\ Broadband \end{array}\right)}{5}$$

Part 2: Country Tables

A. New Member and Candidate Countries

Bulgaria

Bulgaria: Alignment with EU-15

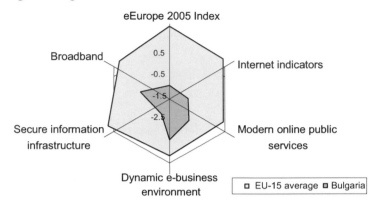

Bulgaria ranks 25th in the eEurope 2005 Index and 73rd out of 104 countries in the Networked Readiness Index 2004. Bulgaria is one of the countries with the lowest GDP per capita among the 25 countries studied in this research project and is hence one of the least developed countries. It is one of the three group V countries that still require significant development before their information and communications technology (ICT) industries can come into line with those of the EU-15 countries. This can be seen from the chart, which plots the degree of Bulgaria's alignment relative to the weighted average for the EU-15 across the five key indicators in the eEurope 2005 framework.

Among the NMS and candidate countries, Bulgaria has one of the lowest GDP per capita figures (€2,154). Internet usage is yet to take off. According to 2003 data from the International Telecommunications Union, 13 percent of its inhabitants use the Internet, compared to an EU-15 average of 46 percent. Internet usage is constrained by an underdeveloped infrastructure. Many people still share telephone lines.

To meet the requirements for accession to the European Union, and in order to further the country's economic development, the government is making efforts to develop its communications and high-technology industries. According to Sibis (2003), some of the key objectives identified by the government are:

1. To promote investment in the ICT sector,
2. To create a competitive, export-oriented software industry,

3. To encourage small and medium-sized businesses to compete in the ICT sector,
4. To encourage young graduates to start their own businesses in Bulgaria.

ICT is one of the most sought-after areas of study by technical students. Currently, the country is benefiting from a healthy supply of trained personnel. Bulgaria is nevertheless also suffering from a brain drain. According to the National Statistical Institute, over 300,000 professionals have left the ICT sector in the past 10 years.

Bulgaria

Key Indicators		eEurope 2005 Index
Population (millions)	7,891	**25**
Gross Domestic Product (€ billions)	17	Networked Readiness Index, 2004 73
GDP per capita (€)	2154	
Internet users per 100 inhabitants, 2003	13.3	Group V, significant development required

Internet indicators	25		Modern online public services (cont.)	
1.01	Home Internet access	21	4.03	Online book search	21
1.02	Internet usage	22	4.04	Government prioritization of ICT	24
1.03	Internet usage intensity	18	4.05	Online tax returns	21
1.04	E-mail	21	4.06	Government ICT promotion	24
1.05	Internet users	24	5.01	Internet access in schools	25
1.06	DSL Internet subscribers	18	5.02	Online learning	23
1.07	ISDN subscribers	25	5.03	Offline electronic learning	23
1.08	Home Internet usage	21	6.01	Online health services	24
1.09	Internet usage at work	22	6.02	Internet usage by the disabled	23
1.10	Internet access in schools	25			
1.11	Households online	23	**Dynamic e-business environment**	**24**
1.12	Personal computers	25	7.01	Online purchases	20
2.01	Employees with Internet access	22	7.02	B2C e-commerce	23
2.02	Business PC	24	8.01	Laws relating to IT	23
2.03	Teleworking usage, 2002/03	19			
2.04	Teleworking intensity	14	**Secure information infrastructure**	**24**
3.01	Residential telephone connection charge	24	9.01	Online privacy	24
3.02	Business telephone monthly subscription	23	9.02	Secure online commerce	24
3.03	Business telephone connection charge	23			
			Broadband	**21**
Modern online public services	**25**	10.01	DSL broadband access	18
4.01	Government online presence segmented	12	10.02	Broadband subscribers	21
4.02	Government online services measured for	20			

Czech Republic

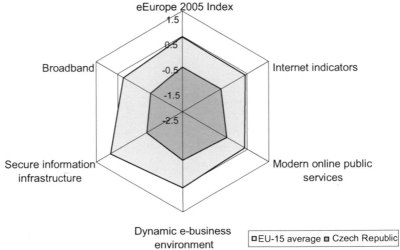

The Czech Republic ranks 20th in the eEurope 2005 Index and 40th out of 104 countries in the Networked Readiness Index 2004. The Czech Republic is positioned in the middle of the group IV countries that require some development before their ICT industries can come into line with those of the EU-15 countries. This can be seen from the chart, which plots the degree of the Czech Republic's alignment relative to the weighted average for the EU-15 across the five key indicators in the eEurope 2005 framework. The Czech Republic is evidently one of the leading nations in Central and Eastern Europe with respect to ICT development.

The Czech Republic has GDP per capita of €7,205. Internet usage is moderate. According to 2003 data from the International Telecommunications Union, 33 percent of its inhabitants use the Internet, compared to an EU-15 average of 47 percent. While infrastructure is good and demand for telecommunications services satisfied, Internet access remains quite expensive at €4.50 per 20 hours of access. By comparison, mobile telephony – a market with three competing operators – has witnessed a high level of development over the past few years.

It is also noticeable that, while Internet bandwidth per capita is relatively high at 2,189 bits (rank 12), broadband usage has yet to take off. The Czech Republic thus ranks 21st with respect to the use of DSL broadband access.

The Ministry of Information defines its mission and objective as creating conditions that will establish the Czech Republic as the leader in Central and Eastern Europe's information and communications technologies sector. Programs are now underway in several areas, such as e-government, e-health and e-education. More than 6,200 schools are now online, for instance.

Czech Repulic

Key indicators		eEurope 2005 Index	
Population (millions)	10,270		20
Gross Domestic Product (€ billions)	74	Networked Readiness Index, 2004	40
GDP per capita (€)	7205		
Internet users per 100 inhabitants, 2003	22.1	Group IV, development required	

Internet indicators	19	Modern online public services (cont.)	
1.01 Home Internet access	16	4.03 Online book search	12
1.02 Internet usage	16	4.04 Government prioritization of ICT	17
1.03 Internet usage intensity	16	4.05 Online tax returns	12
1.04 E-mail	16	4.06 Government ICT promotion	22
1.05 Internet users	19	5.01 Internet access in schools	11
1.06 DSL Internet subscribers	21	5.02 Online learning	15
1.07 ISDN subscribers	18	5.03 Offline electronic learning	19
1.08 Home Internet usage	16	6.01 Online health services	12
1.09 Internet usage at work	14	6.02 Internet usage by the disabled	13
1.10 Internet access in schools	11		
1.11 Households online	19	Dynamic e-business environment	16
1.12 Personal computers	17	7.01 Online purchases	16
2.01 Employees with Internet access	14	7.02 B2C e-commerce	20
2.02 Business PC	15	8.01 Laws relating to IT	15
2.03 Teleworking usage, 2002/03	21		
2.04 Teleworking intensity	25	Secure information infrastructure	20
3.01 Residential telephone connection charge	22	9.01 Online privacy	20
3.02 Business telephone monthly subscription	15	9.02 Secure online commerce	19
3.03 Business telephone connection charge	22		
		Broadband	22
Modern online public services	17	10.01 DSL broadband access	21
4.01 Government online presence segmented	23	10.02 Broadband subscribers	20
4.02 Government online services measured for	18		

Estonia

Estonia: Alignment with EU-15

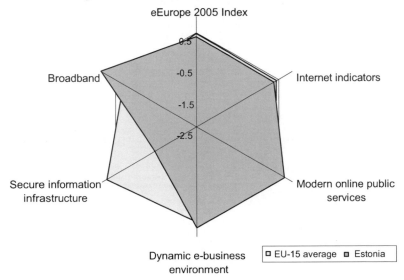

Estonia ranks 10th in the eEurope 2005 Index and 25th out of 104 countries in the Networked Readiness Index 2004. Estonia, the leading performer among the NMS with respect to the eEurope 2005 Index, is the only NMS in group II, which lines up with the EU-15 average. Estonia is fully aligned with the eEurope 2005 objectives with respect to its information and technology industries. This can be seen from the chart, which plots the degree of Estonia's alignment relative to the weighted average for the EU-15 across the five key indicators in the eEurope 2005 framework.

Estonia has GDP per capita of €5,143. Given this level of GDP per capita, its performance in the eEurope 2005 Index and the Networked Readiness Index 2004 is outstanding. According to 2003 data from the International Telecommunications Union, 44.6 percent of its inhabitants use the Internet, compared to an EU-15 average of 47 percent – another indication of its complete alignment. Infrastructure is good and has been completely upgraded. Internet access, however, remains expensive at €3.90 per 20 hours of access (the EU-15 average is €1.15).

It is also noticeable that, while Internet bandwidth per capita is relatively modest at 410 bits (EU-15 average: 3,761 bits per inhabitant), broadband usage in the form of DSL broadband access and the number of broadband subscribers is on a par with EU-15 levels.

On ICT, the government is currently focusing mainly on IT education, e-government and public services. Several programs are in place, such as the Tiger Leap Plus Program for ICT in schools. This program aims to improve the level of ICT in educational institutions and has several goals, such as: 1. Development of ICT skills; 2. Development of virtual learning practices; and 3. Development of infrastructure, notably access infrastructure in schools.

Estonia

Key indicators		eEurope 2005 Index	
Population (millions)	1,361		10
Gross Domestic Product (€ billions)	7	Networked Readiness Index, 2004	25
GDP per capita (€)	5134		
Internet users per 100 inhabitants, 2003	44.6	Group II, totally aligned	

Internet indicators		11	Modern online public services (cont.)		
1.01	Home Internet access	14	4.03	Online book search	11
1.02	Internet usage	8	4.04	Government prioritization of ICT	3
1.03	Internet usage intensity	4	4.05	Online tax returns	10
1.04	E-mail	10	4.06	Government ICT promotion	1
1.05	Internet users	8	5.01	Internet access in schools	4
1.06	DSL Internet subscribers	8	5.02	Online learning	10
1.07	ISDN subscribers	19	5.03	Offline electronic learning	7
1.08	Home Internet usage	14	6.01	Online health services	9
1.09	Internet usage at work	5	6.02	Internet usage by the disabled	10
1.10	Internet access in schools	4			
1.11	Households online	4	Dynamic e-business environment		7
1.12	Personal computers	14	7.01	Online purchases	10
2.01	Employees with Internet access	5	7.02	B2C e-commerce	14
2.02	Business PC	13	8.01	Laws relating to IT	1
2.03	Teleworking usage, 2002/03	8			
2.04	Teleworking intensity	4	Secure information infrastructure		22
3.01	Residential telephone connection charge	18	9.01	Online privacy	22
3.02	Business telephone monthly subscription	13	9.02	Secure online commerce	18
3.03	Business telephone connection charge	18			
			Broadband		6
Modern online public services		8	10.01	DSL broadband access	8
4.01	Government online presence segmented	2	10.02	Broadband subscribers	3
4.02	Government online services measured for	7			

Hungary

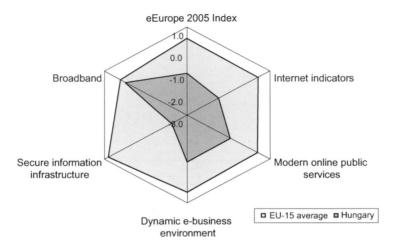

Hungary: Alignment with EU-15

eEurope 2005 Index

Broadband

Internet indicators

Secure information
infrastructure

Modern online public
services

Dynamic e-business
environment

□ EU-15 average □ Hungary

Hungary ranks 24th in the eEurope 2005 Index and 38th out of 104 countries in the Networked Readiness Index 2004. Hungary is one of the group V countries that still have significant efforts to make to bring their information and communications technology (ICT) industries into line with those of the EU-15 countries. This can be seen from the chart, which plots the degree of Hungary's alignment relative to the weighted average for the EU-15 across the five key indicators in the eEurope 2005 framework.

Hungary has GDP per capita of €6,880. Internet usage is moderate. According to 2003 data from the International Telecommunications Union, 23.4 percent of its inhabitants use the Internet, compared to an EU-15 average of 47 percent. While Internet access remains fairly expensive at €2.30 per 20 hours of access (EU-15 average: €1.15 per 20 hours), it is cheaper than that the charge in most other NMS.

It is also noticeable that Internet bandwidth per capita is relatively high compared to most NMS, at 1,048 bits (rank 16; the EU-15 average is 3,160 bits per inhabitant). Broadband users represent 25 percent of all Internet users. In addition, Hungary ranks 18th with respect to the use of DSL broadband access.

The Hungarian government has launched several programs to promote the development of information and communications technologies and to advance alignment with the EU-15 countries. Of note is the *Szechenyi Plan*, launched in December 2000 as a medium-term economic development plan. Its objectives include the modernization of the ICT infrastructure and the promotion of ICT usage within the country. Other more recent plans, such as the *National Development Plan, 2002 (NFT)* are designed to establish electronic public administration and e-government services.

Hungary

Key indicators		eEurope 2005 Index	
Population (millions)	10,175	**24**	
Gross Domestic Product (€ billions)	70	Networked Readiness Index, 2004	38
GDP per capita (€)	6880		
Internet users per 100 inhabitants, 2003	23.4	Group V, significant development required	

Internet indicators	**24**	Modern online public services (cont.)	
1.01 Home Internet access	20	4.03 Online book search	24
1.02 Internet usage	24	4.04 Government prioritization of ICT	15
1.03 Internet usage intensity	23	4.05 Online tax returns	20
1.04 E-mail	23	4.06 Government ICT promotion	8
1.05 Internet users	17	5.01 Internet access in schools	13
1.06 DSL Internet subscribers	18	5.02 Online learning	21
1.07 ISDN subscribers	15	5.03 Offline electronic learning	19
1.08 Home Internet usage	20	6.01 Online health services	22
1.09 Internet usage at work	24	6.02 Internet usage by the disabled	24
1.10 Internet access in schools	13		
1.11 Households online	24	Dynamic e-business environment	**21**
1.12 Personal computers	21	7.01 Online purchases	23
2.01 Employees with Internet access	24	7.02 B2C e-commerce	21
2.02 Business PC	20	8.01 Laws relating to IT	20
2.03 Teleworking usage, 2002/03	23		
2.04 Teleworking intensity	19	Secure information infrastructure	**25**
3.01 Residential telephone connection charge	23	9.01 Online privacy	25
3.02 Business telephone monthly subscription	16	9.02 Secure online commerce	23
3.03 Business telephone connection charge	25		
		Broadband	**12**
Modern online public services	**21**	10.01 DSL broadband access	18
4.01 Government online presence segmented	15	10.02 Broadband subscribers	5
4.02 Government online services measured for	16		

Latvia

Latvia: Alignment with EU-15

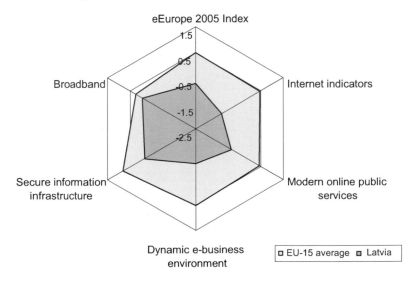

Latvia ranks 19th in the eEurope 2005 Index and 56th out of 104 countries in the Networked Readiness Index 2004. Latvia is positioned in the middle of the group IV consisting of countries that are somewhat aligned with those of the EU-15 countries. This can be seen from the chart, which plots the degree of Latvia's alignment relative to the weighted average for the EU-15 across the five key indicators in the eEurope 2005 framework.

Latvia has GDP per capita of €3,836. Internet usage is moderate. According to 2003 data from the International Telecommunications Union, 14.7 percent of its inhabitants use the Internet, compared to an EU-15 average of 47 percent. While Latvia was among the most advanced countries in the former Soviet Union in terms of its telecommunications development, Internet access remains extremely expensive at €20 per 20 hours of access. It is also noticeable that Internet bandwidth per capita is very low, at 182 bits (rank 21; the EU-15 average is 3,160 bits per inhabitant). Broadband users represent 26.5 percent of all Internet users. All in all, however broadband usage has yet to take off. Accordingly, Latvia ranks 21st with respect to the use of DSL broadband access.

ICT is among the fastest-growing sectors in the country and is one of the top three national economic priorities, alongside timber and light industry. In parallel to the eEurope initiative launched in December 2000, guidelines were laid down in a document entitled "Conceptual guidelines of the eLatvia socioeconomic program". The program has three principal objectives: 1. To enable cheaper access to a faster Internet; 2. To invest in and develop the skills of citizens; and 3. To stimulate the use of the Internet.

Latvia

Key indicators		eEurope 2005 Index	
Population (millions)	2,346		19
Gross Domestic Product (€ billions)	9	Networked Readiness Index, 2004	56
GDP per capita (€)	3836		
Internet users per 100 inhabitants, 2003	14.7	Group IV, development required	

Internet indicators		23	Modern online public services (cont.)		
1.01	Home Internet access	24	4.03	Online book search	23
1.02	Internet usage	18	4.04	Government prioritization of ICT	23
1.03	Internet usage intensity	21	4.05	Online tax returns	12
1.04	E-mail	18	4.06	Government ICT promotion	23
1.05	Internet users	23	5.01	Internet access in schools	19
1.06	DSL Internet subscribers	21	5.02	Online learning	16
1.07	ISDN subscribers	24	5.03	Offline electronic learning	11
1.08	Home Internet usage	24	6.01	Online health services	20
1.09	Internet usage at work	15	6.02	Internet usage by the disabled	17
1.10	Internet access in schools	19			
1.11	Households online	22	Dynamic e-business environment		25
1.12	Personal computers	18	7.01	Online purchases	20
2.01	Employees with Internet access	15	7.02	B2C e-commerce	18
2.02	Business PC	18	8.01	Laws relating to IT	25
2.03	Teleworking usage, 2002/03	16			
2.04	Teleworking intensity	15	Secure information infrastructure		16
3.01	Residential telephone connection charge	25	9.01	Online privacy	8
3.02	Business telephone monthly subscription	18	9.02	Secure online commerce	19
3.03	Business telephone connection charge	24			
			Broadband		13
Modern online public services		20	10.01	DSL broadband access	21
4.01	Government online presence segmented	12	10.02	Broadband subscribers	4
4.02	Government online services measured for	23			

Lithuania

Lithuania: Alignment with EU-15

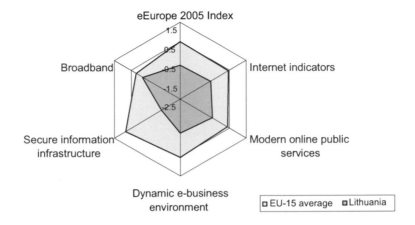

Lithuania gained independence from the former USSR in 1991. Since then, it has concentrated on integration in the European Union and the development of a market economy. The country's long-term economic development strategy, published in 2001, established the goal of making information and communications technology a dominant part of the economy by the year 2015.

Lithuania ranks 18th in the eEurope 2005 Index and 43rd out of 104 countries in the Networked Readiness Index 2004. Lithuania is positioned amongst the group IV countries that still have some efforts to make before their ICT industries can come into line with those of the EU-15 countries. This can be seen from the chart, which plots the degree of Lithuania's alignment relative to the weighted average for the EU-15 across the five key indicators in the eEurope 2005 framework.

Lithuania has GDP per capita of €4,315. Internet usage is moderate. According to 2003 data from the International Telecommunications Union, 22.4 percent of its inhabitants use the Internet, compared to an EU-15 average of 47 percent. Internet access remains very expensive at €11.20 per 20 hours of access, compared to the EU-15 average of €1.15 per 20 hours.

It is also noticeable that Internet bandwidth per capita is very low at 94.7 bits, and that broadband (DSL) usage has yet to take off. Only about one percent of individuals access the Internet via broadband.

Significant efforts are being made to increase computer literacy, as witnessed by the increase in computer penetration in schools. According to Sibis, the penetration of computers in schools rose from one computer per 100 secondary students in 1996 to 2.5 in 2001. More efforts must still be made in promote online public services and e-business.

Lithuania

Key indicators		eEurope 2005 Index	
Population (millions)	3,476		18
Gross Domestic Product (€ billions)	15	Networked Readiness Index, 2004	43
GDP per capita (€)	4315		
Internet users per 100 inhabitants, 2003	22.4	Group IV, development required	

Internet indicators		18	Modern online public services (cont.)		
1.01	Home Internet access	21	4.03	Online book search	19
1.02	Internet usage	17	4.04	Government prioritization of ICT	13
1.03	Internet usage intensity	21	4.05	Online tax returns	16
1.04	E-mail	17	4.06	Government ICT promotion	16
1.05	Internet users	18	5.01	Internet access in schools	17
1.06	DSL Internet subscribers	18	5.02	Online learning	10
1.07	ISDN subscribers	22	5.03	Offline electronic learning	23
1.08	Home Internet usage	21	6.01	Online health services	17
1.09	Internet usage at work	17	6.02	Internet usage by the disabled	18
1.10	Internet access in schools	17			
1.11	Households online	13	Dynamic e-business environment		18
1.12	Personal computers	20	7.01	Online purchases	23
2.01	Employees with Internet access	17	7.02	B2C e-commerce	17
2.02	Business PC	22	8.01	Laws relating to IT	19
2.03	Teleworking usage, 2002/03	13			
2.04	Teleworking intensity	7	Secure information infrastructure		23
3.01	Residential telephone connection charge	21	9.01	Online privacy	23
3.02	Business telephone monthly subscription	14	9.02	Secure online commerce	21
3.03	Business telephone connection charge	21			
			Broadband		14
Modern online public services		18	10.01	DSL broadband access	18
4.01	Government online presence segmented	23	10.02	Broadband subscribers	9
4.02	Government online services measured for	24			

Poland

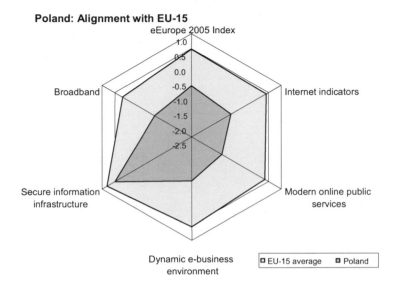

Poland: Alignment with EU-15

Poland ranks 21st in the eEurope 2005 Index and 72nd out of 104 countries in the Networked Readiness Index 2004. Poland is positioned in the middle of the group IV countries that still need some development before their ICT industries can come into line with those of the EU-15 countries. This can be seen from the chart, which plots the degree of Poland's alignment relative to the weighted average for the EU-15 across the five key indicators in the eEurope 2005 framework.

Poland has GDP per capita of €5,177. Internet usage is yet to take off. According to 2003 data from the International Telecommunications Union, 16.3 percent of its inhabitants use the Internet, compared to an EU-15 average of 47 percent. Internet access remains expensive at €4.10 per 20 hours of access, compared to the EU-15 average of €1.15 per 20 hours.

It is also noticeable that Internet bandwidth per capita is very low at 163.6 bits, and that broadband usage has yet to take off.

The document "ePolska – Strategy for the Development of an Information Society in Poland in 2001-2006" outlines a plan of action that will shape the future of the country's information society. Some objectives are: to create an electronic economy; to create legal regulations comparable to those of the European Union; to ensure online security; to provide support to the Polish ICT industry; and to facilitate e-procurement by the government.

Programs such as Pionier (Polish Optical Internet – Advanced Applications, Services and Technologies for the Information Society) aim to build a Polish optical network. The 1999 "Internet at School: Project of the Polish President" initiative aims to increase computer penetration in schools.

While ambitious goals and targets have been set by the Polish government, their realization remains constrained by available finance and by the need for infrastructure improvements.

Poland

Key indicators		eEurope 2005 Index
Population (millions)	38,633	2
Gross Domestic Product (€ billions)	200	Networked Readiness Index, 2004 72
GDP per capita (€)	5177	
Internet users per 100 inhabitants, 2003	16.3	Group IV, development required

Internet indicators	21	Modern online public services (cont.)	
1.01 Home Internet access	19	4.03 Online book search	12
1.02 Internet usage	23	4.04 Government prioritization of ICT	25
1.03 Internet usage intensity	18	4.05 Online tax returns	22
1.04 E-mail	23	4.06 Government ICT promotion	25
1.05 Internet users	22	5.01 Internet access in schools	24
1.06 DSL Internet subscribers	21	5.02 Online learning	25
1.07 ISDN subscribers	21	5.03 Offline electronic learning	14
1.08 Home Internet usage	19	6.01 Online health services	22
1.09 Internet usage at work	22	6.02 Internet usage by the disabled	20
1.10 Internet access in schools	24		
1.11 Households online	21	Dynamic e-business environment	2
1.12 Personal computers	22	7.01 Online purchases	20
2.01 Employees with Internet access	22	7.02 B2C e-commerce	22
2.02 Business PC	19	8.01 Laws relating to IT	21
2.03 Teleworking usage, 2002/03	15		
2.04 Teleworking intensity	16	Secure information infrastructure	10
3.01 Residential telephone connection charge	19	9.01 Online privacy	1
3.02 Business telephone monthly subscription	24	9.02 Secure online commerce	17
3.03 Business telephone connection charge	19		
		Broadband	23
Modern online public services	24	10.01 DSL broadband access	21
4.01 Government online presence segmented	15	10.02 Broadband subscribers	21
4.02 Government online services measured for	24		

Romania

Romania: Alignment with EU-15

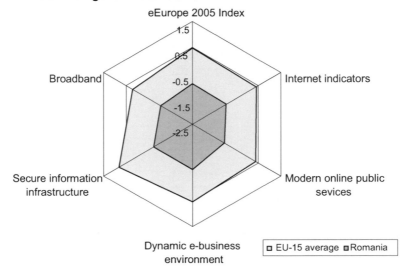

eEurope 2005 Index

Broadband

Internet indicators

Secure information infrastructure

Modern online public sevices

Dynamic e-business environment

☐ EU-15 average ☐ Romania

Romania has historically assumed a leading role among East European countries in the field of ICT. It was a significant exporter of both hardware and software in Eastern Europe during the 1990s. Nevertheless, Romania today ranks 23rd in the eEurope 2005 Index and 53rd out of 104 countries in the Networked Readiness Index 2004. Romania is positioned in the middle of the group V countries that still have significant efforts to make before their ICT industries can come into line with those of the EU-15 countries. This can be seen from the chart, which plots the degree of Romania's alignment relative to the weighted average for the EU-15 across the five key indicators in the eEurope 2005 framework.

Romania has GDP per capita of €2,144. Internet usage is low. According to 2003 data from the International Telecommunications Union, 9.4 percent of its inhabitants use the Internet, compared to an EU-15 average of 47 percent. Internet access is extremely expensive at €17.10 per 20 hours of access, compared to the EU-15 average €1.15.

It is also noticeable that Internet bandwidth per capita is a mere 89.8 bits, and that broadband usage has yet to take off (with respect to the use of DSL broadband access). Several programs are in place to develop Romania's e-society in the following areas: e-government, e-health, ICT skills, and PC penetration and Internet access in schools.

Until 2003, RomTel was the only company that provided a terrestrial communications infrastructure. The liberalization of the telecommunications infrastructure in 2003 is expected to give a major boost to the telecommunications sector. Increased competition could lower connection costs and hence stimulate a rise in the number of individuals connecting to and benefiting from the Internet.

Romania

Key indicators		eEurope 2005 Index	
Population (millions)	22,386		23
Gross Domestic Product (€ billions)	48	Networked Readiness Index, 2004	53
GDP per capita (€)	2144		
Internet users per 100 inhabitants, 2003	9.4	Group IV, development required	

Internet indicators		20	Modern online public services (cont.)		
1.01	Home Internet access	25	4.03	Online book search	20
1.02	Internet usage	25	4.04	Government prioritization of ICT	16
1.03	Internet usage intensity	25	4.05	Online tax returns	24
1.04	E-mail	25	4.06	Government ICT promotion	12
1.05	Internet users	25	5.01	Internet access in schools	22
1.06	DSL Internet subscribers	21	5.02	Online learning	18
1.07	ISDN subscribers	23	5.03	Offline electronic learning	23
1.08	Home Internet usage	25	6.01	Online health services	24
1.09	Internet usage at work	25	6.02	Internet usage by the disabled	25
1.10	Internet access in schools	22			
1.11	Households online	25	Dynamic e-business environment		20
1.12	Personal computers	24	7.01	Online purchases	25
2.01	Employees with Internet access	25	7.02	B2C e-commerce	25
2.02	Business PC	25	8.01	Laws relating to IT	17
2.03	Teleworking usage, 2002/03	25			
2.04	Teleworking intensity	23	Secure information infrastructure		19
3.01	Residential telephone connection charge	13	9.01	Online privacy	11
3.02	Business telephone monthly subscription	17	9.02	Secure online commerce	25
3.03	Business telephone connection charge	13			
			Broadband		23
Modern online public services		23	10.01	DSL broadband access	21
4.01	Government online presence segmented	15	10.02	Broadband subscribers	21
4.02	Government online services measured for	12			

Slovak Republic

Slovak Republic: Alignment with EU-15

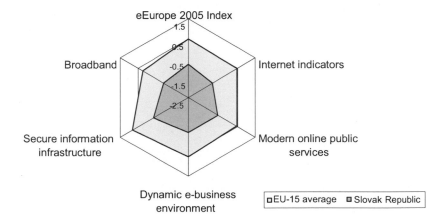

The Slovak Republic was handicapped in the past by a legacy of disproportionately low investment compared to the Czech Republic when the two were part of the former Czechoslovakia. It today ranks 22nd in the eEurope 2005 Index and 48th out of 104 countries in the Networked Readiness Index 2004. The Slovak Republic is positioned in the middle of the group IV countries that still need some development before their ICT industries can come into line with those of the EU-15 countries. This can be seen from the chart, which plots the degree of Slovak Reublic's alignment relative to the weighted average for the EU-15 across the five key indicators in the eEurope 2005 framework.

The Slovak Republic has GDP per capita of €4,647. Internet usage is moderate. According to 2003 data from the International Telecommunications Union, 17.3 percent of its inhabitants use the Internet, compared to an EU-15 average of 47 percent. Internet access remains fairly expensive at €6.30 per 20 hours of access.

It is also noticeable that, while Internet bandwidth per capita is relatively high at 1,516 bits, broadband usage has yet to take off (with respect to the use of DSL broadband access). ADSL roll-out has been hindered by limited access to local loops by interested companies. Liberalization of the telecommunications infrastructure began in 2003, although Slovak Telecom, the fixed-line operator, still has a 100 percent share of the voice telephony market.

The Infovek program, conceived in 1998, has served as the backbone of e-education in the Slovak Republic. The objectives of this program are to prepare Slovak citizens for EU integration and to link all schools to the Internet. According to Sibis, lack of funding meant that only 855 schools out of around 2,500 had been linked to the Internet by 2002. On the e-government front, the Govnet program has been instrumental in linking different parts of the government together through e-mail, text messaging and Internet access.

Slovak Republic

Key indicators

		eEurope 2005 Index
Population (millions)	5,380	**22**
Gross Domestic Product (€ billions)	25	Networked Readiness Index, 2004 48
GDP per capita (€)	4647	
Internet users per 100 Inhabitants, 2003	17.3	Group IV, development required

Internet indicators	22	Modern online public services (cont.)	
1.01 Home Internet access	23	4.03 Online book search	14
1.02 Internet usage	20	4.04 Government prioritization of ICT	21
1.03 Internet usage intensity	23	4.05 Online tax returns	24
1.04 E-mail	18	4.06 Government ICT promotion	21
1.05 Internet users	20	5.01 Internet access in schools	20
1.06 DSL Internet subscribers	21	5.02 Online learning	18
1.07 ISDN subscribers	20	5.03 Offline electronic learning	14
1.08 Home Internet usage	23	6.01 Online health services	14
1.09 Internet usage at work	20	6.02 Internet usage by the disabled	19
1.10 Internet access in schools	20		
1.11 Households online	16	Dynamic e-business environment	19
1.12 Personal computers	16	7.01 Online purchases	18
2.01 Employees with Internet access	20	7.02 B2C e-commerce	24
2.02 Business PC	23	8.01 Laws relating to IT	18
2.03 Teleworking usage, 2002/03	22		
2.04 Teleworking intensity	20	Secure information infrastructure	18
3.01 Residential telephone connection charge	19	9.01 Online privacy	17
3.02 Business telephone monthly subscription	25	9.02 Secure online commerce	16
3.03 Business telephone connection charge	20		
		Broadband	23
Modern online public services	19	10.01 DSL broadband access	21
4.01 Government online presence segmented	20	10.02 Broadband subscribers	21
4.02 Government online services measured for	16		

Slovenia

Slovenia: Alignment with EU-15

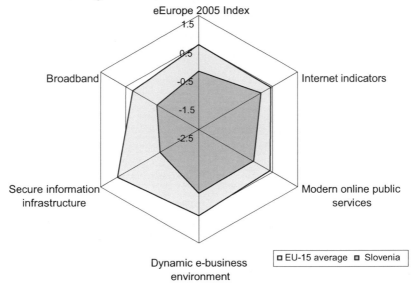

Slovenia ranks 17th in the eEurope 2005 Index and 32nd out of 104 countries in the Networked Readiness Index 2004. Slovenia leads the group III countries, whose ICT industries are partially aligned with those of the EU-15 countries. This can be seen from the chart, which plots the degree of Slovenia's alignment relative to the weighted average for the EU-15 across the five key indicators in the eEurope 2005 framework.

Slovenia has GDP per capita of €11,535, the highest among the NMS. Internet usage is relatively high,. According to 2003 data from the International Telecommunications Union, 43.2 percent of its inhabitants use the Internet, compared to an EU-15 average of 47 percent. Infrastructure is good and demand for telecommunications services is satisfied. However, Internet access, while among the cheapest in the NMS, still remains relatively expensive at €3.10 per 20 hours of access, compared to the EU-15 average of €1.15.

It is also noticeable that Internet bandwidth per capita is modest at 540 bits, and that less than 2 percent of individuals use broadband. Broadband usage has thus yet to take off.

Slovenia's national telephone networks are among the best of the former Yugoslavian states and are comparable with those in the European Union.

Analog networks were replaced by digital switches and fiber-optic cables by the end of 2000. One of the top priorities of the Slovenian government is higher education. The government is hence committed to investing in youth for the digital age. In spite of all schools having Internet access and informatics being a required course in the curriculum, the country still lacks ICT professionals.

Slovenia

Key indicators		eEurope 2005 Index	
Population (millions)	1,994		17
Gross Domestic Product (€ billions)	23	Networked Readiness Index, 2004	32
GDP per capita (€)	11535		
Internet users per 100 inhabitants, 2003	43.2	Group III, somewhat aligned	

Internet indicators	13	Modern online public services (cont.)	
1.01 Home Internet access	13	4.03 Online book search	15
1.02 Internet usage	12	4.04 Government prioritization of ICT	19
1.03 Internet usage intensity	12	4.05 Online tax returns	1
1.04 E-mail	12	4.06 Government ICT promotion	14
1.05 Internet users	9	5.01 Internet access in schools	9
1.06 DSL Internet subscribers	15	5.02 Online learning	18
1.07 ISDN subscribers	9	5.03 Offline electronic learning	14
1.08 Home Internet usage	13	6.01 Online health services	11
1.09 Internet usage at work	12	6.02 Internet usage by the disabled	15
1.10 Internet access in schools	9		
1.11 Households online	15	Dynamic e-business environment	13
1.12 Personal computers	11	7.01 Online purchases	14
2.01 Employees with Internet access	12	7.02 B2C e-commerce	19
2.02 Business PC	14	8.01 Laws relating to IT	11
2.03 Teleworking usage, 2002/03	14		
2.04 Teleworking intensity	12	Secure information infrastructure	21
3.01 Residential telephone connection charge	17	9.01 Online privacy	18
3.02 Business telephone monthly subscription	7	9.02 Secure online commerce	22
3.03 Business telephone connection charge	16		
		Broadband	18
Modern online public services	15	10.01 DSL broadband access	15
4.01 Government online presence segmented	23	10.02 Broadband subscribers	17
4.02 Government online services measured for	20		

Part 2: Country Tables

B. EU-15 Countries

Austria

Key indicators		eEurope 2005 Index
Population (millions)	8,139	7
Gross Domestic Product (€ billions)	217	Networked Readiness Index, 2004 19
GDP per capita (€)	26662	
Internet users per 100 inhabitants, 2003	46.5	Group I, global leader

Internet indicators		8	Modern online public services (cont.)		
1.01	Home Internet access	7	4.03	Online book search	4
1.02	Internet usage	6	4.04	Government prioritization of ICT	9
1.03	Internet usage intensity	6	4.05	Online tax returns	7
1.04	E-mail	6	4.06	Government ICT promotion	7
1.05	Internet users	6	5.01	Internet access in schools	5
1.06	DSL Internet subscribers	5	5.02	Online learning	6
1.07	ISDN subscribers	5	5.03	Offline electronic learning	2
1.08	Home Internet usage	7	6.01	Online health services	9
1.09	Internet usage at work	7	6.02	Internet usage by the disabled	8
1.10	Internet access in schools	5			
1.11	Households online	8	Dynamic e-business environment		6
1.12	Personal computers	9	7.01	Online purchases	8
2.01	Employees with Internet access	7	7.02	B2C e-commerce	6
2.02	Business PC	8	8.01	Laws relating to IT	8
2.03	Teleworking usage, 2002/03	7			
2.04	Teleworking intensity	11	Secure information infrastructure		14
3.01	Residential telephone connection charge	7	9.01	Online privacy	15
3.02	Business telephone monthly subscription	9	9.02	Secure online commerce	12
3.03	Business telephone connection charge	7			
			Broadband		2
Modern online public services		7	10.01	DSL broadband access	5
4.01	Government online presence segmented	6	10.02	Broadband subscribers	2
4.02	Government online services measured for	3			

Belgium

Key indicators		eEurope 2005 Index
Population (millions)	10,310	8
Gross Domestic Product (€ billions)	261	Networked Readiness Index, 2004 26
GDP per capita (€)	25315	
Internet users per 100 inhabitants, 2003	42.2	Group II, totally aligned

Internet indicators		9		Modern online public services (cont.)	
1.01	Home Internet access	10	4.03	Online book search	18
1.02	Internet usage	11	4.04	Government prioritization of ICT	20
1.03	Internet usage intensity	6	4.05	Online tax returns	17
1.04	E-mail	11	4.06	Government ICT promotion	18
1.05	Internet users	10	5.01	Internet access in schools	12
1.06	DSL Internet subscribers	1	5.02	Online learning	13
1.07	ISDN subscribers	8	5.03	Offline electronic learning	7
1.08	Home Internet usage	10	6.01	Online health services	9
1.09	Internet usage at work	10	6.02	Internet usage by the disabled	11
1.10	Internet access in schools	12			
1.11	Households online	10	Dynamic e-business environment		12
1.12	Personal computers	12	7.01	Online purchases	12
2.01	Employees with Internet access	10	7.02	B2C e-commerce	12
2.02	Business PC	11	8.01	Laws relating to IT	13
2.03	Teleworking usage, 2002/03	11			
2.04	Teleworking intensity	8	Secure information infrastructure		13
3.01	Residential telephone connection charge	5	9.01	Online privacy	13
3.02	Business telephone monthly subscription	10	9.02	Secure online commerce	14
3.03	Business telephone connection charge	5			
			Broadband		1
Modern online public services		11	10.01	DSL broadband access	1
4.01	Government online presence segmented	15	10.02	Broadband subscribers	1
4.02	Government online services measured for	10			

Denmark

Key indicators		eEurope 2005 Index
Population (millions)	5,368	1
Gross Domestic Product (€ billions)	183	Networked Readiness Index, 2004 4
GDP per capita (€)	34091	
Internet users per 100 inhabitants, 2003	66.9	Group I, global leader

Internet indicators		4	Modern online public services (cont.)		
1.01	Home Internet access	2	4.03	Online book search	9
1.02	Internet usage	1	4.04	Government prioritization of ICT	1
1.03	Internet usage intensity	1	4.05	Online tax returns	2
1.04	E-mail	1	4.06	Government ICT promotion	3
1.05	Internet users	1	5.01	Internet access in schools	3
1.06	DSL Internet subscribers	1	5.02	Online learning	5
1.07	ISDN subscribers	3	5.03	Offline electronic learning	7
1.08	Home Internet usage	2	6.01	Online health services	1
1.09	Internet usage at work	1	6.02	Internet usage by the disabled	1
1.10	Internet access in schools	3			
1.11	Households online	2	Dynamic e-business environment		2
1.12	Personal computers	3	7.01	Online purchases	1
2.01	Employees with Internet access	1	7.02	B2C e-commerce	4
2.02	Business PC	3	8.01	Laws relating to IT	4
2.03	Teleworking usage, 2002/03	3			
2.04	Teleworking intensity	5	Secure information infrastructure		8
3.01	Residential telephone connection charge	16	9.01	Online privacy	8
3.02	Business telephone monthly subscription	19	9.02	Secure online commerce	8
3.03	Business telephone connection charge	12			
			Broadband		5
Modern online public services		1	10.01	DSL broadband access	1
4.01	Government online presence segmented	1	10.02	Broadband subscribers	11
4.02	Government online services measured for	1			

Finland

Key indicators		eEurope 2005 Index
Population (millions)	5,195	■
Gross Domestic Product (€ billions)	140	Networked Readiness Index, 2004 3
GDP per capita (€)	26949	
Internet users per 100 inhabitants, 2003	50.6	Group I, global leader

Internet indicators		2	Modern online public services (cont.)		
1.01	Home Internet access	4	4.03	Online book search	7
1.02	Internet usage	3	4.04	Government prioritization of ICT	2
1.03	Internet usage intensity	10	4.05	Online tax returns	4
1.04	E-mail	4	4.06	Government ICT promotion	2
1.05	Internet users	5	5.01	Internet access in schools	1
1.06	DSL Internet subscribers	9	5.02	Online learning	1
1.07	ISDN subscribers	6	5.03	Offline electronic learning	14
1.08	Home Internet usage	4	6.01	Online health services	8
1.09	Internet usage at work	2	6.02	Internet usage by the disabled	8
1.10	Internet access in schools	1			
1.11	Households online	5	Dynamic e-business environment		4
1.12	Personal computers	5	7.01	Online purchases	5
2.01	Employees with Internet access	2	7.02	B2C e-commerce	3
2.02	Business PC	5	8.01	Laws relating to IT	2
2.03	Teleworking usage, 2002/03	2			
2.04	Teleworking intensity	3	Secure information infrastructure		9
3.01	Residential telephone connection charge	8	9.01	Online privacy	10
3.02	Business telephone monthly subscription	2	9.02	Secure online commerce	7
3.03	Business telephone connection charge	8			
			Broadband		8
Modern online public services		4	10.01	DSL broadband access	9
4.01	Government online presence segmented	15	10.02	Broadband subscribers	7
4.02	Government online services measured for	9			

France

Key indicators		eEurope 2005 Index
Population (millions)	59,344	**12**
Gross Domestic Product (€ billions)	1521	Networked Readiness Index, 2004 20
GDP per capita (€)	25630	
Internet users per 100 inhabitants, 2003	34.6	Group II, totally aligned

Internet indicators	12	Modern online public services (cont.)	
1.01 Home Internet access	12	4.03 Online book search	2
1.02 Internet usage	14	4.04 Government prioritization of ICT	12
1.03 Internet usage intensity	16	4.05 Online tax returns	12
1.04 E-mail	12	4.06 Government ICT promotion	5
1.05 Internet users	13	5.01 Internet access in schools	14
1.06 DSL Internet subscribers	11	5.02 Online learning	21
1.07 ISDN subscribers	4	5.03 Offline electronic learning	19
1.08 Home Internet usage	12	6.01 Online health services	18
1.09 Internet usage at work	15	6.02 Internet usage by the disabled	12
1.10 Internet access in schools	14		
1.11 Households online	11	**Dynamic e-business environment**	**10**
1.12 Personal computers	10	7.01 Online purchases	11
2.01 Employees with Internet access	15	7.02 B2C e-commerce	9
2.02 Business PC	10	8.01 Laws relating to IT	7
2.03 Teleworking usage, 2002/03	17		
2.04 Teleworking intensity	8	**Secure information infrastructure**	**12**
3.01 Residential telephone connection charge	3	9.01 Online privacy	15
3.02 Business telephone monthly subscription	4	9.02 Secure online commerce	9
3.03 Business telephone connection charge	3		
		Broadband	**10**
Modern online public services	**12**	10.01 DSL broadband access	11
4.01 Government online presence segmented	6	10.02 Broadband subscribers	10
4.02 Government online services measured for	6		

Germany

Key indicators		eEurope 2005 Index
Population (millions)	82,440	**5**
Gross Domestic Product (€ billions)	2108	Networked Readiness Index, 2004 14
GDP per capita (€)	25570	
Internet users per 100 inhabitants, 2003	66.2	Group I, global leader

Internet indicators		6	Modern online public services (cont.)		
1.01	Home Internet access	6	4.03	Online book search	1
1.02	Internet usage	7	4.04	Government prioritization of ICT	8
1.03	Internet usage intensity	6	4.05	Online tax returns	12
1.04	E-mail	9	4.06	Government ICT promotion	13
1.05	Internet users	2	5.01	Internet access in schools	10
1.06	DSL Internet subscribers	7	5.02	Online learning	3
1.07	ISDN subscribers	2	5.03	Offline electronic learning	5
1.08	Home Internet usage	6	6.01	Online health services	6
1.09	Internet usage at work	9	6.02	Internet usage by the disabled	5
1.10	Internet access in schools	10			
1.11	Households online	6	**Dynamic e-business environment**		**5**
1.12	Personal computers	6	7.01	Online purchases	5
2.01	Employees with Internet access	9	7.02	B2C e-commerce	5
2.02	Business PC	9	8.01	Laws relating to IT	5
2.03	Teleworking usage, 2002/03	6			
2.04	Teleworking intensity	12	**Secure information infrastructure**		**4**
3.01	Residential telephone connection charge	2	9.01	Online privacy	4
3.02	Business telephone monthly subscription	3	9.02	Secure online commerce	4
3.03	Business telephone connection charge	2			
			Broadband		**9**
Modern online public services		**6**	10.01	DSL broadband access	7
4.01	Government online presence segmented	12	10.02	Broadband subscribers	13
4.02	Government online services measured for	2			

Greece

Key indicators		eEurope 2005 Index
Population (millions)	10,598	16
Gross Domestic Product (€ billions)	141	Networked Readiness Index, 2004 42
GDP per capita (€)	13304	
Internet users per 100 inhabitants, 2003	16.4	Group III, somewhat aligned

Internet indicators		14	Modern online public services (cont.)		
1.01	Home Internet access	18	4.03	Online book search	25
1.02	Internet usage	20	4.04	Government prioritization of ICT	18
1.03	Internet usage intensity	18	4.05	Online tax returns	7
1.04	E-mail	22	4.06	Government ICT promotion	15
1.05	Internet users	21	5.01	Internet access in schools	21
1.06	DSL Internet subscribers	15	5.02	Online learning	23
1.07	ISDN subscribers	11	5.03	Offline electronic learning	11
1.08	Home Internet usage	18	6.01	Online health services	21
1.09	Internet usage at work	18	6.02	Internet usage by the disabled	22
1.10	Internet access in schools	21			
1.11	Households online	17	Dynamic e-business environment		22
1.12	Personal computers	23	7.01	Online purchases	18
2.01	Employees with Internet access	18	7.02	B2C e-commerce	16
2.02	Business PC	21	8.01	Laws relating to IT	24
2.03	Teleworking usage, 2002/03	9			
2.04	Teleworking intensity	10	Secure information infrastructure		5
3.01	Residential telephone connection charge	4	9.01	Online privacy	6
3.02	Business telephone monthly subscription	8	9.02	Secure online commerce	6
3.03	Business telephone connection charge	4			
			Broadband		20
Modern online public services		22	10.01	DSL broadband access	15
4.01	Government online presence segmented	4	10.02	Broadband subscribers	21
4.02	Government online services measured for	19			

Ireland

Key indicators

		eEurope 2005 Index
Population (millions)	3,883	**9**
Gross Domestic Product (€ billions)	128	Networked Readiness Index, 2004 22
GDP per capita (€)	32964	
Internet users per 100 inhabitants, 2003	33.0	Group II, totally aligned

Internet indicators		10	Modern online public services (cont.)		
1.01	Home Internet access	9	4.03	Online book search	6
1.02	Internet usage	10	4.04	Government prioritization of ICT	4
1.03	Internet usage intensity	12	4.05	Online tax returns	17
1.04	E-mail	8	4.06	Government ICT promotion	4
1.05	Internet users	14	5.01	Internet access in schools	16
1.06	DSL Internet subscribers	15	5.02	Online learning	7
1.07	ISDN subscribers	16	5.03	Offline electronic learning	7
1.08	Home Internet usage	9	6.01	Online health services	2
1.09	Internet usage at work	7	6.02	Internet usage by the disabled	6
1.10	Internet access in schools	16			
1.11	Households online	12	**Dynamic e-business environment**		**9**
1.12	Personal computers	7	7.01	Online purchases	7
2.01	Employees with Internet access	7	7.02	B2C e-commerce	8
2.02	Business PC	6	8.01	Laws relating to IT	9
2.03	Teleworking usage, 2002/03	10			
2.04	Teleworking intensity	20	**Secure information infrastructure**		**2**
3.01	Residential telephone connection charge	9	9.01	Online privacy	2
3.02	Business telephone monthly subscription	6	9.02	Secure online commerce	4
3.03	Business telephone connection charge	9			
			Broadband		**19**
Modern online public services		**9**	10.01	DSL broadband access	15
4.01	Government online presence segmented	20	10.02	Broadband subscribers	19
4.02	Government online services measured for	8			

Italy

Key indicators		eEurope 2005 Index
Population (millions)	58,018	**14**
Gross Domestic Product (€ billions)	1258	Networked Readiness Index, 2004 45
GDP per capita (€)	21683	
Internet users per 100 inhabitants, 2003	40.9	Group III, somewhat aligned

Internet indicators	**15**	Modern online public services (cont.)	
1.01	Home Internet access	11	4.03	Online book search	8
1.02	Internet usage	12	4.04	Government prioritization of ICT	22
1.03	Internet usage intensity	12	4.05	Online tax returns	17
1.04	E-mail	14	4.06	Government ICT promotion	19
1.05	Internet users	11	5.01	Internet access in schools	23
1.06	DSL Internet subscribers	12	5.02	Online learning	10
1.07	ISDN subscribers	7	5.03	Offline electronic learning	2
1.08	Home Internet usage	11	6.01	Online health services	12
1.09	Internet usage at work	13	6.02	Internet usage by the disabled	13
1.10	Internet access in schools	23			
1.11	Households online	14	**Dynamic e-business environment**	**17**
1.12	Personal computers	13	7.01	Online purchases	12
2.01	Employees with Internet access	13	7.02	B2C e-commerce	11
2.02	Business PC	12	8.01	Laws relating to IT	22
2.03	Teleworking usage, 2002/03	12			
2.04	Teleworking intensity	18	**Secure information infrastructure**	**3**
3.01	Residential telephone connection charge	6	9.01	Online privacy	6
3.02	Business telephone monthly subscription	22	9.02	Secure online commerce	1
3.03	Business telephone connection charge	6			
			Broadband	**17**
Modern online public services	**13**	10.01	DSL broadband access	12
4.01	Government online presence segmented	10	10.02	Broadband subscribers	17
4.02	Government online services measured for	11			

Luxembourg

Key indicators		eEurope 2005 Index	
Population (millions)	0,444		**11**
Gross Domestic Product (€ billions)	22	Networked Readiness Index, 2004	17
GDP per capita (€)	49550		
Internet users per 100 inhabitants, 2003	27.7	Group II toally aligned	

Internet indicators		**7**	Modern online public services (cont.)		
1.01	Home Internet access	7	4.03	Online book search	22
1.02	Internet usage	8	4.04	Government prioritization of ICT	10
1.03	Internet usage intensity	9	4.05	Online tax returns	22
1.04	E-mail	7	4.06	Government ICT promotion	10
1.05	Internet users	16	5.01	Internet access in schools	7
1.06	DSL Internet subscribers	12	5.02	Online learning	7
1.07	ISDN subscribers	1	5.03	Offline electronic learning	2
1.08	Home Internet usage	7	6.01	Online health services	5
1.09	Internet usage at work	11	6.02	Internet usage by the disabled	7
1.10	Internet access in schools	7			
1.11	Households online	9	**Dynamic e-business environment**		**11**
1.12	Personal computers	2	7.01	Online purchases	9
2.01	Employees with Internet access	11	7.02	B2C e-commerce	10
2.02	Business PC	2	8.01	Laws relating to IT	10
2.03	Teleworking usage, 2002/03	18			
2.04	Teleworking intensity	17	**Secure information infrastructure**		**7**
3.01	Residential telephone connection charge	1	9.01	Online privacy	13
3.02	Business telephone monthly subscription	1	9.02	Secure online commerce	3
3.03	Business telephone connection charge	1			
			Broadband		**16**
Modern online public services		**10**	10.01	DSL broadband access	12
4.01	Government online presence segmented	6	10.02	Broadband subscribers	16
4.02	Government online services measured for	20			

Netherlands

Key indicators		eEurope 2005 Index	
Population (millions)	16,105		6
Gross Domestic Product (€ billions)	444	Networked Readiness Index, 2004	16
GDP per capita (€)	27569		
Internet users per 100 inhabitants, 2003	61.4	Group I, global leader	

Internet indicators		1	Modern online public services (cont.)		
1.01	Home Internet access	1	4.03	Online book search	5
1.02	Internet usage	3	4.04	Government prioritization of ICT	7
1.03	Internet usage intensity	5	4.05	Online tax returns	6
1.04	E-mail	2	4.06	Government ICT promotion	17
1.05	Internet users	3	5.01	Internet access in schools	6
1.06	DSL Internet subscribers	3	5.02	Online learning	7
1.07	ISDN subscribers	10	5.03	Offline electronic learning	1
1.08	Home Internet usage	1	6.01	Online health services	3
1.09	Internet usage at work	6	6.02	Internet usage by the disabled	2
1.10	Internet access in schools	6			
1.11	Households online	1	Dynamic e-business environment		8
1.12	Personal computers	4	7.01	Online purchases	4
2.01	Employees with Internet access	6	7.02	B2C e-commerce	7
2.02	Business PC	4	8.01	Laws relating to IT	12
2.03	Teleworking usage, 2002/03	1			
2.04	Teleworking intensity	1	Secure information infrastructure		17
3.01	Residential telephone connection charge	11	9.01	Online privacy	18
3.02	Business telephone monthly subscription	20	9.02	Secure online commerce	15
3.03	Business telephone connection charge	10			
			Broadband		3
Modern online public services		2	10.01	DSL broadband access	3
4.01	Government online presence segmented	2	10.02	Broadband subscribers	6
4.02	Government online services measured for	12			

Portugal

Key indicators   eEurope 2005 Index

Population (millions)	10,336

Gross Domestic Product (€ billions)	129	Networked Readiness Index, 2004	30
GDP per capita (€)	12481		
Internet users per 100 inhabitants, 2003	36.4	Group III somewhat aligned	

Internet indicators		17	Modern online public services (cont.)		
1.01	Home Internet access	16	4.03	Online book search	17
1.02	Internet usage	18	4.04	Government prioritization of ICT	11
1.03	Internet usage intensity	15	4.05	Online tax returns	2
1.04	E-mail	20	4.06	Government ICT promotion	6
1.05	Internet users	12	5.01	Internet access in schools	15
1.06	DSL Internet subscribers	12	5.02	Online learning	16
1.07	ISDN subscribers	13	5.03	Offline electronic learning	14
1.08	Home Internet usage	16	6.01	Online health services	18
1.09	Internet usage at work	21	6.02	Internet usage by the disabled	21
1.10	Internet access in schools	15			
1.11	Households online	18	Dynamic e-business environment		14
1.12	Personal computers	19	7.01	Online purchases	14
2.01	Employees with Internet access	21	7.02	B2C e-commerce	15
2.02	Business PC	16	8.01	Laws relating to IT	14
2.03	Teleworking usage, 2002/03	24			
2.04	Teleworking intensity	20	Secure information infrastructure		11
3.01	Residential telephone connection charge	15	9.01	Online privacy	11
3.02	Business telephone monthly subscription	11	9.02	Secure online commerce	13
3.03	Business telephone connection charge	15			
			Broadband		15
Modern online public services		16	10.01	DSL broadband access	12
4.01	Government online presence segmented	5	10.02	Broadband subscribers	15
4.02	Government online services measured for	14			

Spain

Key indicators		eEurope 2005 Index
Population (millions)	40,409	**13**
Gross Domestic Product (€ billions)	694	Networked Readiness Index, 2004 29
GDP per capita (€)	17174	
Internet users per 100 inhabitants, 2003	29.7	Group III, somewhat aligned

Internet indicators	16	Modern online public services (cont.)	
1.01 Home Internet access	15	4.03 Online book search	16
1.02 Internet usage	15	4.04 Government prioritization of ICT	14
1.03 Internet usage intensity	10	4.05 Online tax returns	5
1.04 E-mail	15	4.06 Government ICT promotion	20
1.05 Internet users	15	5.01 Internet access in schools	18
1.06 DSL Internet subscribers	9	5.02 Online learning	13
1.07 ISDN subscribers	14	5.03 Offline electronic learning	5
1.08 Home Internet usage	15	6.01 Online health services	14
1.09 Internet usage at work	18	6.02 Internet usage by the disabled	15
1.10 Internet access in schools	18		
1.11 Households online	20	**Dynamic e-business environment**	**15**
1.12 Personal computers	15	7.01 Online purchases	16
2.01 Employees with Internet access	18	7.02 B2C e-commerce	13
2.02 Business PC	17	8.01 Laws relating to IT	16
2.03 Teleworking usage, 2002/03	20		
2.04 Teleworking intensity	23	**Secure information infrastructure**	**6**
3.01 Residential telephone connection charge	14	9.01 Online privacy	5
3.02 Business telephone monthly subscription	5	9.02 Secure online commerce	9
3.03 Business telephone connection charge	14		
		Broadband	**11**
Modern online public services	**14**	10.01 DSL broadband access	9
4.01 Government online presence segmented	6	10.02 Broadband subscribers	14
4.02 Government online services measured for	14		

Sweden

Key indicators		eEurope 2005 Index	
Population (millions)	8,909		3
Gross Domestic Product (€ billions)	255	Networked Readiness Index, 2004	6
GDP per capita (€)	28623		
Internet users per 100 inhabitants, 2003	58.4	Group I, global leader	

Internet indicators		3
1.01	Home Internet access	3
1.02	Internet usage	2
1.03	Internet usage intensity	3
1.04	E-mail	2
1.05	Internet users	4
1.06	DSL Internet subscribers	3
1.07	ISDN subscribers	12
1.08	Home Internet usage	3
1.09	Internet usage at work	3
1.10	Internet access in schools	2
1.11	Households online	3
1.12	Personal computers	1
2.01	Employees with Internet access	3
2.02	Business PC	1
2.03	Teleworking usage, 2002/03	4
2.04	Teleworking intensity	2
3.01	Residential telephone connection charge	12
3.02	Business telephone monthly subscription	20
3.03	Business telephone connection charge	11

Modern online public services		5
4.01	Government online presence segmented	20
4.02	Government online services measured for	5

Modern online public services (cont.)		
4.03	Online book search	10
4.04	Government prioritization of ICT	5
4.05	Online tax returns	7
4.06	Government ICT promotion	11
5.01	Internet access in schools	2
5.02	Online learning	2
5.03	Offline electronic learning	19
6.01	Online health services	6
6.02	Internet usage by the disabled	3

Dynamic e-business environment		3
7.01	Online purchases	2
7.02	B2C e-commerce	1
8.01	Laws relating to IT	6

Secure information infrastructure		15
9.01	Online privacy	21
9.02	Secure online commerce	11

Broadband		4
10.01	DSL broadband access	3
10.02	Broadband subscribers	8

United Kingdom

Key indicators		eEurope 2005 Index
Population (millions)	60,114	**2**
Gross Domestic Product (€ billions)	1660	Networked Readiness Index, 2004 12
GDP per capita (€)	27614	
Internet users per 100 inhabitants, 2003	46.0	Group I, global leader

Internet indicators		5	Modern online public services (cont.)		
1.01	Home Internet access	5	4.03	Online book search	3
1.02	Internet usage	5	4.04	Government prioritization of ICT	6
1.03	Internet usage intensity	2	4.05	Online tax returns	10
1.04	E-mail	4	4.06	Government ICT promotion	9
1.05	Internet users	7	5.01	Internet access in schools	8
1.06	DSL Internet subscribers	6	5.02	Online learning	3
1.07	ISDN subscribers	17	5.03	Offline electronic learning	11
1.08	Home Internet usage	5	6.01	Online health services	4
1.09	Internet usage at work	4	6.02	Internet usage by the disabled	4
1.10	Internet access in schools	8			
1.11	Households online	7	Dynamic e-business environment		1
1.12	Personal computers	8	7.01	Online purchases	3
2.01	Employees with Internet access	4	7.02	B2C e-commerce	2
2.02	Business PC	7	8.01	Laws relating to IT	3
2.03	Teleworking usage, 2002/03	5			
2.04	Teleworking intensity	6	Secure information infrastructure		1
3.01	Residential telephone connection charge	10	9.01	Online privacy	3
3.02	Business telephone monthly subscription	12	9.02	Secure online commerce	2
3.03	Business telephone connection charge	17			
			Broadband		7
Modern online public services		3	10.01	DSL broadband access	6
4.01	Government online presence segmented	11	10.02	Broadband subscribers	12
4.02	Government online services measured for	4			

Part 3: Data Tables

1.01 Home Internet access, 2002/3

Percentage of individuals having access to the Internet at home

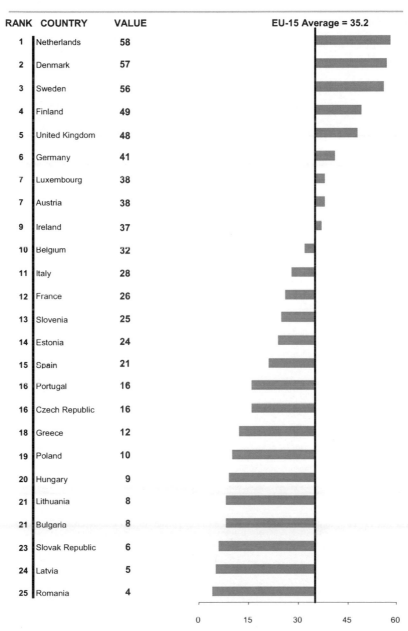

RANK	COUNTRY	VALUE
1	Netherlands	58
2	Denmark	57
3	Sweden	56
4	Finland	49
5	United Kingdom	48
6	Germany	41
7	Luxembourg	38
7	Austria	38
9	Ireland	37
10	Belgium	32
11	Italy	28
12	France	26
13	Slovenia	25
14	Estonia	24
15	Spain	21
16	Portugal	16
16	Czech Republic	16
18	Greece	12
19	Poland	10
20	Hungary	9
21	Lithuania	8
21	Bulgaria	8
23	Slovak Republic	6
24	Latvia	5
25	Romania	4

EU-15 Average = 35.2

Source: Sibis 2002/3

1.02 Internet usage, 2002/3

Regular and occasional Internet usage by Individuals

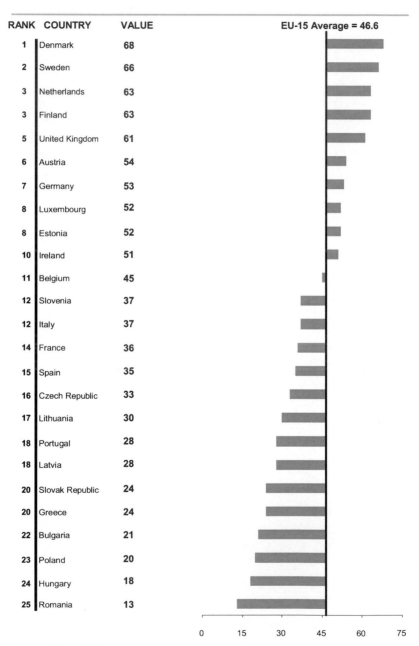

RANK	COUNTRY	VALUE
1	Denmark	68
2	Sweden	66
3	Netherlands	63
3	Finland	63
5	United Kingdom	61
6	Austria	54
7	Germany	53
8	Luxembourg	52
8	Estonia	52
10	Ireland	51
11	Belgium	45
12	Slovenia	37
12	Italy	37
14	France	36
15	Spain	35
16	Czech Republic	33
17	Lithuania	30
18	Portugal	28
18	Latvia	28
20	Slovak Republic	24
20	Greece	24
22	Bulgaria	21
23	Poland	20
24	Hungary	18
25	Romania	13

EU-15 Average = 46.6

Source: Sibis 2002/3

1.03 Internet usage intensity, 2002/3

Percentage of people spending more than six hours per week on the Internet

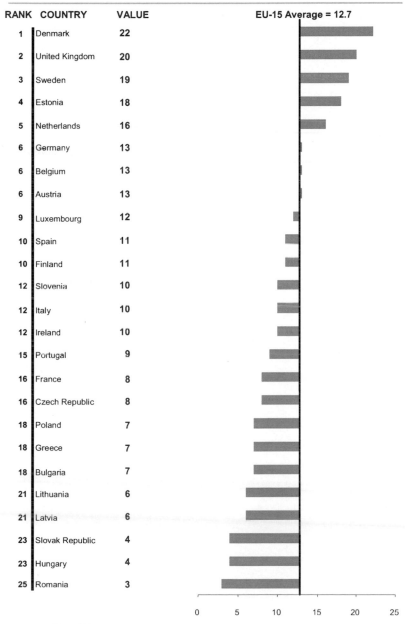

RANK	COUNTRY	VALUE	EU-15 Average = 12.7
1	Denmark	22	
2	United Kingdom	20	
3	Sweden	19	
4	Estonia	18	
5	Netherlands	16	
6	Germany	13	
6	Belgium	13	
6	Austria	13	
9	Luxembourg	12	
10	Spain	11	
10	Finland	11	
12	Slovenia	10	
12	Italy	10	
12	Ireland	10	
15	Portugal	9	
16	France	8	
16	Czech Republic	8	
18	Poland	7	
18	Greece	7	
18	Bulgaria	7	
21	Lithuania	6	
21	Latvia	6	
23	Slovak Republic	4	
23	Hungary	4	
25	Romania	3	

Source: Sibis 2002/3

1.04 E-mail, 2002/3

Percentage of individuals having sent an e-mail in the last four weeks

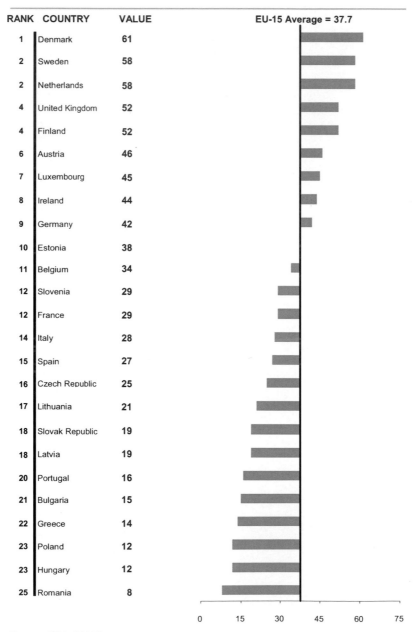

RANK	COUNTRY	VALUE
1	Denmark	61
2	Sweden	58
2	Netherlands	58
4	United Kingdom	52
4	Finland	52
6	Austria	46
7	Luxembourg	45
8	Ireland	44
9	Germany	42
10	Estonia	38
11	Belgium	34
12	Slovenia	29
12	France	29
14	Italy	28
15	Spain	27
16	Czech Republic	25
17	Lithuania	21
18	Slovak Republic	19
18	Latvia	19
20	Portugal	16
21	Bulgaria	15
22	Greece	14
23	Poland	12
23	Hungary	12
25	Romania	8

EU-15 Average = 37.7

Source: Sibis 2002/3

1.05 Internet users, 2003

Internet users per 100 inhabitants

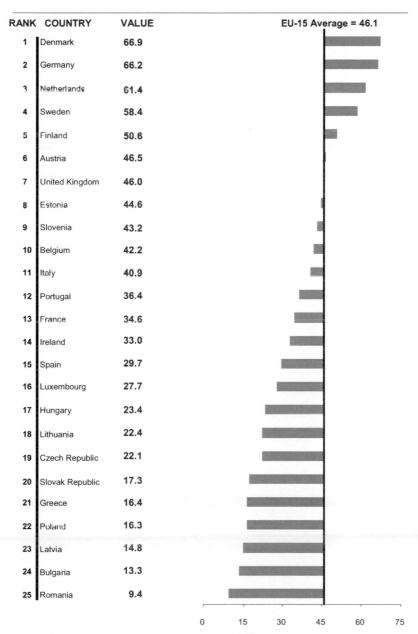

RANK	COUNTRY	VALUE
1	Denmark	66.9
2	Germany	66.2
3	Netherlands	61.4
4	Sweden	58.4
5	Finland	50.6
6	Austria	46.5
7	United Kingdom	46.0
8	Estonia	44.6
9	Slovenia	43.2
10	Belgium	42.2
11	Italy	40.9
12	Portugal	36.4
13	France	34.6
14	Ireland	33.0
15	Spain	29.7
16	Luxembourg	27.7
17	Hungary	23.4
18	Lithuania	22.4
19	Czech Republic	22.1
20	Slovak Republic	17.3
21	Greece	16.4
22	Poland	16.3
23	Latvia	14.8
24	Bulgaria	13.3
25	Romania	9.4

EU-15 Average = 46.1

Source: Euromonitor/International Telecommunication Union, 2003

1.06 DSL Internet subscribers, 2004

DSL Internet subscribers per 100 inhabitants

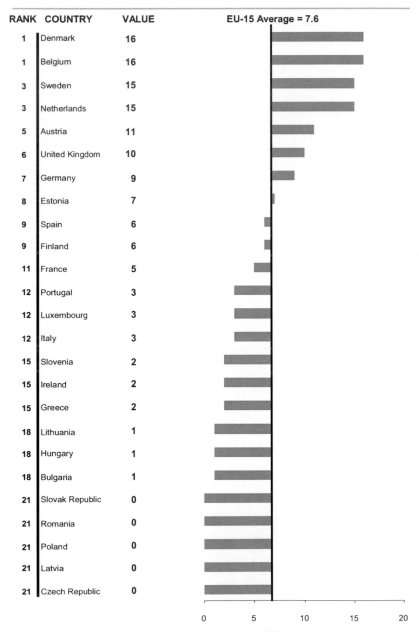

RANK	COUNTRY	VALUE	EU-15 Average = 7.6
1	Denmark	16	
1	Belgium	16	
3	Sweden	15	
3	Netherlands	15	
5	Austria	11	
6	United Kingdom	10	
7	Germany	9	
8	Estonia	7	
9	Spain	6	
9	Finland	6	
11	France	5	
12	Portugal	3	
12	Luxembourg	3	
12	Italy	3	
15	Slovenia	2	
15	Ireland	2	
15	Greece	2	
18	Lithuania	1	
18	Hungary	1	
18	Bulgaria	1	
21	Slovak Republic	0	
21	Romania	0	
21	Poland	0	
21	Latvia	0	
21	Czech Republic	0	

Source: International Telecommunication Union, June 2004

1.07 ISDN subscribers, 2003

ISDN subscribers per 100 inhabitants

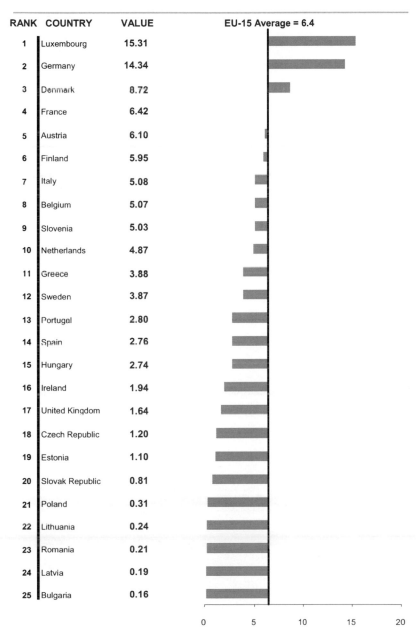

RANK	COUNTRY	VALUE	EU-15 Average = 6.4
1	Luxembourg	15.31	
2	Germany	14.34	
3	Denmark	8.72	
4	France	6.42	
5	Austria	6.10	
6	Finland	5.95	
7	Italy	5.08	
8	Belgium	5.07	
9	Slovenia	5.03	
10	Netherlands	4.87	
11	Greece	3.88	
12	Sweden	3.87	
13	Portugal	2.80	
14	Spain	2.76	
15	Hungary	2.74	
16	Ireland	1.94	
17	United Kingdom	1.64	
18	Czech Republic	1.20	
19	Estonia	1.10	
20	Slovak Republic	0.81	
21	Poland	0.31	
22	Lithuania	0.24	
23	Romania	0.21	
24	Latvia	0.19	
25	Bulgaria	0.16	

Source: Euromonitor/ International Telecommunication Union, 2003

1.08 Home Internet usage, 2002/3

Percentage of individuals using the Internet at home

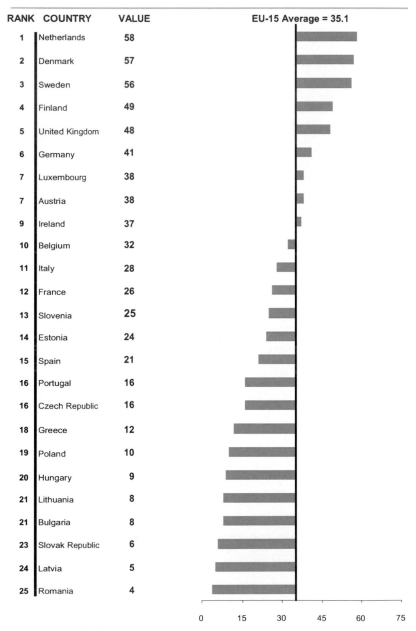

RANK	COUNTRY	VALUE	EU-15 Average = 35.1
1	Netherlands	58	
2	Denmark	57	
3	Sweden	56	
4	Finland	49	
5	United Kingdom	48	
6	Germany	41	
7	Luxembourg	38	
7	Austria	38	
9	Ireland	37	
10	Belgium	32	
11	Italy	28	
12	France	26	
13	Slovenia	25	
14	Estonia	24	
15	Spain	21	
16	Portugal	16	
16	Czech Republic	16	
18	Greece	12	
19	Poland	10	
20	Hungary	9	
21	Lithuania	8	
21	Bulgaria	8	
23	Slovak Republic	6	
24	Latvia	5	
25	Romania	4	

Source: Sibis 2002/3

1.09 Internet usage at work, 2002/3

Percentage of individuals using the Internet at work

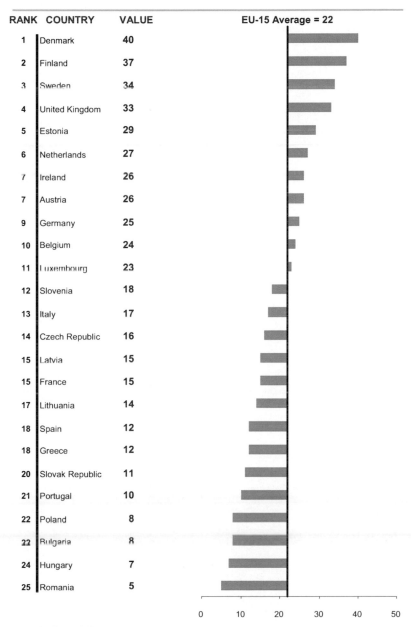

RANK	COUNTRY	VALUE
1	Denmark	40
2	Finland	37
3	Sweden	34
4	United Kingdom	33
5	Estonia	29
6	Netherlands	27
7	Ireland	26
7	Austria	26
9	Germany	25
10	Belgium	24
11	Luxembourg	23
12	Slovenia	18
13	Italy	17
14	Czech Republic	16
15	Latvia	15
15	France	15
17	Lithuania	14
18	Spain	12
18	Greece	12
20	Slovak Republic	11
21	Portugal	10
22	Poland	8
22	Bulgaria	8
24	Hungary	7
25	Romania	5

EU-15 Average = 22

Source: Sibis 2002/3

1.10 Internet access in schools, 2004

Internet access in schools is (1- very limited, 7 - pervasive – most children have frequent access)

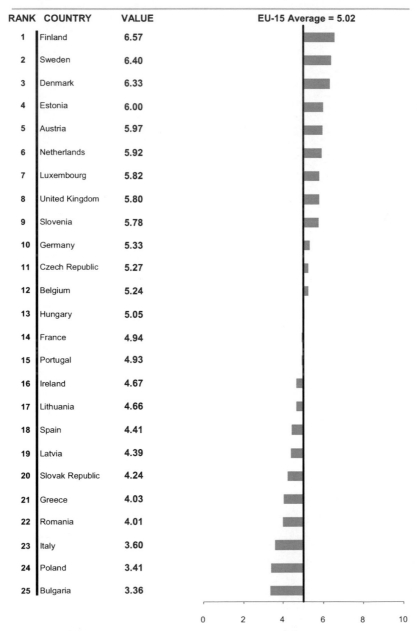

RANK	COUNTRY	VALUE
1	Finland	6.57
2	Sweden	6.40
3	Denmark	6.33
4	Estonia	6.00
5	Austria	5.97
6	Netherlands	5.92
7	Luxembourg	5.82
8	United Kingdom	5.80
9	Slovenia	5.78
10	Germany	5.33
11	Czech Republic	5.27
12	Belgium	5.24
13	Hungary	5.05
14	France	4.94
15	Portugal	4.93
16	Ireland	4.67
17	Lithuania	4.66
18	Spain	4.41
19	Latvia	4.39
20	Slovak Republic	4.24
21	Greece	4.03
22	Romania	4.01
23	Italy	3.60
24	Poland	3.41
25	Bulgaria	3.36

EU-15 Average = 5.02

Source: World Economic Forum, Executive Opinion Survey 2004

1.11 Households online, 2003

Percentage of all households online

RANK	COUNTRY	VALUE	EU-15 Average = 39.5
1	Netherlands	58.6	
2	Denmark	54.9	
3	Sweden	53.4	
4	Estonia	51.6	
5	Finland	51.2	
6	Germany	48.5	
7	United Kingdom	42.2	
8	Austria	41.3	
9	Luxembourg	39.4	
10	Belgium	36.6	
11	France	35.8	
12	Ireland	34.4	
13	Lithuania	33.7	
14	Italy	33.0	
15	Slovenia	32.6	
16	Slovak Republic	30.0	
17	Greece	29.4	
18	Portugal	28.6	
19	Czech Republic	24.6	
20	Spain	23.6	
21	Poland	21.2	
22	Latvia	20.3	
23	Bulgaria	17.7	
24	Hungary	14.9	
25	Romania	8.7	

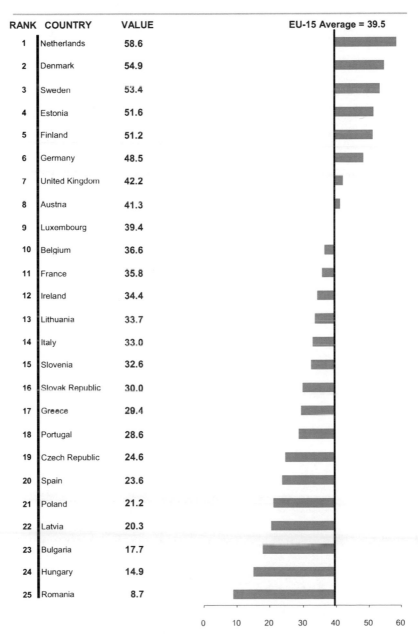

Source: Euromonitor/Jupiter, 2003

1.12 Personal computers, 2002

Personal computer penetration per 100 inhabitants

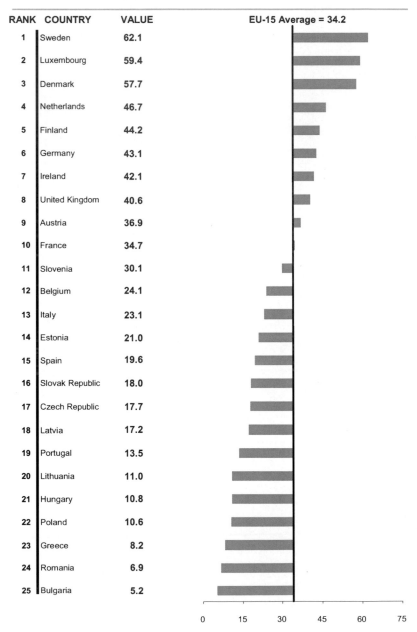

RANK	COUNTRY	VALUE	EU-15 Average = 34.2
1	Sweden	62.1	
2	Luxembourg	59.4	
3	Denmark	57.7	
4	Netherlands	46.7	
5	Finland	44.2	
6	Germany	43.1	
7	Ireland	42.1	
8	United Kingdom	40.6	
9	Austria	36.9	
10	France	34.7	
11	Slovenia	30.1	
12	Belgium	24.1	
13	Italy	23.1	
14	Estonia	21.0	
15	Spain	19.6	
16	Slovak Republic	18.0	
17	Czech Republic	17.7	
18	Latvia	17.2	
19	Portugal	13.5	
20	Lithuania	11.0	
21	Hungary	10.8	
22	Poland	10.6	
23	Greece	8.2	
24	Romania	6.9	
25	Bulgaria	5.2	

Source: International Telecommunication Union, 2002

2.01 Employees with Internet access, 2002/3

Employees with Internet access at the workplace

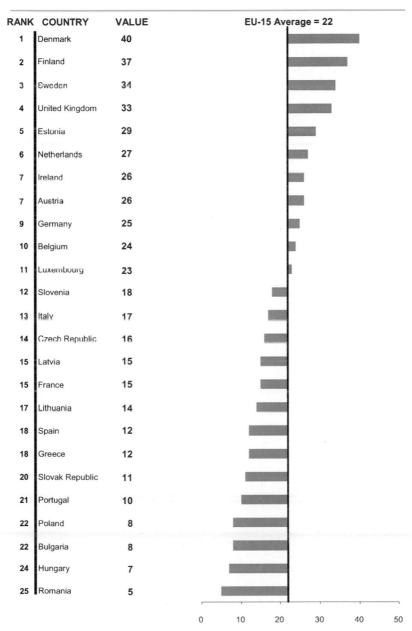

RANK	COUNTRY	VALUE
1	Denmark	40
2	Finland	37
3	Sweden	34
4	United Kingdom	33
5	Estonia	29
6	Netherlands	27
7	Ireland	26
7	Austria	26
9	Germany	25
10	Belgium	24
11	Luxembourg	23
12	Slovenia	18
13	Italy	17
14	Czech Republic	16
15	Latvia	15
15	France	15
17	Lithuania	14
18	Spain	12
18	Greece	12
20	Slovak Republic	11
21	Portugal	10
22	Poland	8
22	Bulgaria	8
24	Hungary	7
25	Romania	5

EU-15 Average = 22

Source: Sibis 2002/3

2.02 Business PCs, 2002

Business PC installed base per 100 inhabitants

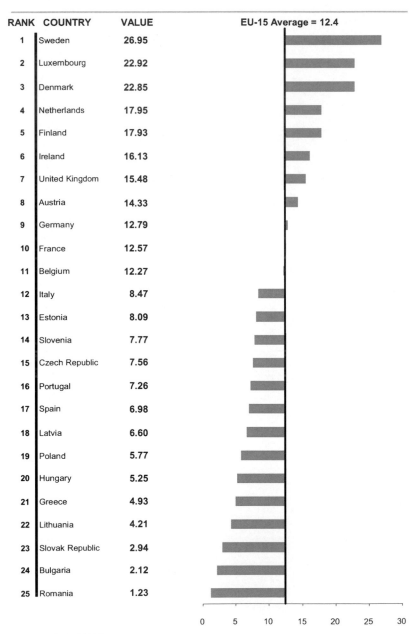

RANK	COUNTRY	VALUE	EU-15 Average = 12.4
1	Sweden	26.95	
2	Luxembourg	22.92	
3	Denmark	22.85	
4	Netherlands	17.95	
5	Finland	17.93	
6	Ireland	16.13	
7	United Kingdom	15.48	
8	Austria	14.33	
9	Germany	12.79	
10	France	12.57	
11	Belgium	12.27	
12	Italy	8.47	
13	Estonia	8.09	
14	Slovenia	7.77	
15	Czech Republic	7.56	
16	Portugal	7.26	
17	Spain	6.98	
18	Latvia	6.60	
19	Poland	5.77	
20	Hungary	5.25	
21	Greece	4.93	
22	Lithuania	4.21	
23	Slovak Republic	2.94	
24	Bulgaria	2.12	
25	Romania	1.23	

Source: Sibis 2002/3

2.03 Teleworking usage, 2002/3

Share of employed population teleworking

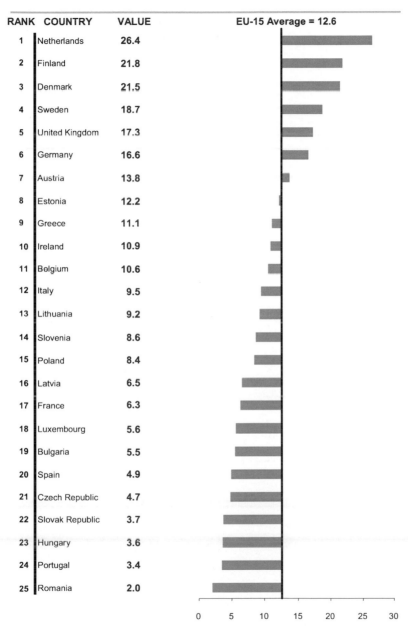

RANK	COUNTRY	VALUE
1	Netherlands	26.4
2	Finland	21.8
3	Denmark	21.5
4	Sweden	18.7
5	United Kingdom	17.3
6	Germany	16.6
7	Austria	13.8
8	Estonia	12.2
9	Greece	11.1
10	Ireland	10.9
11	Belgium	10.6
12	Italy	9.5
13	Lithuania	9.2
14	Slovenia	8.6
15	Poland	8.4
16	Latvia	6.5
17	France	6.3
18	Luxembourg	5.6
19	Bulgaria	5.5
20	Spain	4.9
21	Czech Republic	4.7
22	Slovak Republic	3.7
23	Hungary	3.6
24	Portugal	3.4
25	Romania	2.0

EU-15 Average = 12.6

Source: Sibis 2002/3

2.04 Teleworking intensity, 2002/3

Percentage of people who spend more than one day per week teleworking

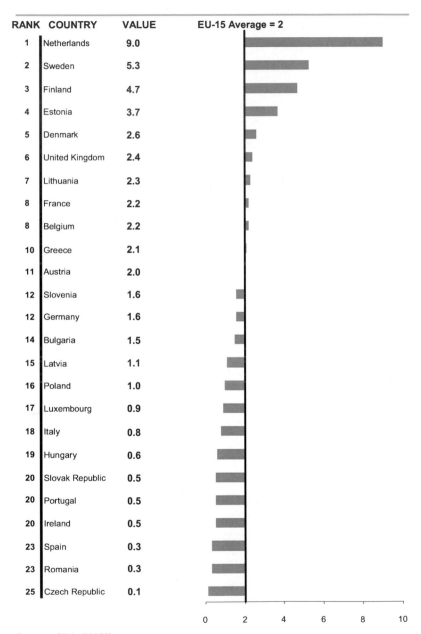

RANK	COUNTRY	VALUE
1	Netherlands	9.0
2	Sweden	5.3
3	Finland	4.7
4	Estonia	3.7
5	Denmark	2.6
6	United Kingdom	2.4
7	Lithuania	2.3
8	France	2.2
8	Belgium	2.2
10	Greece	2.1
11	Austria	2.0
12	Slovenia	1.6
12	Germany	1.6
14	Bulgaria	1.5
15	Latvia	1.1
16	Poland	1.0
17	Luxembourg	0.9
18	Italy	0.8
19	Hungary	0.6
20	Slovak Republic	0.5
20	Portugal	0.5
20	Ireland	0.5
23	Spain	0.3
23	Romania	0.3
25	Czech Republic	0.1

EU-15 Average = 2

Source: Sibis 2002/3

3.01 Residential telephone connection charge, 2002

Residential telephone connection charge (US$) (adjusted against GDP per capita / 1000)

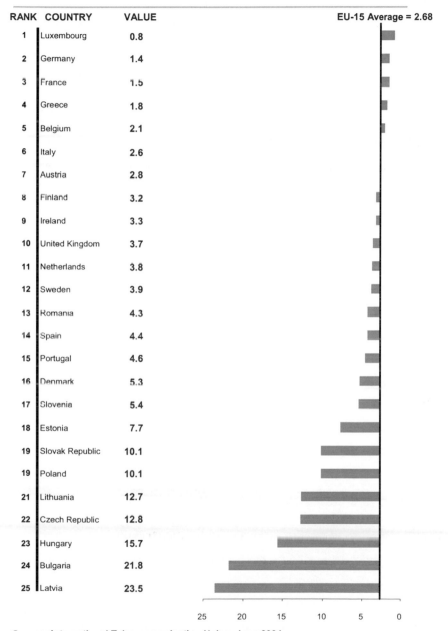

RANK	COUNTRY	VALUE
1	Luxembourg	0.8
2	Germany	1.4
3	France	1.5
4	Greece	1.8
5	Belgium	2.1
6	Italy	2.6
7	Austria	2.8
8	Finland	3.2
9	Ireland	3.3
10	United Kingdom	3.7
11	Netherlands	3.8
12	Sweden	3.9
13	Romania	4.3
14	Spain	4.4
15	Portugal	4.6
16	Denmark	5.3
17	Slovenia	5.4
18	Estonia	7.7
19	Slovak Republic	10.1
19	Poland	10.1
21	Lithuania	12.7
22	Czech Republic	12.8
23	Hungary	15.7
24	Bulgaria	21.8
25	Latvia	23.5

EU-15 Average = 2.68

Source: International Telecommunication Union, June 2004

3.02 Business telephone monthly subscription, 2002/3

Business monthly telephone subscription charge (adjusted against GDP per capita / 1000)

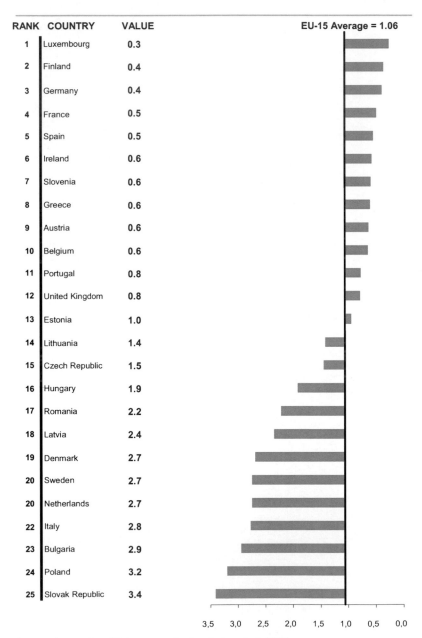

RANK	COUNTRY	VALUE
1	Luxembourg	0.3
2	Finland	0.4
3	Germany	0.4
4	France	0.5
5	Spain	0.5
6	Ireland	0.6
7	Slovenia	0.6
8	Greece	0.6
9	Austria	0.6
10	Belgium	0.6
11	Portugal	0.8
12	United Kingdom	0.8
13	Estonia	1.0
14	Lithuania	1.4
15	Czech Republic	1.5
16	Hungary	1.9
17	Romania	2.2
18	Latvia	2.4
19	Denmark	2.7
20	Sweden	2.7
20	Netherlands	2.7
22	Italy	2.8
23	Bulgaria	2.9
24	Poland	3.2
25	Slovak Republic	3.4

EU-15 Average = 1.06

Source: International Telecommunication Union, June 2004

3.03 Business telephone connection charge, 2002/3

Business monthly telephone subscription charge (adjusted against GDP per capita / 1000)

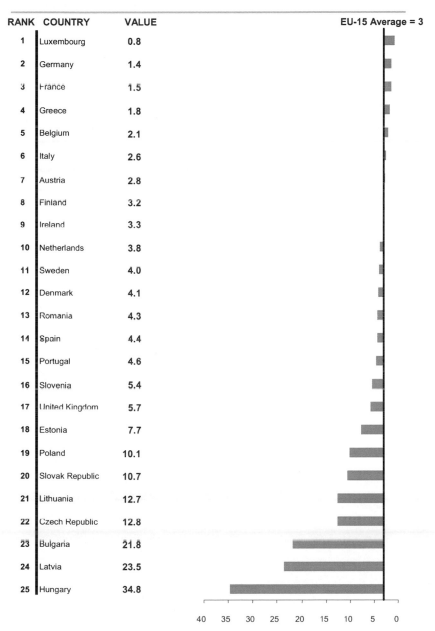

RANK	COUNTRY	VALUE
1	Luxembourg	0.8
2	Germany	1.4
3	France	1.5
4	Greece	1.8
5	Belgium	2.1
6	Italy	2.6
7	Austria	2.8
8	Finland	3.2
9	Ireland	3.3
10	Netherlands	3.8
11	Sweden	4.0
12	Denmark	4.1
13	Romania	4.3
14	Spain	4.4
15	Portugal	4.6
16	Slovenia	5.4
17	United Kingdom	5.7
18	Estonia	7.7
19	Poland	10.1
20	Slovak Republic	10.7
21	Lithuania	12.7
22	Czech Republic	12.8
23	Bulgaria	21.8
24	Latvia	23.5
25	Hungary	34.8

EU-15 Average = 3

Source: International Telecommunication Union, June 2004

4.01 Government online presence, 2003

Government online presence segmented into the executive, legislative, judiciary,
ministries and embassies branches

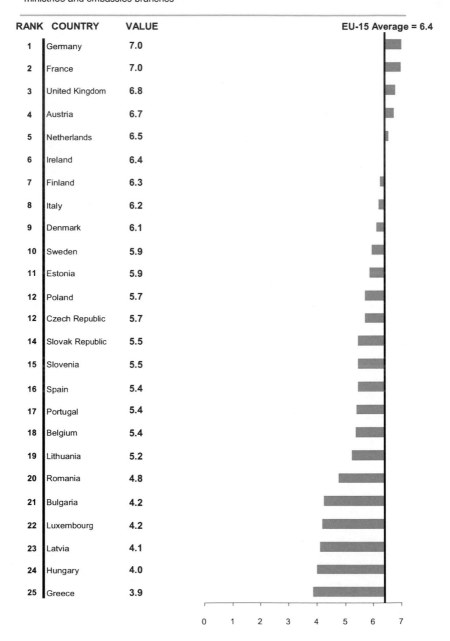

RANK	COUNTRY	VALUE
1	Germany	7.0
2	France	7.0
3	United Kingdom	6.8
4	Austria	6.7
5	Netherlands	6.5
6	Ireland	6.4
7	Finland	6.3
8	Italy	6.2
9	Denmark	6.1
10	Sweden	5.9
11	Estonia	5.9
12	Poland	5.7
12	Czech Republic	5.7
14	Slovak Republic	5.5
15	Slovenia	5.5
16	Spain	5.4
17	Portugal	5.4
18	Belgium	5.4
19	Lithuania	5.2
20	Romania	4.8
21	Bulgaria	4.2
22	Luxembourg	4.2
23	Latvia	4.1
24	Hungary	4.0
25	Greece	3.9

EU-15 Average = 6.4

Source: World Economic Forum, 2003

4.02 Government online services, 2003

Government online services as measured by personal tax, car registration, passport, business permit and e-procurement

RANK	COUNTRY	VALUE	EU-15 Average = 4.08
1	Denmark	5.3	
2	Germany	4.9	
3	Austria	4.7	
4	United Kingdom	4.6	
5	Sweden	4.5	
6	France	4.3	
7	Estonia	4.1	
8	Ireland	3.9	
9	Finland	3.8	
10	Belgium	3.7	
11	Italy	3.5	
12	Romania	3.1	
12	Netherlands	3.1	
14	Spain	3.0	
14	Portugal	3.0	
16	Slovak Republic	2.9	
16	Hungary	2.9	
18	Czech Republic	2.7	
19	Greece	2.6	
20	Slovenia	2.5	
20	Luxembourg	2.5	
20	Bulgaria	2.5	
23	Latvia	2.3	
24	Poland	2.2	
24	Lithuania	2.2	

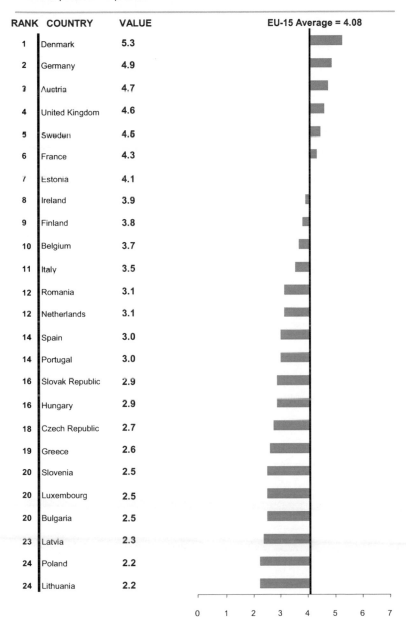

Source: World Economic Forum, 2003

4.03 Online book search, 2002/3

Percentage of people that have tried to use the Internet to search for books in public libraries

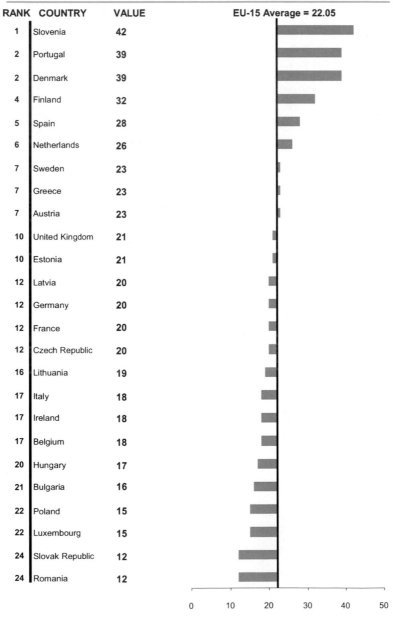

RANK	COUNTRY	VALUE
1	Slovenia	42
2	Portugal	39
2	Denmark	39
4	Finland	32
5	Spain	28
6	Netherlands	26
7	Sweden	23
7	Greece	23
7	Austria	23
10	United Kingdom	21
10	Estonia	21
12	Latvia	20
12	Germany	20
12	France	20
12	Czech Republic	20
16	Lithuania	19
17	Italy	18
17	Ireland	18
17	Belgium	18
20	Hungary	17
21	Bulgaria	16
22	Poland	15
22	Luxembourg	15
24	Slovak Republic	12
24	Romania	12

EU-15 Average = 22.05

Source: Sibis 2002/3

4.04 Government prioritization of ICT, 2004

ICT are an overall priority for the government: 1 - strongly disagree, 7 - strongly agree

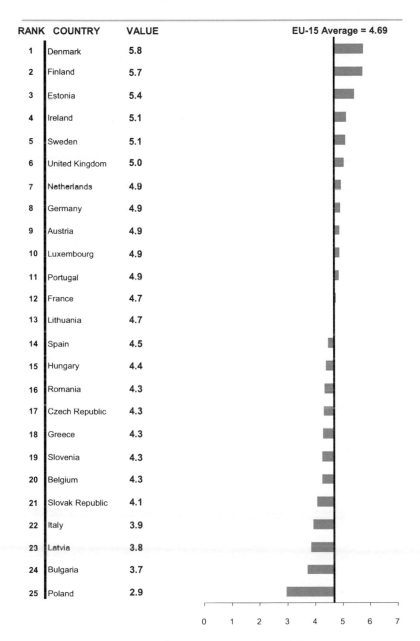

RANK	COUNTRY	VALUE
1	Denmark	5.8
2	Finland	5.7
3	Estonia	5.4
4	Ireland	5.1
5	Sweden	5.1
6	United Kingdom	5.0
7	Netherlands	4.9
8	Germany	4.9
9	Austria	4.9
10	Luxembourg	4.9
11	Portugal	4.9
12	France	4.7
13	Lithuania	4.7
14	Spain	4.5
15	Hungary	4.4
16	Romania	4.3
17	Czech Republic	4.3
18	Greece	4.3
19	Slovenia	4.3
20	Belgium	4.3
21	Slovak Republic	4.1
22	Italy	3.9
23	Latvia	3.8
24	Bulgaria	3.7
25	Poland	2.9

EU-15 Average = 4.69

Source: World Economic Forum Executive Opinion Survey, 2004

4.05 Online tax returns, 2002/3

Percent people that have tried to use the Internet to fill the income tax return / tax declaration

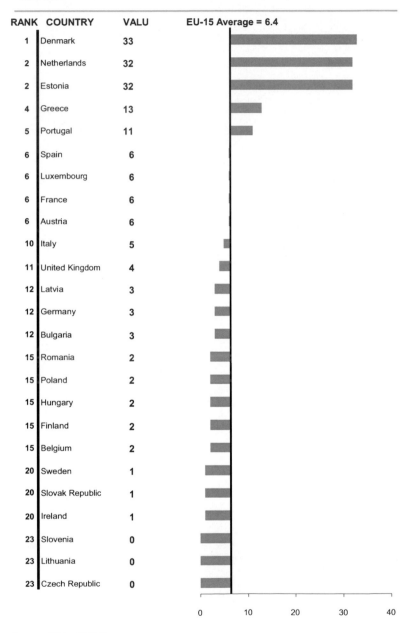

RANK	COUNTRY	VALU
1	Denmark	33
2	Netherlands	32
2	Estonia	32
4	Greece	13
5	Portugal	11
6	Spain	6
6	Luxembourg	6
6	France	6
6	Austria	6
10	Italy	5
11	United Kingdom	4
12	Latvia	3
12	Germany	3
12	Bulgaria	3
15	Romania	2
15	Poland	2
15	Hungary	2
15	Finland	2
15	Belgium	2
20	Sweden	1
20	Slovak Republic	1
20	Ireland	1
23	Slovenia	0
23	Lithuania	0
23	Czech Republic	0

EU-15 Average = 6.4

Source: Sibis, 2002/3

4.06 Government ICT promotion, 2004

Government programmes promoting the use of ICT are: 1- not very successful, 7 - highly successful

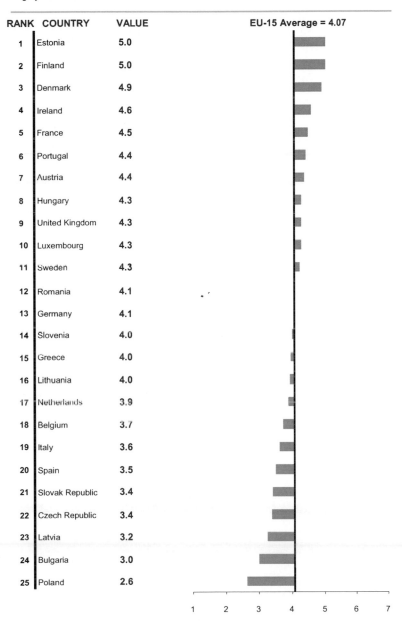

RANK	COUNTRY	VALUE	EU-15 Average = 4.07
1	Estonia	5.0	
2	Finland	5.0	
3	Denmark	4.9	
4	Ireland	4.6	
5	France	4.5	
6	Portugal	4.4	
7	Austria	4.4	
8	Hungary	4.3	
9	United Kingdom	4.3	
10	Luxembourg	4.3	
11	Sweden	4.3	
12	Romania	4.1	
13	Germany	4.1	
14	Slovenia	4.0	
15	Greece	4.0	
16	Lithuania	4.0	
17	Netherlands	3.9	
18	Belgium	3.7	
19	Italy	3.6	
20	Spain	3.5	
21	Slovak Republic	3.4	
22	Czech Republic	3.4	
23	Latvia	3.2	
24	Bulgaria	3.0	
25	Poland	2.6	

Source: World Economic Forum Executive Opinion Survey, 2004

5.01 Internet access in schools, 2004

Internet access in schools is (1- very limited, 7 - pervasive – most children have frequent access)

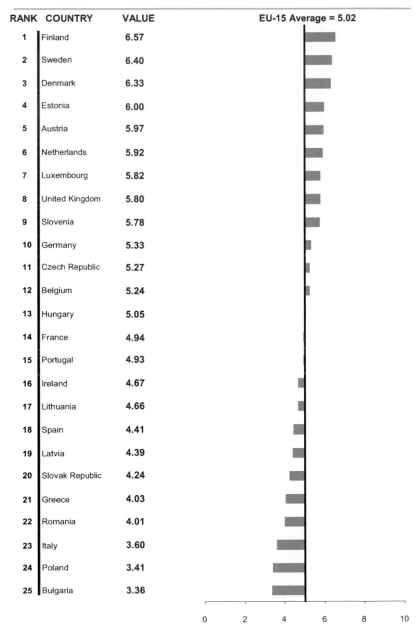

RANK	COUNTRY	VALUE	EU-15 Average = 5.02
1	Finland	6.57	
2	Sweden	6.40	
3	Denmark	6.33	
4	Estonia	6.00	
5	Austria	5.97	
6	Netherlands	5.92	
7	Luxembourg	5.82	
8	United Kingdom	5.80	
9	Slovenia	5.78	
10	Germany	5.33	
11	Czech Republic	5.27	
12	Belgium	5.24	
13	Hungary	5.05	
14	France	4.94	
15	Portugal	4.93	
16	Ireland	4.67	
17	Lithuania	4.66	
18	Spain	4.41	
19	Latvia	4.39	
20	Slovak Republic	4.24	
21	Greece	4.03	
22	Romania	4.01	
23	Italy	3.60	
24	Poland	3.41	
25	Bulgaria	3.36	

Source: World Economic Forum, Executive Opinion Survey 2004

5.02 Online learning, 2002

Share of employed population who used online electronic learning material for work-related learning

RANK	COUNTRY	VALUE	
1	Finland	16	
2	Sweden	14	
3	United Kingdom	13	
3	Germany	13	
5	Denmark	12	
6	Austria	10	
7	Netherlands	9	
7	Luxembourg	9	
7	Ireland	9	
10	Lithuania	8	
10	Italy	8	
10	Estonia	8	
13	Spain	7	
13	Belgium	7	
15	Czech Republic	6	
16	Portugal	5	
16	Latvia	5	
18	Slovenia	4	
18	Slovak Republic	4	
18	Romania	4	
21	Hungary	3	
21	France	3	
23	Greece	2	
23	Bulgaria	2	
25	Poland	1	

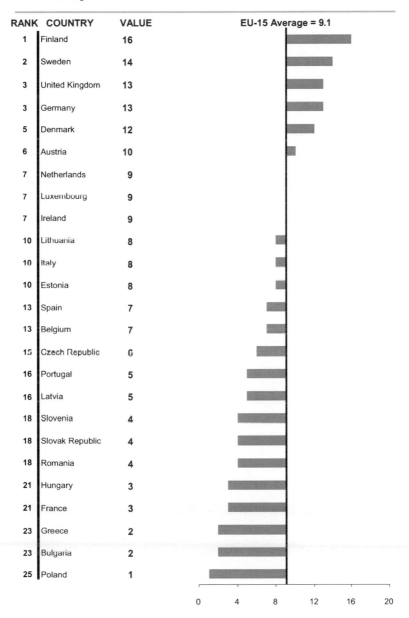

EU-15 Average = 9.1

0   4   8   12   16   20

Source: Sibis, 2002/3

5.03 Offline electronic learning, 2002/3

Share of employed population who used offline electronic learning material for work-related learning

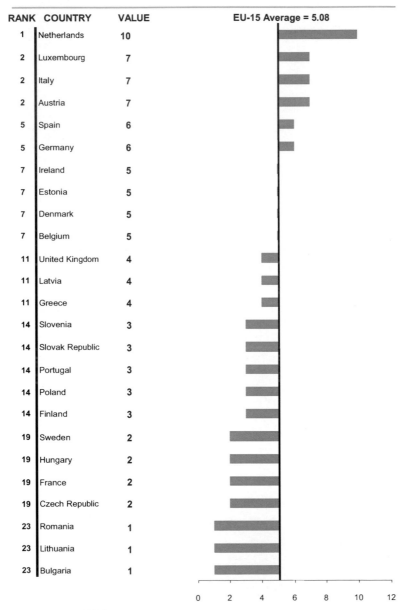

RANK	COUNTRY	VALUE
1	Netherlands	10
2	Luxembourg	7
2	Italy	7
2	Austria	7
5	Spain	6
5	Germany	6
7	Ireland	5
7	Estonia	5
7	Denmark	5
7	Belgium	5
11	United Kingdom	4
11	Latvia	4
11	Greece	4
14	Slovenia	3
14	Slovak Republic	3
14	Portugal	3
14	Poland	3
14	Finland	3
19	Sweden	2
19	Hungary	2
19	France	2
19	Czech Republic	2
23	Romania	1
23	Lithuania	1
23	Bulgaria	1

EU-15 Average = 5.08

Source: Sibis, 2002/3

6.01 Online health searches, 2002/3

Percentage of individuals using Internet effecting online searches for health-related information in the last 12 months

RANK	COUNTRY	VALUE	EU-15 Average = 19.7
1	Denmark	35	
2	Ireland	32	
3	Netherlands	31	
4	United Kingdom	30	
5	Luxembourg	26	
6	Sweden	24	
6	Germany	24	
8	Finland	22	
9	Estonia	20	
9	Belgium	20	
9	Austria	20	
12	Italy	14	
12	Czech Republic	14	
14	Spain	13	
14	Slovenia	13	
14	Slovak Republic	13	
17	Lithuania	12	
18	Portugal	11	
18	France	11	
20	Latvia	9	
21	Greece	8	
22	Poland	7	
22	Hungary	7	
24	Romania	6	
24	Bulgaria	6	

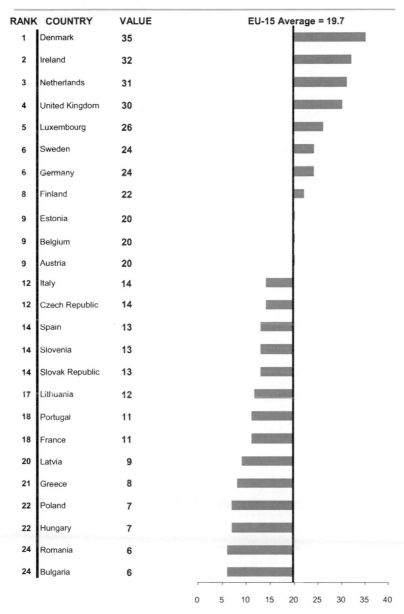

Source: Sibis, 2002/3

6.02 Internet use by the disabled, 2002/3

Percentage of disabled people using the Internet

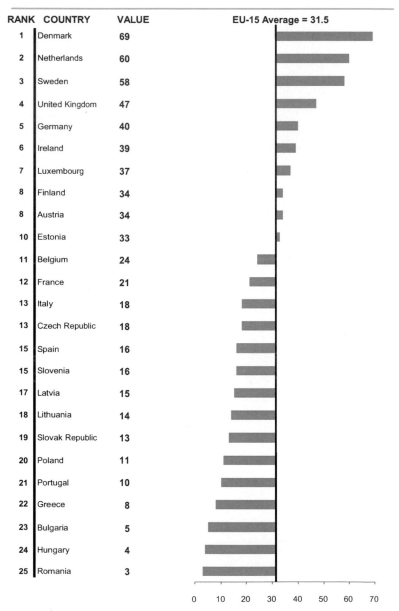

RANK	COUNTRY	VALUE
1	Denmark	69
2	Netherlands	60
3	Sweden	58
4	United Kingdom	47
5	Germany	40
6	Ireland	39
7	Luxembourg	37
8	Finland	34
8	Austria	34
10	Estonia	33
11	Belgium	24
12	France	21
13	Italy	18
13	Czech Republic	18
15	Spain	16
15	Slovenia	16
17	Latvia	15
18	Lithuania	14
19	Slovak Republic	13
20	Poland	11
21	Portugal	10
22	Greece	8
23	Bulgaria	5
24	Hungary	4
25	Romania	3

EU-15 Average = 31.5

Source: Sibis 2002/3

7.01 Online purchases, 2002/3

Percentage of individuals making purchases over the Internet

RANK	COUNTRY	VALUE	
			EU-15 Average = 19.9
1	Denmark	40	
2	Sweden	37	
3	United Kingdom	36	
4	Netherlands	27	
5	Germany	26	
5	Finland	26	
7	Ireland	24	
8	Austria	23	
9	Luxembourg	21	
10	Estonia	15	
11	France	12	
12	Italy	11	
12	Belgium	11	
14	Slovenia	7	
14	Portugal	7	
16	Spain	6	
16	Czech Republic	6	
18	Slovak Republic	5	
18	Greece	5	
20	Poland	4	
20	Latvia	4	
20	Bulgaria	4	
23	Lithuania	3	
23	Hungary	3	
25	Romania	2	

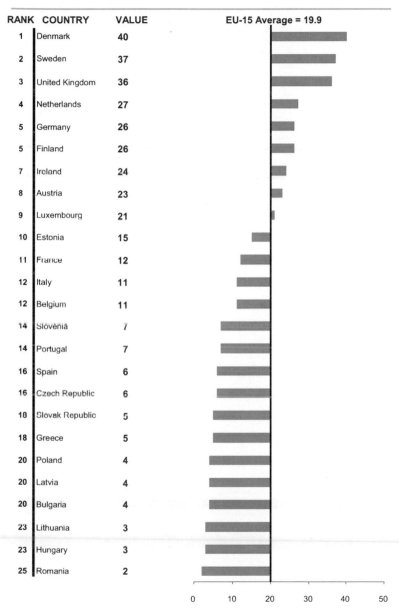

Source: Sibis 2002/3

7.02 B to C E-commerce, 2002

Volume of B to C E-commerce per inhabitant (US $)

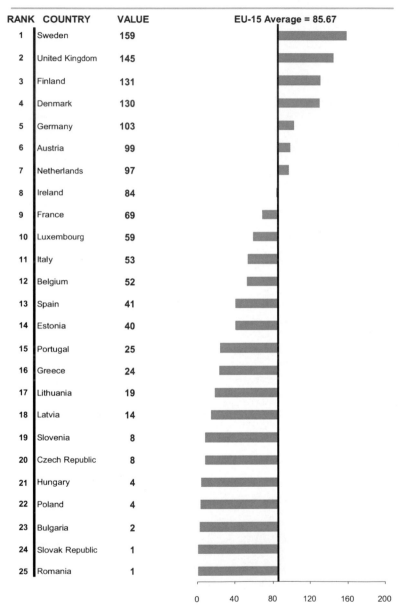

RANK	COUNTRY	VALUE
1	Sweden	159
2	United Kingdom	145
3	Finland	131
4	Denmark	130
5	Germany	103
6	Austria	99
7	Netherlands	97
8	Ireland	84
9	France	69
10	Luxembourg	59
11	Italy	53
12	Belgium	52
13	Spain	41
14	Estonia	40
15	Portugal	25
16	Greece	24
17	Lithuania	19
18	Latvia	14
19	Slovenia	8
20	Czech Republic	8
21	Hungary	4
22	Poland	4
23	Bulgaria	2
24	Slovak Republic	1
25	Romania	1

EU-15 Average = 85.67

Source: Witsa 2002

8.01 Laws relating to ICT, 2003

Laws relating to information technology (electronic commerce, digital signatures, consumer protection) are: 1 - non-existent, 7 - well-developed and enforced

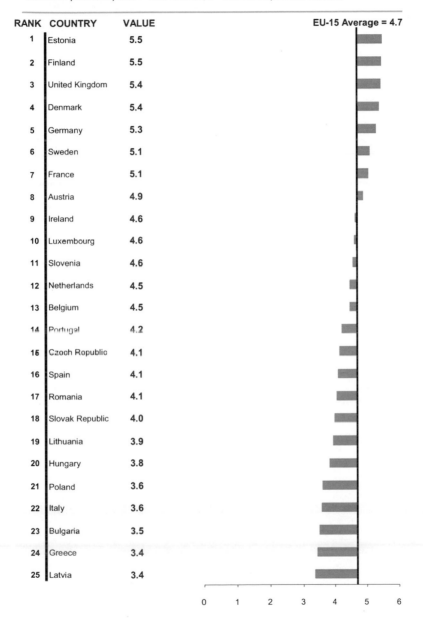

RANK	COUNTRY	VALUE
1	Estonia	5.5
2	Finland	5.5
3	United Kingdom	5.4
4	Denmark	5.4
5	Germany	5.3
6	Sweden	5.1
7	France	5.1
8	Austria	4.9
9	Ireland	4.6
10	Luxembourg	4.6
11	Slovenia	4.6
12	Netherlands	4.5
13	Belgium	4.5
14	Portugal	4.2
15	Czech Republic	4.1
16	Spain	4.1
17	Romania	4.1
18	Slovak Republic	4.0
19	Lithuania	3.9
20	Hungary	3.8
21	Poland	3.6
22	Italy	3.6
23	Bulgaria	3.5
24	Greece	3.4
25	Latvia	3.4

EU-15 Average = 4.7

Source: World Economic Forum Executive Opinion Survey, 2004

9.01 Online privacy, 2002/3

Percentage of individuals using Internet concerned with online privacy and security

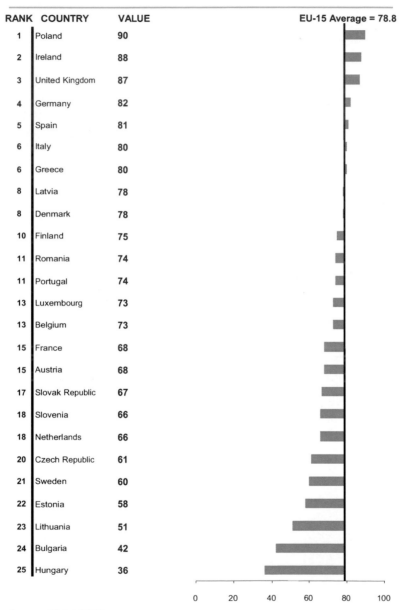

RANK	COUNTRY	VALUE	EU-15 Average = 78.8
1	Poland	90	
2	Ireland	88	
3	United Kingdom	87	
4	Germany	82	
5	Spain	81	
6	Italy	80	
6	Greece	80	
8	Latvia	78	
8	Denmark	78	
10	Finland	75	
11	Romania	74	
11	Portugal	74	
13	Luxembourg	73	
13	Belgium	73	
15	France	68	
15	Austria	68	
17	Slovak Republic	67	
18	Slovenia	66	
18	Netherlands	66	
20	Czech Republic	61	
21	Sweden	60	
22	Estonia	58	
23	Lithuania	51	
24	Bulgaria	42	
25	Hungary	36	

0   20   40   60   80   100

Source: Sibis 2002/3

9.02 Secure online commerce , 2002/3

Percentage of individuals using Internet effecting online purchases that have refrained from making purchases due to concerns about security

RANK	COUNTRY	VALUE
1	Italy	61
2	United Kingdom	57
3	Luxembourg	56
4	Ireland	54
4	Germany	54
6	Greece	53
7	Finland	51
8	Denmark	49
9	Spain	47
9	France	47
11	Sweden	45
12	Austria	44
13	Portugal	43
14	Belgium	39
15	Netherlands	36
16	Slovak Republic	27
17	Poland	26
18	Estonia	22
19	Latvia	21
19	Czech Republic	21
21	Lithuania	18
22	Slovenia	13
23	Hungary	10
24	Bulgaria	8
25	Romania	7

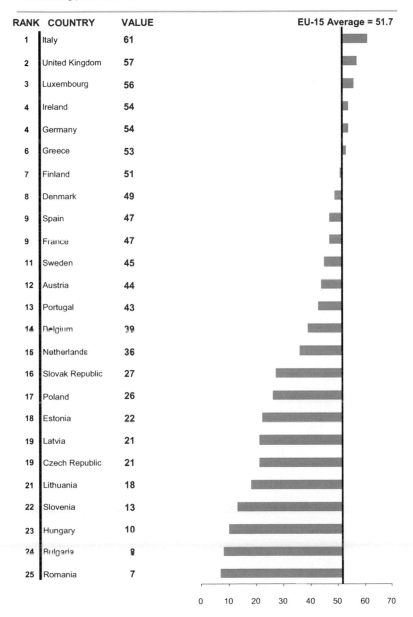

EU-15 Average = 51.7

Source: Sibis 2002/3

10.01 DSL broadband access, 2002/3

Percentage of individuals with DSL broadband access

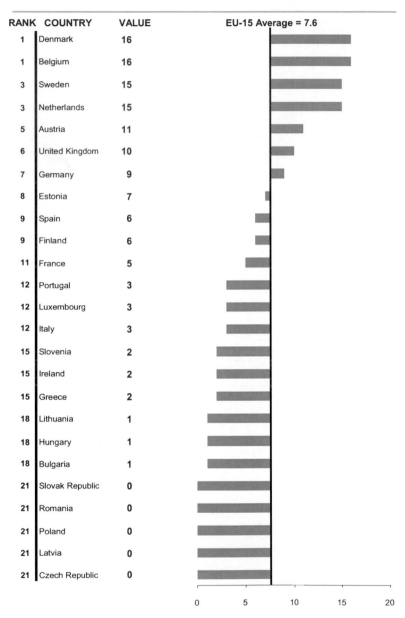

RANK	COUNTRY	VALUE
1	Denmark	16
1	Belgium	16
3	Sweden	15
3	Netherlands	15
5	Austria	11
6	United Kingdom	10
7	Germany	9
8	Estonia	7
9	Spain	6
9	Finland	6
11	France	5
12	Portugal	3
12	Luxembourg	3
12	Italy	3
15	Slovenia	2
15	Ireland	2
15	Greece	2
18	Lithuania	1
18	Hungary	1
18	Bulgaria	1
21	Slovak Republic	0
21	Romania	0
21	Poland	0
21	Latvia	0
21	Czech Republic	0

EU-15 Average = 7.6

Source: Sibis 2002/3

10.02 Broadband subscribers, 2002/3

Broadband subscribers as a percentage of total Internet subscribers

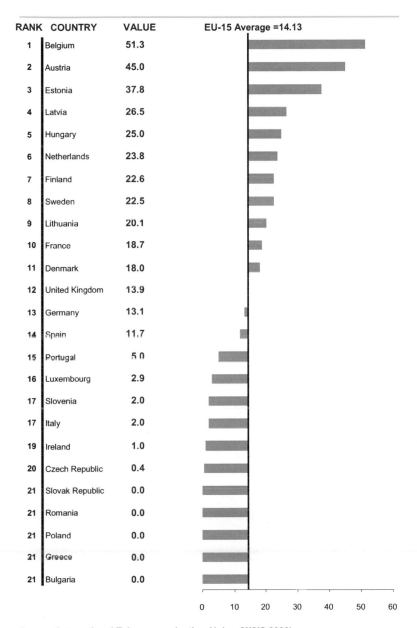

RANK	COUNTRY	VALUE
1	Belgium	51.3
2	Austria	45.0
3	Estonia	37.8
4	Latvia	26.5
5	Hungary	25.0
6	Netherlands	23.8
7	Finland	22.6
8	Sweden	22.5
9	Lithuania	20.1
10	France	18.7
11	Denmark	18.0
12	United Kingdom	13.9
13	Germany	13.1
14	Spain	11.7
15	Portugal	5.0
16	Luxembourg	2.9
17	Slovenia	2.0
17	Italy	2.0
19	Ireland	1.0
20	Czech Republic	0.4
21	Slovak Republic	0.0
21	Romania	0.0
21	Poland	0.0
21	Greece	0.0
21	Bulgaria	0.0

Source: International Telecommunication Union (WSIS 2003)

Authors' Biographies

Kai BENDER

Kai Bender studied information management at the European Business School (ebs) in Oestrich-Winkel, ebs London and San Diego State University. He holds a Ph.D. in computer science from the Technical University of Dresden. His academic work focused on applying software analysis and design patterns to more application and strategy oriented fields. Bender joined Roland Berger Strategy Consultants in 1999. He currently serves as Senior Project Manager and specializes in the fields of IT strategy development, IT implementation management and IT organization. One of his recent projects was the successful launch of the German Truck Toll project.

Kai_Bender@de.rolandberger.com

Soumitra DUTTA

Soumitra Dutta is the Roland Berger Professor of E-Business and Information Technology and Dean of Executive Education at INSEAD. He is the faculty director of Elab@INSEAD, an INSEAD initiative, launched in collaboration with leading international organizations such as Morgan Stanley, SAP, Roland Berger and Intel, to build a center of excellence for teaching and research in the digital economy. Prior to joining the faculty at INSEAD, he spent periods with Schlumberger in Japan and General Electric in the USA. Professor Dutta earned his Ph.D. in computer science and his M.Sc. in business administration from the University of California at Berkeley.

Dutta's research and consulting have focused on breakthrough approaches to the inter-relationships between innovation, technology and organizational design. He has also conducted research into national ICT strategies and leads an annual research project on global ICT benchmarking in collaboration with the World Economic Forum. His latest book is *"The Global Information Technology Report"* (Palgrave/MacMillan, Feb 2005). His previous books include *"The Global Information Technology Report: Towards an Equitable Information Society"* (Oxford University Press, January 2004), *"The Global Information Technology Report: Readiness for the Networked Future"* (Oxford University Press, January 2003), *"The Bright Stuff: How Innovative People and Technology can Make the Old Economy New"* (Financial Times/Prentice Hall, 2002), *"Embracing the Net: Get.Competitive"* (Financial Times/Prentice Hall, 2001) and *"Process*

Reengineering, Organizational Change and Performance Improvement" (Mc-Graw Hill, 1999). In addition, he has published over 50 articles in leading international journals.

A fellow of the World Economic Forum, Dutta has won several awards for research and pedagogy. His research has been showcased on international media such as CNN, the BBC and CNBC. He has taught in and consulted with leading international corporations across the world.

Soumitra.Dutta@insead.edu

Karsten GAREIS

Karsten Gareis is senior researcher at Empirica, Bonn. His main field of interest is the way information and communications technologies impact human resources systems, the locational behavior of firms and social disparities. He has worked extensively on conceptualizing, preparing, overseeing and analyzing European surveys of the general population and of decision-makers in establishments, focusing on information society phenomena such as multi-locational work, e-commerce, e-business and cooperation over ICT networks.

Karsten.Gareis@empirica.com

Julia HOERAUF

Julia Hoerauf studied industrial engineering and management at the University of Karlsruhe, Germany, and at the Escuela superior de Ingenieros in Seville, Spain. The technical focus of her studies was information and telecommunications technology. She wrote her thesis in cooperation with T-Systems on the market development of e-payment from the perspective of a systems integrator. During her studies, she worked for companies such as Siemens ICN in the United States and Bosch Telecom. Hoerauf joined Roland Berger Strategy Consultants in March 2004, where she currently works as a consultant in the InfoCom Competence Center. Her work centers around information management.

Julia_Hoerauf@de.rolandberger.com

Tobias HÜSING

Tobias Hüsing is a researcher at Empirica. His educational background is in economics and sociology. He has worked in quantitative empirical research and has been responsible for survey methodology and statistical analysis in a variety of large-scale, pan-European projects. Among other projects, he has played a part in the European research projects Senior-Watch, BISER, SIBIS, e-business W@tch and eUser. He also shouldered responsibility for a project with Eurostat to draw up the methodological report for the 2002 and 2003 European ICT household surveys. His main research interests are the digital divide and societal implications of ICT, as well as methods of empirical ICT research and statistical analysis.

Tobias.Huesing@empirica.com

Amit JAIN

Amit Jain is a Research Program Manager at INSEAD, and a visiting Professor at the Université de Paris, Dauphine. He has worked at INSEAD on various research projects in information and communications technology and knowledge management, and formerly served as Technical Director of INSEAD Online, INSEAD's e-learning initiative. Before joining INSEAD, Jain worked with Schlumberger in the Middle East and has pursued several entrepreneurial opportunities in the information technology space. He earned a D.E.A. in strategy and organizations from the Université de Paris, an M.B.A. from INSEAD and a bachelor of technology degree in mechanical engineering from the Indian Institute of Technology.

Amit.Jain@insead.edu

George KARAGEORGOS

George Karageorgos has been responsible for the *e-Business W@tch* implemented by the European Commission, Enterprise Directorate General, since late 2001. Before moving to Brussels, he worked in the private and public sectors in Greece, managing, preparing and implementing EU-supported programs and projects in the ICT, manufacturing and regional development areas. He holds a degree in mathematics (University of Athens, 1983), M.Sc. in operational research and another in analysis, design and management of information systems (University of London, LSE, 1984 and 1985 respectively).

Georgios.Karageorgos@ccc.cu.int

Werner B. KORTE

Werner B. Korte shares the directorship of Empirica with Simon Robinson and is responsible for managing many of the largest Empirica research and development projects in relation to the information society, statistical indicators for benchmarking and regional development. He has been and still is project manager of large-scale international Empirica projects in these areas, providing policy evaluation and assessment to public and private customers, including different DGs of the European Commission, national ministries, federal and regional governments and ministries, and local governments since the early 1980s. He has been responsible for several market research monitoring and benchmarking studies. Since 1989, he has served as an external expert to the European Commission to help develop the work program. Concurrently, he has worked as evaluator and technical reviewer for the ESPRIT Program. From 1996 through 1999, he was responsible for coordinating workgroups and directing all operations in the "Forum Info 2000: Germany's Way into the Information Society", a major government initiative supported by the economics and research ministers. Some recent projects he has managed include "SIBIS – Statistical Indicators Benchmarking the Information Society", "EUFORIA – European Foresight Project" and "SUSTEL – Sustainable Teleworking". He is currently deployed as project coordinator for the eUser project to develop a knowledge base and evidence-based support for the design and delivery of user-centric online public services in Europe. Korte has rich experience in analyzing the implications of the information society and related developments for local and regional territories, and in advising policy-makers about adequate strategies to benefit from these advances.

Werner.Korte@empirica.com

Arnoud De MEYER

Arnoud De Meyer is Professor of Technology Management and Deputy Dean in charge of Administration and External Relations at INSEAD. He is also Akzo Nobel Fellow in Strategic Management and is director of several hi-tech companies.

Arnoud.de.Meyer@insead.edu

Gérard RICHTER

Gérard Richter is partner at Roland Berger Strategy Consultants and responsible for information management at the Infocom Competence Center. He studied business in Frankfurt and Paris, and began his consulting career in 1997 at Roland Berger Strategy Consultants. His work includes cross-industry IT consulting (information management) as well as strategic consulting projects in the IT industry. He has carried out numerous national and international IT and e-business projects in several industries, including

IT, telecommunications, media, aerospace, consumer goods, construction and financial services. His area of expertise includes optimizing the value contribution of technology and IT within companies.

Gerard_Richter@de.rolandberger.com

Petri ROUVINEN

Petri Rouvinen is a research director at ETLA, the Research Institute of the Finnish Economy. For the 2004-5 academic year and upon writing the chapter for this volume – he was a Jean Monnet Fellow at the European University Institute (Florence, Italy). He holds a Ph.D. in economics from Vanderbilt University (Nashville, USA). In recent years, he has participated in ICT-related projects organized by the EU, OECD, the Ministry of Trade and Industry, UNU/WIDER, and the World Bank. Dr. Rouvinen's research interests include ICT and technology in general, innovation, R&D, globalization, competitiveness, entrepreneurship and economic policy. He has served as a referee for several scholarly journals including Industrial and Corporate Change, Journal of Economic Behavior and Organization and Research Policy. He has published many books and contributed to several collective volumes by well-known publishers. His scholarly work has been published in Economics of Innovation and New Technology, Information Economics and Policy, and the Journal of Applied Economics among others.

pro@etla.fi

Hannes SELHOFER

Hannes Selhofer is project manager at Empirica GmbH, a research and consulting company based in Bonn, Germany. He has been coordinator of the *e-Business W@tch* since 2002, a project carried out by Empirica GmbH with international partners on behalf of the European Commission, DG Enterprise and Industry.

Selhofer holds a master's degree in communication and media research from the University of Salzburg (1992). Prior to joining Empirica in early 2001, he worked for research organizations in Salzburg. His main areas of work are socioeconomic studies on the knowledge society and economy and studies on the media industry. He has been involved in numerous policy-oriented research and consulting projects since the mid-1990s. His clients include the European Commission and Federal Ministries in Germany and Austria.

Hannes.Selhofer@empirica.com

Pekka YLÄ-ANTTILA

Pekka Ylä-Anttila is Research Director at ETLA (the Research Institute of the Finnish Economy) and Managing Director of Etlatieto Ltd. (a project research and information services unit of ETLA). He is author or co-author of about 25 books and dozens of articles in the fields of competitiveness analysis, industrial and technology policies, industrial economics, technological change and the internationalization of business. He was a member of the Executive Committee of EARIE (the European Association for Research in Industrial Economics) from 1984 through 1992 and a member of the Scientific Advisory Board of Statistics Finland (Central Statistical Office) from 1996 through 2002.

Ylä-Anttila directed "Advantage Finland – the Future of Finnish Industries", a major cluster study program carried out in 1992-1995. He was principal adviser to the Ministry of Trade and Industry as it prepared the National Industrial Strategy for Finland in 1992-93, and filled a consulting role during the formulation of industrial and innovation policy guidelines in 2001. He was also a steering group member of the prime minister's task force "Finland in the Global Economy" in 2004. Ylä-Anttila has participated in several groups evaluating innovation and industrial policies, including the evaluation of the Finnish innovation support system in 2003.

He recently took part in international ICT-related projects at OECD and UNU/WIDER. He is also a team leader in the ETLA – BRIE (Berkeley Roundtable on the International Economy at University of California, Berkeley) collaborative research program on the wireless economy.

Ylä-Anttila is a member of several international research teams and networks. His current research interests include innovation policies, the internationalization of R&D and multinational companies in small economies.

Pekka.Yla-Anttila@etla.fi

Printing and Binding: Strauss GmbH, Mörlenbach